INSIGHT INTO EMPTINESS

INSIGHT
INTO
EMPTINESS

Khensur Rinpoche Jampa Tegchok

Interpreted by the Buddhist monk Steve Carlier
Edited by Bhikshuni Thubten Chodron

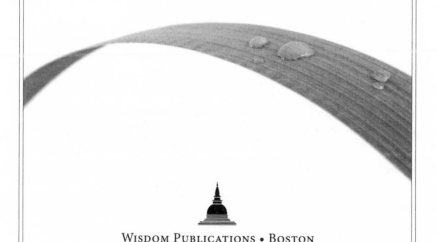

WISDOM PUBLICATIONS • BOSTON

Wisdom Publications
199 Elm Street
Somerville, MA 02144 USA
www.wisdompubs.org

Library of Congress Cataloging-in-Publication Data

Jampa Tegchok, Geshe, 1930–
 Insight into emptiness / Khensur Jampa Tegchok ; interpreted by the Buddhist monk Steve
Carlier ; edited by Thubten Chodron.
    pages cm
 This book is a compilation of talks on emptiness given by Khensur Rinpoche at Land of
Medicine Buddha, a Buddhist center in Soquel, California, from October 2006 to December
2007.
 Includes bibliographical references and index.
 ISBN 1-61429-013-X (pbk. : alk. paper)
 1. Sunyata. I. Title.
 BQ4275.J36 2012
 294.3'42—dc23

                         2012010359

ISBN 9781614290131
eBook ISBN 9781614290223

16 15 14 13 12
5 4 3 2 1

Cover design by Phil Pascuzzo. Interior design by Gopa & Ted2, Inc. Set in Minion Pro
10.5/14.125.

Wisdom Publications' books are printed on acid-free paper and meet the guidelines for
permanence and durability of the Production Guidelines for Book Longevity of the Council
on Library Resources.

Printed in the United States of America.

  This book was produced with environmental mindfulness. We have
elected to print this title on 30% PCW recycled paper. As a result,
we have saved the following resources: 18 trees, 7 million BTUs of
energy, 1,827 lbs. of greenhouse gases, 8,237 gallons of water, and 522 lbs. of solid waste. For
more information, please visit our website, www.wisdompubs.org. This paper is also FSC®
certified. For more information, please visit www.fscus.org.

Contents

Charts

Introduction

A dewdrop poised delicately on the tip of a blade of grass. It looks so real and "solid," but how long will it remain there? As soon as the sun rises, it will be gone. Where did it go? Where did it come from? While it was here, was it as real as it appeared?

Perhaps this image of the dewdrop on the cover of *Insight into Emptiness* drew you to pick up this book. Although all of us—you, me, and everyone around—appear so real and truly existent, we are as illusory and transient as that sparkling dewdrop. What is the actual way in which we exist?

With clarity, precision, and grace, Khensur Jampa Tegchok Rinpoche will explain this to us. *Insight into Emptiness* is about the nature of reality—both our ultimate and conventional natures, for the two are inseparable. Through contemplating what he compassionately teaches us in *Insight into Emptiness*, we will come to understand that dependently arising appearances and their emptiness of having an inherently existent nature are noncontradictory and mutually supportive. We live in the midst of these two; they are our nature.

Khensur Jampa Tegchok Rinpoche had the idea for this book in his mind for many years before conditions became suitable for him to give the Dharma teachings that led to this publication. Rinpoche knew that his Western and other non-Tibetan students sought deeper teachings on emptiness, explained in an easily understandable way, so that they could discern the important points for meditation. Of course, when I heard of this idea I instantly volunteered to edit the teachings into a book. This was not entirely altruistic on my part, for having edited Khensur Rinpoche's book *Transforming Adversity into Joy and Courage*, I knew how much I would learn by doing this work. In addition, there is a certain joy that arises in the heart from offering service to our teacher when we know that teacher's motivation is to benefit all sentient beings. So editing a book is an offering to my teacher and to sentient beings at the same time.

This book is designed for people who have some background in Buddhism—those who have heard teachings on karma and its effects, the four noble truths, and the altruistic intention of bodhichitta. With this foundation, such people become interested in liberation from cyclic existence and naturally seek the method to cultivate the wisdom realizing the ultimate nature. They are appropriate students who will benefit from learning, reflecting on, and meditating on reality—the emptiness of inherent existence.

This book presents the essential concepts to facilitate our investigation into how things actually exist. When learning about the nature of reality, we will encounter some technical vocabulary as well as concepts that are new to us. The philosophical terms are explained, and a glossary can be found at the end of the book. The new concepts are also unpacked in a clear manner. Thus this book is an excellent, in-depth introduction to the topic of emptiness that will help prepare the reader for the study of translations of the great Indian and Tibetan works. This clear explanation also includes instructions on how to reflect and meditate on emptiness.

While an excellent teacher is essential, understanding this material also depends on our own enthusiasm and diligence. Emptiness is not a simple topic; if it were easy to realize, we would have done so many lifetimes ago. Because our minds are obscured by ignorance, we need to make effort to familiarize ourselves with a new way of thinking. What is challenging in this process is that we are so familiar with the view painted by ignorance that when we hear the correct view, we may become confused. But if we persevere, continuing to question whether things exist in the way they appear to us, progress is inevitable and enlightenment will come.

An Overview

We begin our journey into the nature of reality by cultivating the altruistic intention of bodhichitta and by learning the benefits of understanding the emptiness of inherent existence. This is the essence of chapter 1. Chapter 2 sets the stage for the commentary to come, presenting the three levels of capacity of spiritual practitioners and the importance of taking refuge in the Three Jewels as our spiritual guides. We then examine our current situation of being born again and again in cyclic existence under the control of afflictions and karma. We trace the root of this predicament to ignorance, the mind that not only doesn't know reality but also actively misapprehends the way persons and phenomena exist. We then come to understand that the wisdom realizing emptiness is in direct opposition to ignorance and leads to liberation from cyclic existence.

Chapter 3 expands upon the importance of realizing emptiness and the benefits of exerting ourselves to do so. Just having a doubt, thinking that perhaps things are empty of inherent existence, begins to challenge samsara. In chapter 4, we are introduced to the four seals, the various levels of selflessness, and the importance of using reasoning to uncover them. Here we learn that emptiness is an obscure object—not something that will just pop into our awareness as we sit quietly and still our minds.

Chapters 5 and 6 continue this theme, examining, "What is a person?" Are we permanent, unitary, and independent entities? Is there a self-sufficient, substantially existent person? What is an inherently existent person and do we exist that way? Chapter 7 continues to explore what the I is and examines both the valid apprehension of the conventionally existent I and the erroneous grasping at a truly existent person. Chapter 8 presents selflessness in terms of the four schools of philosophical tenets in general and the two Middle Way schools in particular. We come to see that the I exists by mere imputation, by mere name, but not from its own side.

Chapter 9 leads us into a continuing exploration of the view. Here we look at the well-known example of a fluid appearing differently to a human, a celestial being, and a hungry ghost. Chapter 10 encourages us by explaining that our afflictions are adventitious and not the nature of the mind. Therefore they can be eliminated, and all sentient beings can attain the enlightenment of a buddha.

Chapter 11 reviews some of the important points covered so far and then presents various ways of apprehending phenomena. This chapter sets the stage for the vital topic of dependent arising explained in chapter 12.

It is said that if the Buddha had a slogan, it would be "dependent arising." Realizing that everything—ourselves, others, our environment, even the nature of reality itself—arises dependent on other factors is the key to understanding the nature of reality. Thus this topic is presented in depth and is put forth as the foremost reasoning to prove the lack of inherent existence.

Chapter 13 presents another important reasoning to negate inherent existence—the four essential points. These points encourage us to identify what exactly we think we are by examining the strong feeling that there is a solid I inside of us somewhere. We then try to find this I. Chapter 14 explains another important reasoning that proves emptiness by encouraging us to question how things come into being. Do they arise from themselves, from things that are other than themselves, from both, or without any causes whatsoever? Is arising in any of those four ways actually possible? Usually we take for granted that a sprout grows from a seed or that a human being arises from a fertilized egg. But how does that actually happen?

Chapter 15 presents the three turnings of the Dharma wheel and illustrates the immense skill that the Buddha had as a teacher in teaching selflessness in ways that are appropriate to various audiences. In doing so, he presented a wide variety of views, and we must scrutinize these carefully to see which is the most accurate. Chapter 16 tells us that all persons and phenomena are empty, yet they exist nominally, on the level of appearances. They are falsities in that they do not exist inherently in the way they appear, yet they still appear and function. Emptiness does not mean nothing exists.

Chapter 17 contains some beautiful similes illustrating the transitory and empty nature of our five aggregates—the components that form the basis of designation of the I. This chapter continues by disproving both our body and our perceptions being truly existent. We are then warned of extremist views of reality—those that negate too much and fall to nihilism, and those that negate too little and fall to absolutism. In other words, emptiness does not mean total nonexistence, and conventional existence does not entail inherent existence.

Chapter 18 explains the two truths—conventional and ultimate—while chapters 19 and 20 consist of an in-depth explanation of a verse from the *Diamond Cutter Sutra*. The nine similes in this verse poetically explain the relationship and compatibility of dependent arising and emptiness from diverse angles. Chapter 21 again reminds us of our fortune in learning about emptiness and encourages us to continue on with the search for the ultimate nature of reality, the realization of which will free us from the bonds of cyclic existence.

THE ORIGINS OF THIS BOOK

This book is a compilation of talks on emptiness given by Khensur Rinpoche at Land of Medicine Buddha, a Buddhist center in Soquel, California, from October 2006 to December 2007. The Buddhist monk Steve Carlier, who studied with Khensur Rinpoche both at Nalanda Monastery in France and at Sera Je Monastery in India, was the interpreter for these teachings. They were faithfully recorded and transcribed by students there, after which Steve rechecked the translations. The transcripts were then given to me to edit.

Working with the material in the transcripts, I could often feel Khensur Rinpoche's compassion in giving these teachings. He was amazingly patient, repeating points again and again to make sure that the audience understood them correctly. He would speak about a topic from different angles to give a broader perspective. He continually stressed the importance of thinking about the teachings deeply over a period of time, and in this way encouraged us to persist with joyous effort and confidence in ourselves and in the Dharma.

Khensur Rinpoche believes in his students. He believes that we can not only benefit from hearing these profound teachings but also gain a correct understanding of them. I heard that in the 1970s, when Lama Thubten Yeshe first asked Khensur Rinpoche to go to England to instruct Westerners in the Dharma, Rinpoche wondered why people who knew nothing about the Dharma would need to be taught by geshes, the most learned of the monastic scholars. It seemed to him that the geshes were needed to teach the monks in the monasteries in India and that someone else could go to the West to teach people simple beginning topics. But after a year or so of teaching in the West, Rinpoche apparently said, "Now I know why geshes are needed to teach here! These people have received a good secular education; they know how to think and they ask probing and complex questions!"

The nature of reality is not easy to understand and realize. So this book is not a "one-read" book, where we receive some useful information and go on to something else afterward. The topic of emptiness entails great effort in study and contemplation, and thus rereading this book will enable us to derive more and more benefit. Each time we read the material, new understandings will develop in our mind, even though the words are the same. This happens due to the mental purification and accumulation of merit that we have done between one reading and the next.

A Note on Terminology

Some Sanskrit and Tibetan terms do not have a corresponding English word that correctly conveys their meaning. This fact means that, depending on the situation, a translator may use different words to translate the same Sanskrit term. It also means that the reader must be aware of the Buddhist meaning of certain English words.

For example, the Sanskrit term *duhkha* is usually translated into English as "suffering." This often leads people to incorrect conclusions, such as thinking that the Buddha says that all life is suffering, when we clearly do experience times of happiness. When used in phrases such as "the truth of suffering," *duhkha* has the connotation of "unsatisfactory." In our present state, although we are not in a constant state of suffering, we can say that our lives are unsatisfactory and we lack complete security and fulfillment. However, in the discussion of the three types of feeling, *duhkha* means pain or suffering. For our purposes here, I will differentiate these two meanings by using "duhkha" or "unsatisfactory" when referring to the first meaning and using "pain" or "suffering" when referring to unpleasant feeling.

Selflessness (*nairatmya*) is another confusing word. In Buddhist usage it refers to the absence of a certain type of fantasized way of existence. The usual English meaning of putting others' needs first does not apply here.

Appreciation

First and foremost, appreciation goes to Khensur Jampa Tegchok Rinpoche and the lineage of masters in the Nalanda tradition that traces its roots back to the Buddha. The monk Steve Carlier (Thubten Sherab) did a magnificent job translating these talks. Ven. Tenzin Tsomo, Sharon Gross, and Bhikshu Steve Carlier transcribed the talks, and Steve also rechecked the translation. Bhiksuni Sangye Khadro made many helpful suggestions and clarified several points. Appreciation goes to David Kittelstrom, Namdrol Miranda Adams, and the monastics at Sravasti Abbey for their help in editing and proofreading the manuscript. All errors are my own.

Bhikshuni Thubten Chodron
Sravasti Abbey, February 22, 2012

CHAPTER ONE

The Benefits of Learning about and Meditating on Emptiness

MOTIVATION

Having the right mental approach to whatever we do is of utmost importance. A positive motivation is crucial, because it determines the long-term value of our actions. When we listen to the teachings and reflect and meditate on their meaning for our own purposes alone, the benefit is very small. Each of us is only one being, while the number of sentient beings in cyclic existence is countless. Considering the welfare of others to be equally important to our own, let's cultivate the best possible motivation, which is, "I must accomplish the welfare of all sentient beings. The best way to do that is by taking into account their various dispositions, attitudes, and values, and benefiting them in accordance with those. To accomplish this, I must attain the state of a buddha."

Some people may think, "There is no need to consider all sentient beings. Each of us is responsible for himself or herself; it is not necessary for me to be concerned with others." This way of thinking does not take into account one very important point—all sentient beings have been kind to us and will continue to be kind to us lifetime after lifetime. Our lives today depend on others. Without the food they grow, the clothes they make, the buildings they construct, and the medical care others provide, we would not be able to stay alive. Everything we know—from our ability to use language, to our athletic and artistic abilities, to academic and Dharma knowledge—we have learned from others, who have taught us out of kindness. Although we think of ourselves as independent beings who can take care of ourselves, in fact we are dependent on others to provide everything we need to stay alive. Once we develop a strong awareness of this, we will automatically want to repay their kindness and feel that it is imperative to accomplish their welfare. To do so, we choose to progress on the path to buddhahood, the state of full enlightenment in which our wisdom, compassion, and ability to benefit all beings will be fully developed.

THE SOURCES OF THIS TEACHING

My explanation will not follow a single, specific text but will elucidate the points that are most important for you to understand based on a variety of sources. In general, I follow the interpretation of Je Tsongkhapa Lobsang Dragpa, the founder of the Gelug tradition of Tibetan Buddhism. As preparation, over the years I have read, studied, and contemplated Je Tsongkhapa's five major treatises on the Middle Way: (1) *Great Treatise on the Stages of the Path*, (2) the insight section of *Medium-Length Exposition of the Stages of the Path*, (3) *Elucidation of the Thought* (his commentary on Chandrakirti's *Supplement to the Middle Way*), (4) *Ocean of Reasoning* (his commentary on Nagarjuna's *Treatise of the Middle Way*), and (5) *Essence of Good Explanations: Discriminating the Definitive and Provisional Meanings*. These great texts are very important from beginning to end. No point they make is unimportant.

Furthermore I have studied various stages of the path (*lamrim*) and mind training (*lojong*) texts, and other important texts by great lamas. I have listened to the teachings and commentaries of many learned lamas, especially His Holiness the Dalai Lama, from whom I have received many teachings.

As I read and contemplated these texts, certain passages strongly struck me clearly as important, and I was able to understand them clearly as well. You may have had that experience yourself—you'll be reading a text, something is clear to you, and you think, "Wow! This is really important!" Over the years I wrote these points down, and my explanation of emptiness here is based on these points. Because they are clear to me, I will be able to explain them clearly to you! In addition, I will explain the various levels of emptiness, starting with the coarser levels and progressing to the subtlest and most profound levels.

Emptiness is the actual way in which each and every phenomenon exists. We can understand this only by eliminating all mental superimpositions and deprecations. *Superimpositions* are thinking that something exists when actually it does not, and *deprecations* are thinking something does not exist when in fact it does.

Although some of you are new to the topic of emptiness of inherent existence and the teachings explaining it, I believe that your education has prepared you well to understand this topic. Your secular education has trained your analytical mind, so that now it is as if you have a sharp knife with which you can dissect ideas and cut through misunderstandings regarding any topic you investigate in depth. For this reason, I don't think you will have much trouble understanding emptiness.

THE BENEFITS IN GENERAL

The time and effort we put into an undertaking is directly correlated with the benefit we believe we will receive from doing so. For example, people have the energy and willingness to study hard at university because they understand the many ways in which having a good education will help them attain their goals in life. It's the same for people who work hard in business. Once they are convinced of the value of a certain enterprise, they will be prepared to work day and night to achieve it. When we put our energy wholeheartedly into an activity, we will naturally progress toward our goal.

What follows are some passages from the sutras in which the Buddha extolled the importance and value of learning, thinking about, and meditating on the nature of reality—that all phenomena lack inherent existence.

ADMIRATION FOR THE PROFOUND

In *Ocean of Reasoning*, Je Tsongkhapa quotes a passage from Nagarjuna's *Compendium of Sutras* (*Sutrasamucchaya*):

> Through aspiration towards the profound Dharma all merits are accumulated, because it accomplishes all mundane and supra-mundane benefits until one attains enlightenment.[1]

What is the profound Dharma? It is the ultimate nature, the selflessness of persons and phenomena, the emptiness of inherent existence.

Why is it called "profound"? We say that the correct view is profound because emptiness is a profound object to realize. Just as we have to peel away the top layers of a lettuce to reach its heart, so too do we have to work our way through the more superficial descriptions of emptiness to arrive at the subtler ones. This means we should first work to understand the "outer" layers of explanations of the lower Buddhist tenet schools until we can finally understand the "innermost," subtlest emptiness as described by the Prasangika school.

The Buddhist philosophical systems of Vaibhashika, Sautrantika, Chittamatra, Svatantrika-Madhyamaka, and Prasangika-Madhyamaka all accept selflessness, but they differ as to what they mean by it. As we progress through these philosophical systems, beginning with the Vaibhashika, the meaning of selflessness becomes more subtle and more profound. It is only when we reach the last system, the Prasangika-Madhyamaka, that we arrive at a completely correct explanation. Nonetheless, the explanation of selflessness that we find in the Vaibhashika system helps us to understand the explanation in the Sautrantika system, and that helps understand the explanation in the Chittamatra system, and so on. The tenets of the philosophical schools are like steps of a staircase, each leading up to a subtler view, until finally we arrive at the subtlest view.

"Through aspiration towards the profound Dharma all merits are accumulated" means that if we have admiration and faith in emptiness as well as the aspiration to realize it, we will try to understand it. By exerting effort to understand emptiness, we will gather immeasurable merit. Since even a cursory idea of emptiness creates so much merit, there is no need to mention the merit created when we actually understand it!

Explaining the value of familiarizing ourselves with emptiness, a sutra says that some bodhisattvas may diligently practice just the first five of the six perfections—giving, ethical conduct, fortitude, joyous effort, and meditative stability—for hundreds and thousands of eons. But the merit of even an ordinary practitioner who listens to the topic of emptiness, reflects and meditates on its meaning, writes it out, or explains it to others—even with some hesitation or indecision—is far greater than that. Therefore, imagine the merit if we listen to teachings on emptiness without the doubt that thinks, "I can't say whether everything is empty or not." Then, think of the merit accumulated if we have an accurate and firm conviction, "This is what emptiness means," or if, clearly understanding emptiness, we explain it or discuss it with others, write it out, confer oral transmissions, and so on. The merit would be truly amazing! For that reason, practice of the first five perfections that is reinforced by the wisdom realizing emptiness is called "a practice accompanied by skillful means," while a practice that lacks an understanding of emptiness is known as "a practice unaccompanied by skillful means."

THE THREE DOORS OF LIBERATION

The *Questions of Rashtrapala Sutra* says:

> Due to not knowing the modes of being empty, peaceful, and
>   unborn, beings wander.
> The one endowed with compassion causes them to enter
>   [an understanding of those three doors] with hundreds of
>   methods and reasonings.

The three doors of liberation as taught by the Buddha are empty, peaceful, and unborn. Because sentient beings do not understand these, they wander in cyclic existence, engaging in many destructive actions that lead them to experience unfortunate rebirths as a result. Even when they have fortunate rebirths, they are still trapped in cyclic existence, where they experience so many problems and sufferings. The root of this can be traced to their ignorance of the ultimate nature of phenomena—the emptiness of inherent existence.

To help them understand these three doors of liberation, the Buddha, in his wisdom, taught many scriptures and explained hundreds of lines of reasoning that would enable people to gain access to that understanding. He was moved to do so by his great compassion for all sentient beings (a compassion that finds their suffering unbearable) and by his great love for each of them (a love more intense than a mother feels for her only child).

The three doors of liberation apply to functioning things—conditioned things that arise due to causes and themselves yield results. Functioning things are singled out because it is mainly due to grasping the I and the aggregates[2]—which are functioning things—as truly existent that sentient being wander in cyclic existence.

The three doors of liberation are connected to the conditioned things' natures, their causes, and their effects. In terms of their nature, they are *empty* of inherent existence. In terms of their causes, all signs of true existence of their causes are *pacified*—in the sense that such signs do not exist. That is, their causes are empty of true existence. In terms of their results, no truly existent results arise—that is, truly existent results are *not produced*. We should not wish for results within thinking of them as truly existent.

Sometimes the three doors of liberation are said to be emptiness, signlessness, and wishlessness. *Emptiness* correlates with the nature of functioning things being empty; *signlessness* with their causes being pacified or free from true existence, and *wishlessness* with their results being unborn or not arising.

Through becoming familiar with these three doors of liberation, we cease grasping conditioned things—specifically the I and the aggregates—as truly existent. Since grasping at true existence is the root of our duhkha, understanding of the three doors of liberation is essential for attaining our spiritual goals.

BENEFITS ACCORDING TO THE SUTRAS

In the *Diamond Cutter Sutra* (*Vajracchedika Sutra*), the Buddha teaches that if any man, woman, or virtuous being were to take the number of worlds equal to the particles of sand in the River Ganges[3] and completely fill them with the seven types of precious substances—gold, silver, and so on—and offer this to all buddhas, bodhisattvas, and others worthy of worship, the offerings made would be immeasurable, and the merit created would also be immeasurable. Still, the Buddha says, the merit of reflecting on the meaning of emptiness would be even greater. Although making magnificent offerings creates great merit, this practice alone cannot cut the root of cyclic existence. However, reflecting on emptiness even for a little while begins the process of demolishing the ignorance that keeps us bound in cyclic existence.

Meditating on selflessness and emptiness purifies a tremendous amount of destructive karma. An Abhidharma sutra called *The Tathagata's Treasury Sutra* (*Tathagatakosha Sutra*) says:

> If one who has done all of the ten destructive karmas engages in the meaning of selflessness, has faith in and admiration for the primordial purity of all phenomena, he or she will not be born in the unfortunate realms.[4]

Of the ten destructive karmas, three are done physically (killing, stealing, and unwise sexual behavior), four are done verbally (lying, divisive speech, harsh speech, and idle talk), and three are done mentally (covetousness, maliciousness, and wrong views).

Imagine the karma of someone who has done all ten destructive actions. It's pretty bad, isn't it? Nevertheless, if this person "engages in the meaning of selflessness"—that is, if he reflects that nothing is established as a self and contemplates the meaning of emptiness—and if he "has faith in and admiration for the primordial purity[5] of all phenomena," their selflessness, he will not be born in the unfortunate realms as a hell being, hungry ghost, or animal. This is how powerful meditation on emptiness can be. It will purify all this destructive karma.

How does that work? The objects of the ignorance grasping true existence (true-grasping) mistakenly appear to be truly existent. On that basis, afflictions such as attachment and anger arise, and these afflictions motivate us to engage in destructive behavior. Given that we accumulate the ten nonvirtues based on the assumption that these objects are truly existent, if we were instead to think that these objects are not truly existent, we would harm the grasping at true existence. Harming the grasping at true existence harms everything that is based on it. Thus, self-grasping ignorance, the afflictions, and the destructive karmas are all harmed. It is similar to destroying the canvas on which a picture has been painted; doing so destroys the picture as well. The *Subduer of Demons Sutra* (*Maradamana-paripriccha*) says:

> The monastic who understands that all dharmas are completely pacified, and who understands the emptiness of nature of the extreme of the origin of the infractions, who atones for the infractions committed and expiates them, nullifies even the actions with immediate results. So, what is a minor breach of propriety or a ritual omission?[6]

Someone who has committed the five actions with immediate results—sometimes called the *five uninterrupted karmas* or the *five heinous actions*—and who meditates on their emptiness will be able to purify those karmas. The five karmas with immediate results are: (1) killing one's father, (2) killing one's mother, (3) killing an arhat, (4) maliciously causing a tathagata to bleed, and (5) causing a schism in the sangha. Because these actions are so severely destructive, under normal conditions the person who does them cannot attain liberation in that same life, and after death that person will immediately be reborn in the hell realms. This is why these five are said to be actions with immediate results. If such brutal destructive actions can be purified by meditating on emptiness, surely lesser ethical faults can be as well.

The *Ajatashatru Sutra* relates the account of King Ajatashatru, who killed his father King Bimbisara, thus committing an action with immediate results. The king also abducted the nun Kapilabhadra, who was an arhat, and forced her to have sex with him, which is a secondary uninterrupted karma. When the Buddha talked with the venerable nun afterward, she reported that she had not experienced a single moment of lust, pleasure, or joy during the entire episode. She said that for her the experience had been like having a stick pushed into her. The Buddha confirmed that she was therefore still a pure bhikshuni. Nevertheless, the evil karma the king had done was very heavy. The Buddha then said:

> I would not even call the karma of those who have committed the acts with immediate results but who listen to this holy Dharma, engage with it, and aspire to understand it a "karmic obscuration."[7]

Here the Buddha speaks about a person who has committed uninterrupted karmas. If this person later listens to teachings on emptiness, admires emptiness, and reflects on its meaning, the Buddha says that the karma may no longer be a karma that prevents, or "obscures," liberation. The Buddha still considers the king's actions to be destructive; killing one's father is horrible, as is raping a nun. However, purifying karma by meditating on emptiness changes the situation. After such purification, it would be difficult to say that the karma from killing his father would still bring such a terrible, suffering result.

There are more sutra passages that teach the benefits of learning about emptiness. From time to time I will quote one and explain it so we can encourage ourselves to keep going in our endeavor to understand this topic.

The meaning of these quotations comes to the same point: The main purpose of understanding emptiness is to understand how we are born in cyclic existence and how we are able to leave cyclic existence and attain liberation and enlightenment.

CHAPTER TWO

Why Realizing Emptiness Is Important

BACKGROUND

I would not feel comfortable talking about emptiness without first explaining the context of the practices that lead up to the teaching on emptiness. If I neglected the foundational practices, my explanation would be incomplete. Some of you may already have a solid background in the initial topics, so you do not need much explanation. But some of you may not be as familiar with them, so I would like to give you some background to help you understand where the study and practice of the wisdom realizing emptiness fits into the overall structure of the stages of the path to enlightenment. Without understanding a little about cyclic existence (samsara) or nirvana (the state beyond the sorrow of samsara), these teachings on emptiness will not mean very much to you. Although I will not go into great detail about these now, this explanation will provide you with an adequate base, and you can explore these initial topics more elsewhere.

According to the stages of the path literature from the tradition of Lama Atisha, there are three capacities of persons who practice the path. These capacities are not predetermined, fixed, or eternal but rather represent a person's spiritual capacity and level of practice at this particular time. A person of initial capacity contemplates the preciousness of the human life, its purpose, and its rarity, as well as impermanence and death and the possibility of taking an unfortunate rebirth after death. These meditations stimulate him to aspire to have a fortunate rebirth, and he implements this aspiration by taking refuge in the Three Jewels and observing the law of karma and its effects.

A person of middle capacity builds upon the previous stages by meditating on the four noble truths. By understanding (1) the truth of the duhkha of cyclic existence and (2) the true origins and how these can be eliminated so that one attains (3) the true cessation of duhkha and its origins by practicing

(4) the true path, she generates the motivation to attain liberation from cyclic existence. This in turn motivates her to practice the three higher trainings—the higher trainings in ethical conduct, concentration, and wisdom. Within the higher training in wisdom, the student learns about emptiness, the methods to realize it, and the crucial role this realization plays in the personal attainment of liberation from cyclic existence.

Subsequently, the practitioner becomes a person of advanced capacity. Here, he meditates on one or both methods of generating bodhichitta—the aspiration to attain enlightenment for the benefit of all sentient beings. The two methods of cultivating this altruistic intention are the seven-point instruction of cause and effect and equalizing and exchanging self and others. Both are based on cultivating equanimity for friends, enemies, and strangers.[8]

Having generated the altruistic intention to attain enlightenment, a practitioner now actualizes that aspiration by practicing the six perfections: (1) generosity, (2) ethical conduct, (3) fortitude, (4) joyous effort, (5) meditative stability, and (6) wisdom. The practice of the perfection of wisdom includes the generation of the subtlest wisdom realizing emptiness, the chief means to free oneself from the obscurations preventing omniscience and to attain full enlightenment.

Thus, whether we seek liberation from cyclic existence for ourselves or enlightenment for the benefit of others, the single realization that has the capacity to cut all the obscurations is the wisdom realizing emptiness. As we delve into emptiness in subsequent chapters, it is good to bear the structure of the path in mind so that we will remember the context in which we are pursuing the realization of emptiness.

TAKING REFUGE

The great masters advise that all activities we embark on should be reinforced by the two attitudes of taking refuge and generating bodhichitta. In this way, whatever we do becomes worthwhile. This is particularly important during the activity of listening to or studying the Dharma. For this reason, at the beginning of oral teachings, we recite the following four-line verse, which includes both of these practices:

I take refuge until I am enlightened
in the Buddha, the Dharma, and the Sangha.
By the merit I create by practicing generosity and the other
    perfections,
may I attain buddhahood in order to benefit all sentient beings.

The first two lines of this verse encompass taking refuge, while the last two
are to generate bodhichitta.

Taking refuge means entrusting our spiritual guidance to the Three
Jewels—the Buddha, Dharma, and Sangha. The Tibetan word for buddha,
sangye, and the Tibetan word for enlightenment, *jangchub*, have the same
meaning. The first syllable of each, *sang* and *jang*, refer to the quality of having purified or abandoned all afflictions, negativities, and defilements. *Gye*
and *chub* refer to the quality of having developed all excellent qualities to
their full extent and having attained total knowledge of phenomena. When
we understand the meaning of these syllables, whenever we say them we
will remember their great significance.

The Buddha is the fully enlightened one who gives the spiritual teachings and instructions. The Buddha does this by first explaining, "I practiced
in the same way the great beings of the past have practiced, over a long
period of time, in order to attain the result of enlightenment, which is free
of all faults and possesses all knowledge and qualities. If you would like to
become like me, this is how to do it." And then he gives the teachings.

This is a really nice way of teaching, isn't it? The Buddha says the path
he followed is one that many beings in the past have followed. The fact that
so many beings have attained enlightenment through this path proves that
it works. Therefore, if our disposition, attitudes, interests, and values are
similar to those of the Buddha, we too can become enlightened by practicing in the same way he did. Having thus inspired confidence in us, the
Buddha then teaches us how to practice the path.

The Dharma is the advice or teaching that the Buddha gives. On a deeper
level, the Dharma is the last two noble truths—true paths and true cessations. Actualizing these two in our own minds is the real refuge from all
unsatisfactory circumstances and suffering.

The Sangha is the "supreme assembly." This refers both to the aryas—
those who have practiced as the Buddha instructed and realized emptiness

directly—as well as to the monastic community that practices the teachings and advice of the Buddha. In other words, the Sangha includes those people who have practiced according to the Buddha's advice and already achieved their goal as well as those who are in the process of following his instructions right now.

We call the Three Jewels "objects of refuge" because they protect us. Among them, the Dharma Jewel is the actual protection, because if we follow the instructions given by the Buddha and practice accordingly, our minds will gradually transform into the Dharma Jewel—the true path and true cessation. This internal Dharma Jewel that is the realization of the Dharma in our own minds protects us from the misery of unfortunate rebirths and the misery of all of cyclic existence.

Contemplating the verse above will enable us to develop the right motivation and right attitude toward what we do. The way generating bodhichitta creates a good motivation is pretty straightforward. From the beginning of learning the Mahayana teachings, we imbue our studies and practice with the bodhichitta motivation, "I must attain enlightenment for the sake of all sentient beings. Therefore I am going to engage in this action." This ensures that the ensuing action will be a very powerful virtue, even if the action is one that is seemingly insignificant, such as sweeping the floor.

You might wonder how that works with refuge; that is, how does taking refuge enable us to have a good motivation? To truly develop the wish to take refuge in the Three Jewels and to entrust our spiritual guidance to them, first we must contemplate the suffering of the three unfortunate realms and the drawbacks and difficulties of cyclic existence as a whole. We must realize that there is no lasting and secure happiness to be found in cyclic existence no matter where we are born. Thinking in this way, we will naturally generate thoughts of renunciation, the determination to be free from cyclic existence. We will determine to renounce all the unsatisfactory conditions of cyclic existence as well as its causes and seek the more stable peace and happiness of liberation and enlightenment. When an action is held by or sustained by refuge, it is also reinforced with the motivation of wanting to be free from cyclic existence, renunciation. In this way, refuge changes our orientation from a worldly one to a spiritual one. This is a general outline of the practice of taking refuge. Please follow up on it and bring the practice to its culmination.

Cyclic Existence:
The Five Aggregates and Six Realms

We take refuge in the Three Jewels in order to be free from the duhkha of cyclic existence in general and unfortunate rebirths in particular. Cyclic existence involves taking on one set of mental and physical aggregates after another, continuously, without any fixed order. "Without any fixed order" means that there is no predetermined order of rebirth such that we will continuously have increasingly better rebirths. In fact, we've been born into each realm countless times, with no fixed order and without choice. This circling is due to afflictions (destructive thoughts and emotions) and karma (physical, verbal, and mental actions). After living one life with its set of aggregates, we die and take another set of aggregates.

The five aggregates are form, feeling, discrimination, volitional factors, and consciousness. Together, they are the basis of a person. In the context of a person, the form aggregate is the physical body. The feeling aggregate consists of pleasant, unpleasant, and neutral feelings, and it accompanies all of our consciousnesses. The aggregate of discrimination identifies different features of an object and distinguishes one object from another, without mixing them up. The aggregate of consciousness refers to the six types of consciousness of a person, the five sense consciousnesses and the mental consciousness. The five sense consciousnesses correspond to the five types of sense objects and sense powers. One quality of the mental consciousness is that it thinks. The aggregate of volitional factors includes everything not included in the other four: all the various mental factors—emotions, attitudes, views, and so forth—as well as qualities such as being impermanent and being produced depending upon causes and conditions.

Cyclic existence refers to the six types of sentient beings who are born under the control of afflictions and karma. They are also called *migrating beings* because they migrate from one realm to another as they take successive rebirths and *samsaric beings* because they circle under the power of afflictions and karma.

Of the six realms of existence that sentient beings are born into, the three unfortunate realms are those of hell beings, hungry ghosts, and of animals. Literally translated, the term we render as *unfortunate realms* is "bad-gone realms." They are so called for two reasons. First, we experience those rebirths as a result of having engaged in "bad" actions, heavy destructive karma. Second, those rebirths are "bad" in the sense that they are infused with pain and undesirable experiences.

The unfortunate realm with the most intense suffering is the hell realm. In one type of hell realm, the beings suffer from extreme heat and fire, while in another they suffer from unbearable cold. The temporary and neighboring hells also encompass their own particular miseries. In the hungry ghost realms, beings predominantly experience the suffering of hunger and thirst, unbearable cravings that are never sated. In the animal realm, the suffering is principally being preyed upon by other animals, used by human beings for work, and killed and eaten by either human beings or other animals.

The three *fortunate realms* are the realms of the human beings, demigods, and gods. Beings of these realms are still in cyclic existence, and thus their situation remains unsatisfactory. But because they are temporarily experiencing the result of virtuous actions done in the past, they have much more happiness than those beings inhabiting the unfortunate realms. The term "gone-to-happiness" is used to describe them, because they have gone to an abode of happiness and because in that lifetime, it is easier to go from happiness to happiness, instead of from suffering to suffering as in the unfortunate realms.

The form and formless realms, into which beings are born as a result of having attained various levels of meditative absorptions, are included in the fortunate realms.

In terms of the comparable number of beings in these realms, it is said that the greatest population by far exists in the hell realms, in comparison to which the population of the hungry ghost realm fades into insignificance. The population in the hungry ghost realm is huge compared with that of the animal realm. Similarly, when we compare the population of animals to the population in the fortunate realms of human beings and gods, the number of sentient beings in the fortunate realms is tiny in comparison.

In cyclic existence, we could be reborn in the human realm with human aggregates—that is, a human body and mind. After passing away from that rebirth and leaving the human aggregates, we could then be born in the animal realms with the aggregates of a bird, and after that life, we could be born in the hungry ghost realm or the celestial realm. We could say that we take one body after another in any of the six realms of samsaric rebirth. However, it is more accurate to say that we take one set of aggregates after another, because in the formless realm there is no body, only mental aggregates are present. As long as we are under the influence of afflictions and karma, this process continues without interruption.

In terms of having the opportunity to practice Dharma, the best rebirth by far is that of a human being, with its eighteen freedoms and fortunes,[9] where we have all the internal and external conditions that enable us to learn and practice the Buddha's teachings. Such a life is so amazing, the opportunity we have is indescribable.

IGNORANCE, AFFLICTIONS, KARMA, AND LIBERATION

Reflecting on the suffering of sentient beings in the unfortunate realms helps us to develop an aversion to those rebirths and the wish to be free of them. This in turn inspires us to seek a refuge that can protect us from that suffering—the Three Jewels—and to devote effort to following the Buddha's advice in order to avoid such rebirths. Furthermore, reflecting on the disadvantages of being born in cyclic existence in general under the control of afflictions and contaminated actions, we develop intense aversion to cyclic existence and turn to the Three Jewels of refuge to guide us from the state of uncontrolled and repeated rebirth to the state of either an arhat—a being who has attained liberation from cyclic existence—or a buddha—one who has eradicated all defilements and seeks to benefit all beings most effectively.

Now, wandering in cyclic existence, being born again and again in the six realms, is not something that we have any choice about. It is not as if we make up our minds, "I think I will be born here this rebirth," or "I want to be reborn in that family during this rebirth." It doesn't work like that. We are born in the various realms of cyclic existence as a result of karma. Due to destructive karma created in the past, we are born in the unfortunate realms; due to constructive karma we are born in the fortunate realms.

This karma was created by our afflictions—disturbing thoughts and emotions. Clearly, if we had a choice, we would be born as human beings life after life; we would not choose to be born in suffering abodes with unfortunate bodies. And if we were really wise, we would not be satisfied with a human rebirth at all but rather seek liberation from the round of existence altogether.

There are 84,000 afflictions described in the Buddhist scriptures. These can be summarized into the six root[10] and twenty auxiliary afflictions.[11] All of these can further be condensed into the three poisons: attachment, anger, and confusion. But the root of all afflictions and karma, the foundation upon which all of cyclic existence rests, the one cause of all rebirths, is self-grasping ignorance, also called the *ignorance grasping at true existence.*

Thus, if we want to be free of all duhkha and rebirth in cyclic existence, we need to eradicate their root—ignorance. The way to do that is through the direct and nonconceptual realization of emptiness. This realization can free us. Now we see the importance of learning, thinking, and meditating on emptiness. Our very well-being and happiness depend on this.

The steps leading us to the direct realization of emptiness must be cultivated gradually, over time. Through learning about emptiness, we get a general idea of the important points. By thinking about what we have learned, our understanding becomes more refined and accurate. When we meditate on emptiness, we first realize it conceptually and later nonconceptually. As we become more familiar with emptiness, we gradually are able to harm and then eventually completely eliminate the self-grasping ignorance, the root of cyclic existence. In this way we become free of duhkha altogether.

If we want to remove a tree, we must do so by destroying its root. Just trimming the branches won't achieve our purpose. In the same way, if we want to get rid of cyclic existence once and for all, we must eliminate its root, self-grasping ignorance. Once we eliminate that ignorance, all the afflicted thoughts and emotions derived from it—such as attachment, anger, jealousy, and pride—will also be eliminated. If we remove these afflictions, it is no longer possible to create karma motivated by them. Without afflictions and karma, rebirth in cyclic existence is no longer possible.

The entire structure on which our continued misery is built can be abolished by means of the wisdom realizing the emptiness of inherent existence. It is vital to cultivate this wisdom, because there is absolutely no other way of attaining liberation. It is very important to understand this; otherwise we will have little interest in learning about emptiness and little energy to practice the teachings that lead to realizing it.

The state of freedom from cyclic existence is called *liberation*. We will also actualize *true cessation* and *nirvana*. What is the difference between these three? *Liberation* is posited from the viewpoint of being free from the duhkha of cyclic existence and unfortunate realms. *True cessation* is posited from the viewpoint of ceasing the causes that impel us to experience the duhkha of cyclic existence and unfortunate rebirths. *Nirvana* is posited from the viewpoint of having gone beyond the duhkha of samsara and unfortunate realms along with their causes. Nirvana is translated as "the state beyond sorrow," *sorrow* referring to the afflicted thoughts and emotions as well as the duhkha of cyclic existence.

Having taken refuge and seen the disadvantages of cyclic existence, we cultivate admiration and appreciation for the state of liberation, which is free of duhkha, and the aspiration to attain that state. Such an attitude will naturally inspire us to practice Dharma, which is the means to eliminate duhkha. As we practice the Dharma, we will gradually become free from duhkha. In this way, the Dharma will truly protect us.

The direct nonconceptual realization of emptiness is known as the "actual" refuge because it completely eliminates the root cyclic existence, the self-grasping ignorance. When the foundation of cyclic existence has been destroyed, everything that depends on that foundation—the afflictions and karma—also crumble.

Renouncing Duhkha and Its Causes

The first step in the process of attaining liberation is to generate renunciation, the determination to be free. The Tibetan term for this state is *ngejung*, which literally means "definite emergence," indicating the wish to definitely emerge from cyclic existence. Renunciation does not mean giving up happiness; it means renouncing duhkha—all the unsatisfactory conditions that constitute cyclic existence—and its causes. It is an attitude of mind; it does not necessitate living unhappily in a cold cave! When our renunciation is strong, Dharma practice becomes much easier because our minds are focused on liberation, not on all the seemingly interesting distractions that cyclic existence offers us.

How do we cultivate renunciation? We begin by asking ourselves, "Where will I be reborn after I die?" In answer, we see two possibilities: in one of the three unfortunate realms or in one of the three fortunate realms. Although suffering is great in the unfortunate realms, there is a lot of misery in the fortunate realms as well, as we know from our own experience. Whichever of the six realms of cyclic existence we will be born in, duhkha awaits. Since all rebirths in cyclic existence are full of duhkha, let's abandon all of them without exception. Understanding that it is impossible to find lasting happiness in cyclic existence, we become disillusioned with it. We think, "Wherever I am born under the control of afflictions and karma, there is nothing but unsatisfactory experiences and problems." This makes us feel really fed up with cyclic existence.

Just as a sick person finds food repulsive and does not want to eat, so too, once we have generated renunciation, we are disinterested in any pleasures samsara dangles before us and instead want to abide in a state of true peace and enduring happiness.

Until we have a firm, authentic attitude of renunciation, there is no way we will be able to overcome the attachment to the marvels, wonders, and pleasures of cyclic existence. What is meant by "the marvels of cyclic existence"? These are the things that we personally consider to be sources of pleasure and happiness as well as the things that society in general considers to be wonderful. They include but are not limited to pleasures such as delicious food, fine clothing, a wonderful sex life, popularity, approval, praise, fame, and power. It's not that these things are bad or that wishing for them is evil. Rather, procuring and possessing these things does not bring lasting happiness and actually may bring a lot of pain. We are seeking something better than the continual struggle for pleasure that most sentient beings are engaged in.

When we take time to ask ourselves, "Do these things really bring lasting enjoyment and fulfillment?" we will see that they don't. We will know that such pleasure isn't true happiness. But when we don't investigate in this way, out of habit we are still liable to see things in a distorted way, believing that pleasurable things exist all around us and that having or experiencing them is real happiness. This distorted belief causes us to seek fabulous possessions, wonderful experiences, praise, and reputation, even though none of these things brings lasting happiness.

The Buddha spoke about three kinds of duhkha. The first is called the *duhkha of pain.* It refers to the physical pain we experience from illness or injury as well as the mental pain we experience when we don't get what we like or when we encounter difficulties. These experiences are unpleasant from the outset, and the more they continue, the worse they become. Everyone, including animals and insects, know that the duhkha of pain is undesirable.

The second kind of duhkha is the *duhkha of change.* This refers to the unsatisfactory condition of seemingly pleasurable experiences becoming unpleasant if we continue doing them for long enough. For example, if the pleasure we experience from food, clothing, music, and so on were true happiness, it would never change into suffering or start giving us problems. It would remain constantly pleasurable—the more we did it and the more we had it, the happier we would become. But this is not the case. In relation to food, for example, if we keep eating we end up feeling sick to our stomachs. If the happiness we receive from eating were real happiness, no matter what, the more we ate the better we would feel.

It is similar with clothing. When we first put on a heavy coat in cold weather, it seems quite cozy. But if we wear it long enough, we'll end up roasting. In the summertime, clothing that initially seems comfortable and cool leaves us shivering later on. The apparent pleasure that we originally experience is not stable and turns into pain in the end. Whether it is food, clothing, sex, or whatever, if we persist in doing it long enough, it eventually becomes uncomfortable, either mentally or physically. We may enjoy watching a movie once, but if we were to watch it nonstop many times in a row, we would get bored and yearn to do something else. Someone massaging us may feel wonderful, but if he or she continues massaging the same area without stopping, we will become sore or annoyed!

The third kind of duhkha is called the *pervasive duhkha of conditioning*. This refers to having a body and mind under the control of afflictions and karma. Our physical body, the form aggregate, is conditioned by afflictions and karma. The same is true for our four mental aggregates—feeling, discrimination, volitional factors, and consciousness. This duhkha is called "pervasive" because we have it wherever we are born in cyclic existence, without choice. It is called "conditioned" because it is conditioned by afflictions and karma; it is under their control.

All births in cyclic existence are bound and tormented by these three types of duhkha. Even a rebirth in one of the fortunate realms is only a temporary respite from the more obvious forms of duhkha. For example, beings born as form or formless realm gods do not experience the duhkha of pain, and those born from the fourth meditative stabilization on up through the formless absorptions do not experience the duhkha of change. However, because they have been reborn under the control of afflictions and karma, eventually the good karma of the higher rebirth will run out. Without choice, they will fall again to a birth in the desire realm, in the body of a hell being, hungry ghost, animal, human being, demigod, or god. The fact that these rebirths continue without interruption under the control of afflictions and karma is the pervasive duhkha of conditioning.

We will know that we have developed renunciation when we do not, even for a second, experience the slightest desire for anything that is considered fantastic within cyclic existence. When, day and night, all we seek is to attain liberation from the duhkha of cyclic existence and the unfortunate realms, then we know our determination to be free is stable.

The Root of Cyclic Existence

Renunciation of cyclic existence is having compassion for ourselves. We want ourselves to be free of true duhkha and true origins, which are the afflictions and karmas that cause those unsatisfactory experiences. Karmas or actions ripen into the rebirths we take and the events we experience in these rebirths. These actions are motivated by the afflictions in our mindstreams—attachment, anger, jealousy, conceit, confusion, and so on. All the faults of cyclic existence arise from these mental afflictions, and all the mental afflictions are derived from the ignorance grasping true existence.

Sometimes we hear that the root of cyclic existence is ignorance. Other times the root of cyclic existence is said to be self-grasping, true-grasping, or the view of the perishing aggregates. It is important not to get confused here, because all of these boil down to one common denominator: grasping at true or inherent existence.

The Tibetan word for ignorance literally means "unknowing"; it is a mind that does not know or is not aware of the true nature of reality. In fact, it is not only unaware of the true nature of reality, but it also grasps things as existing in the opposite way to how they actually exist.

There are two types of self-grasping: (1) self-grasping of the person and (2) self-grasping of phenomena. Both of them are forms of ignorance, and both are the root causes that keep us in cyclic existence. The nature of both the self-grasping of persons and self-grasping of phenomena is ignorance. According to the Prasangikas, these two are differentiated merely in terms of their focal objects. The self-grasping of persons grasps at the inherent existence of persons, while the self-grasping of phenomena grasps at the inherent existence of phenomena.

You may wonder, "Isn't the person also a phenomenon?" Generally speaking, the person is a phenomenon because anything that exists is a phenomenon. A phenomenon is defined as "that which holds its own entity or has its own identity," and this includes the person. It is a phenomenon because it is an object of knowledge, because it is an object realized by omniscient mind, and because it has an identifiable entity or nature.

However, in this instance the person and phenomena are differentiated in order to vividly distinguish the I, which is a person, and the aggregates, which are phenomena. The person, self, or I is the agent, and the aggregates are objects used by the person; they are what the self clings to or appropriates. They are also the basis of designation of the person. Close analysis and examination of the precise relationship between the I and the aggregates is essential to realize emptiness. For this reason, the selflessness of persons and the selflessness of phenomena are investigated separately.

The view of the perishing aggregates is also said to be the root of cyclic existence. It is one type of self-grasping of persons. *Self-grasping of persons* refers to grasping at any person—ourselves or others—as truly existent, while the view of the perishing aggregates grasps only at our own self as truly existent. This view is of two types: the view of the perishing aggregates grasping at "I" and the view of the perishing aggregates grasping at "mine." Both of these are forms of self-grasping because they grasp their object as existing in a way that is precisely opposite to the way in which it actually exists. The view of the perishing aggregates is so-called because the I is merely labeled in dependence on the aggregates, and the aggregates arise and cease in every moment.

In short, when we speak about the root of cyclic existence, we use different names to refer to the same thing. In fact, sometimes we combine terms—"self-grasping ignorance," "ignorance grasping the self of persons," and "ignorance grasping the self of phenomena." These are not contradictory; they arrive at the same point: the mind that grasps at true or inherent existence, the mind that believes we exist in a way that we don't. Ignorance is their shared nature in the sense that they are all obscured with respect to the true nature of reality and grasp things to exist in the exact opposite way from the way they do exist.

THE FOUR NOBLE TRUTHS

The Buddha "turned the Dharma wheel"—that is, he gave sets of teachings—three times. In the first turning of the Dharma wheel in Varanasi in northern

India, he taught the four noble truths. As we saw above in the section on the middling capacity, the four noble truths are true duhkha, true origins, true cessations, and true paths. For each of these four, the Buddha prescribed a particular activity. He said true duhkha—all the unsatisfactory and suffering situations involved in being born under the influence of afflictions and contaminated karma—is to be known and understood. Once we clearly understand the three kinds of duhkha, the natural result is that we will want to be free of them.

The way to be free of them is to eliminate their causes—the afflictive obscurations, which are the afflictions and karma that cause rebirth in samsara without choice. Therefore the Buddha explained true origins, stating, "True origins are to be abandoned."

When we rid ourselves of the origins of all duhkha, we attain true cessation. By means of meditating on the ultimate nature of reality, the afflictions and defilements that are the origin of all our duhkha can be completely removed from the mind in such a way that they never reappear. Thus the Buddha said true cessation, the third of the four noble truths, is to be actualized or manifested. When all afflictions, their seeds, and the karma that causes rebirth have been ceased, we attain liberation, the state of being free of cyclic existence.

Liberation is freedom from all of the duhkha of the six realms of cyclic existence. When we attain liberation, true cessation, which is the extinction of all afflictive obscurations—that is, the nonexistence or purity of the afflictive obscurations—is attained in our mind at the same time. So liberation and cessation come down to the same thing. It is like looking at the same object from different angles.

The way to actualize true cessations is by practicing true paths, the fourth of the four noble truths. Thus the Buddha said true paths are to be cultivated and to be meditated on. The main true path is the direct realization of emptiness. The emptiness of true duhkha is meditated on to abandon afflictions pertaining to true duhkha; the emptiness of true origins is meditated on to abandon afflictions pertaining to true origins, and so on for the rest of the four noble truths. Although there is a slight difference in subtlety between the afflictions pertaining to true duhkha and those pertaining to true origins and in how difficult they are to abandon, there is no difference between the emptiness of those two truths. It is the same with the other truths.

Previously I said that the last two noble truths—true cessation and true path—are the Dharma Jewel that is our real refuge. Now we understand why. Actualizing the eradication of duhkha and defilements in our own mindstream and realizing the paths leading to that is what protects us from duhkha. There is no other door to peace or nirvana. No external being can protect us in this way.

In the second turning of the Dharma wheel the Buddha taught such sutras as the Perfection of Wisdom sutras that explain the emptiness of inherent existence. The *Heart Sutra* that we recite at the beginning of teachings comes from this turning of the Dharma wheel that was done primarily at Vulture's Peak in Rajragriha, India. In the third turning of the Dharma wheel, the Buddha taught sutras such as the *Sutra Unraveling the Thought*, in which he taught the tenets that became the Chittamatra system. At that time, he also taught the *tathagatagarbha*, or buddha nature.

Now those of you who are new to Buddhism also have a basic idea of the Buddhist worldview. While older students will already be familiar with these concepts, it is good to review them. I don't think you will have much trouble understanding these ideas on an intellectual level because you have had a good education that encourages you to investigate and think about things. You can build on this by reading, studying, attending teachings, and contemplating what you have learned.

CHAPTER THREE

Enthusiasm for Emptiness

UNDERSTANDING EMPTINESS IS CRUCIAL

As we saw in the previous chapter, understanding emptiness is crucial to our liberation from cyclic existence. The *8,000 Verse Perfection of Wisdom Sutra* (*Ashtasahasrika Prajnaparamita*) takes emptiness as its main subject matter. Throughout this sutra, and particularly in the chapter entitled "The Complete Transmission of the Teaching," it is said that the Buddha himself considered the realization of emptiness paramount, so much so that before passing into parinirvana, he went to great lengths to emphasize its significance by conferring the responsibility for this teaching to his attendant, Ananda.

> Ananda, therefore I bestow upon you this profound perfection of wisdom...You should hold the perfection of wisdom and not forget it; if for some doctrine other than the perfection of wisdom you were to forget a word and make some mistake, I will not hold you at fault; but if for the perfection of wisdom you forget a word and so forth, I will fault you.

Clearly, the Buddha cherished the teaching on emptiness and wanted others to do so as well. In fact, all the buddhas have gained enlightenment by depending on the wisdom realizing emptiness. As it says in the *Heart Sutra*:

> All the buddhas who perfectly reside in the three times, relying upon the perfection of wisdom, become manifest and complete buddhas in the state of unsurpassed, perfect, and complete enlightenment.

All the buddhas in the past who have attained enlightenment, all the buddhas in the present who are attaining enlightenment, and all the buddhas of the future—including ourselves—will attain enlightenment by depending on the perfection of wisdom.

Meditating on emptiness purifies a great deal of karma, even before we have realized emptiness directly. We may wonder—isn't bodhichitta just as strong a method, if not stronger, to purify destructive karma? In *Engaging in the Bodhisattva's Conduct* (*Bodhisattvacharyavatara*, 1:6), Shantideva says:

> Thus virtue is perpetually ever so feeble,
> while the power of vice is great and extremely dreadful.
> If there were no bodhichitta,
> what other virtue would overcome it?[12]

This quote indicates that bodhichitta has the potential to purify very heavy destructive karmas. But it can only do so when it is reinforced by the wisdom realizing emptiness. Its power is derived from that wisdom.

The wisdom realizing emptiness is so effective in purifying karma and eradicating afflictions because it apprehends phenomena completely opposite to the way ignorance apprehends phenomena. Thus it meets ignorance head on and can inflict harm on ignorance directly, not indirectly as other virtues such as love and compassion do. For example, if we have to go to court, many people may advise us what to say and do when we get there. But what we really need is someone who stands up in court and proves to the judge and jury that what our adversary says is wrong. Similarly, the virtuous qualities such as compassion, fortitude, and concentration assist us on the path to enlightenment, but only the wisdom realizing the emptiness of inherent existence can prove without a doubt that the root of cyclic existence—ignorance grasping inherent existence—apprehends phenomena in a mistaken way.

Ignorance and the wisdom realizing emptiness take the same object as their focus—a table or a person, for example. Ignorance grasps this object as truly existent, as existing from its own side. That is why it is called the *true-grasping mind*. The wisdom realizing emptiness, however, realizes the absence of true existence; it knows that the object does not exist from its own side at all. The wisdom realizing emptiness realizes that the very same object that ignorance believes to be truly existent is completely empty of being truly existent. For this reason, wisdom is said to oppose ignorance head on and to harm it directly.

The practices of bodhichitta, love, compassion, and so on are a great help in overcoming ignorance, but they do not confront it directly. By themselves, they do not understand that phenomena exist completely opposite to the way ignorance believes them to exist.

When we are sick, we can treat our symptoms with a variety of medicines that correspond to the diversity of symptoms. But if we want to treat the fundamental cause of the illness, we have to identify it exactly and then take the medicine that opposes it directly. This medicine will cure all the symptoms. Similarly, we may oppose hatred by meditation on love and counteract attachment by meditation on impermanence, but to root out all afflictions, we must eliminate their common cause, the self-grasping ignorance. This can be done only by meditating on the wisdom realizing that the self that ignorance grasps does not exist in the least.

This wisdom is very profound, and its object, the emptiness of inherent existence, is not easy to realize. For this reason the Buddha did not teach emptiness immediately after he attained enlightenment. In his own words, upon enlightenment, he had "discovered this Dharma which was profound, peaceful, free of elaborations, clear light, and unconditioned." That is, he had realized the ultimate nature of all phenomena, their emptiness of true existence. It was so profound and difficult to understand that he wondered if he would be able to find anybody capable of understanding it. But eventually—and fortunately for us—he was persuaded to teach emptiness.

We may think, "But the first thing the Buddha taught was the four noble truths, not emptiness." This is half right. The first thing he taught was the four noble truths, and the first truth, the truth of duhkha, has four attributes: impermanence, nature of duhkha, empty, and selfless. So emptiness is included in the Buddha's first teaching.

Hearing the benefits and importance of understanding emptiness will inspire us and help us to maintain interest in and appreciation for this teaching, especially for those of us who do not have an extensive background in this topic. We will be energized to learn and reflect on emptiness over a long period of time. This also applies to studying love, compassion, bodhichitta, and the six perfections. Having faith in and admiration toward these practices will inspire us to become familiar with them. Admiration and confidence in these practices will lead to the aspiration to engage in them. This, in turn, will spur joyous effort, and when we practice with enthusiasm and correct understanding, we will progress on the path.

THE DANGER OF MISUNDERSTANDING EMPTINESS

Nagarjuna says in *Treatise on the Middle Way* (*Mulamadhyamakakarika*, 24:11):

> By a misperception of emptiness
> a person of little intelligence is destroyed,
> like a snake incorrectly seized
> or like a spell incorrectly cast.[13]

If someone's wisdom is not sufficiently developed in the topic of emptiness, it could lead to his downfall. Imagine that a person incorrectly thinks that because phenomena are empty, the law of karma and its effects does not exist and thus falls to the nihilistic extreme. This view leads him to be negligent and reckless in his actions, and as a result he creates massive nonvirtue, which leads him to take one unfortunate rebirth after another. For those who are wise, however, the situation is very different. Listening to and understanding the teachings on emptiness will only increase their faith in the functioning of causality.

In fact, whenever we don't know what we are doing, we risk making mistakes. If we try to use a table saw without understanding how it operates, we could lose a finger. Similarly, if we misunderstand emptiness, we place ourselves further from liberation because this realization is indispensable in order to attain liberation and enlightenment.

The Buddha hesitated to teach emptiness because he wasn't sure that people would understand it correctly. If we misunderstand, great damage may occur by falling to either of the two extremes, nihilism or absolutism (eternalism, permanence). Of these two, nihilism is the worst, because it negates the existence of karma and its effects, and it may thus harm our interest and diligence in living ethically. The *Heart Sutra*, for example, says, "There is no eye, no ear, no nose, no tongue, no body, no mind." If we misunderstand the intended meaning of this teaching and take these words literally, we risk concluding that refuge, karma, and cause and effect in general don't exist at all. That would be falling into the great abyss of the nihilistic extreme. Because it is easy to make this mistake, the Buddha was initially reluctant to teach emptiness.

The scriptures say that there is no destructive action that cannot be purified by meditation on emptiness. But if someone listens to teachings on emptiness, misunderstands their meaning, and generates a wrong view about emptiness, that is very dire. Someone could incorrectly conclude that emptiness is worthless because it means that nothing whatsoever exists. Holding such a wrong view about emptiness, the person now lacks a reliable antidote to purify that destructive karma. This is equivalent to a prisoner holding the key to his cell but thinking it is a bomb and throwing it away.

Such an emphatic admonition to be careful in the way in which we reflect upon and meditate on the meaning of a teaching taught by the Buddha is only heard in connection with the teachings on emptiness. We do not hear this warning in relation to compassion, bodhichitta, or other topics that relate to the method side of the path. But misunderstanding the meaning of emptiness may lead us to think that conventional phenomena, dependent arising, and all the qualities cultivated on the method side of the path do not exist. Or we may think that emptiness itself doesn't exist. This is really quite dangerous.

In his *Precious Garland* (*Ratnavali*), Nagarjuna talks about two errors that people make in relation to the teaching on emptiness. One is when someone from the outset has no appreciation for the highest teaching on emptiness and rejects it outright. This includes proponents of the lower philosophical schools whose understanding of emptiness is comparatively coarse. For example, the Chittamatrins think that dependent phenomena are truly existent, so when they hear the teaching that dependent phenomena are empty of true existence, they dismiss it. The Svatantrikas assert that everything is inherently existent on the conventional level, so when they hear the teaching that all phenomena are empty of inherent existence, they reject it. Both the Chittamatrins and the Svatantrikas mistakenly believe that the teaching on the emptiness of inherent existence denies the existence of phenomena that in fact do exist. Believing that the Prasangika teaching on emptiness is a nihilist teaching, they discard it. Thus Chittamatrins and Svatantrikas fall to the extreme of absolutism, because they reject the Prasangika teaching on emptiness, mistakenly thinking that phenomena must exist inherently.

The other error is made by someone who has faith in the teaching on emptiness yet misunderstands it and thinks that because everything is empty, nothing exists at all. In doing so, the person with faith in emptiness falls to the extreme of nihilism because she mistakenly thinks that emptiness means nothing exists. This person is in greater danger, because she could easily proceed to reject ethical conduct, love, compassion, and so on, saying that they do not exist at all. Even Buddhists who make the first kind of error will at least continue to observe the law of karma and its effects and to cultivate love, compassion, and bodhichitta. By understanding the error in these two extreme views, we should try to gain a correct understanding of emptiness.

DOUBT INCLINED TOWARD EMPTINESS

While the consequences of misunderstanding emptiness are severe, the result of having even a doubt whether phenomena are inherently existent is very beneficial. In his *Four Hundred Stanzas* (*Chatuhshataka-karika*, verse 180), Aryadeva says:

> Those with little merit
> do not even doubt this doctrine.
> Entertaining just a doubt
> tears to tatters worldly existence.[14]

There are three types of doubt: (1) doubt inclined to the wrong conclusion, in this case that things inherently exist, (2) doubt that is equal to both sides, and (3) doubt inclined toward the correct conclusion, that phenomena are empty of inherent existence. The doubt Aryadeva speaks of here is the latter, the doubt inclined to the correct conclusion that phenomena lack inherent existence. Although this doubt does not have even the surety of a correct assumption, let alone an inference or a direct perception of emptiness, it still has the power to ruin the fabric of cyclic existence. Considering that perhaps we have never had even a doubt inclined toward emptiness in any of our previous rebirths, we can get a sense of the tremendous force of such a doubt. It sets our train of thought in the totally opposite direction.

If we leave cloth somewhere for many years, and bugs burrow into it and chew at it, it may look like the cloth is still there, but when we pick it up it falls to pieces. Even if we can pick it up, if we shake it, it disintegrates into shreds. Doubt inclined toward emptiness has a similar effect on samsara. Doubt challenges the ignorance on which the entire heap of samsaric duhkha stands; thus it spoils the foundation of cyclic existence.

Just thinking "Maybe things do not exist from their own side" occurs only to a person who has great merit. Otherwise, he or she wouldn't even wonder about it.

The Power of Realizing Emptiness

The full, direct realization of emptiness comes about gradually. Our first realization of emptiness is inferential and occurs by means of a conceptual appearance. This means that emptiness is understood conceptually. At this point, the conceptual appearance acts like a veil between the object—emptiness—and the mind perceiving it, so emptiness does not appear in a totally vivid way to the mind. Although the realization is clear and the mind ascertains emptiness—that is, the mind has reached certainty about the meaning of emptiness through sound reasoning and analysis—we are not yet able to cognize emptiness directly and nonconceptually. Gradually, as we continue meditating on emptiness, the conceptual appearance of emptiness will drop away, and our realization of emptiness will become a nonconceptual, direct perception, and therefore much clearer.

Each level of the path has its own objects to be abandoned, which are various levels of afflictions, so before we go on, it will be helpful to explain the layout of the path. There are three vehicles of Buddhist practice: the vehicles of the hearers, solitary realizers, and bodhisattvas. The aim of the first two is individual liberation from cyclic existence. The aim of the bodhisattva path is full enlightenment in order to guide all sentient beings to full awakening as well. Each of the three vehicles has five paths: the path of accumulation, path of preparation, path of seeing, path of meditation, and path of no-more learning (either the state of an arhat or buddhahood, depending on which vehicle a person follows).

On the first path, the path of accumulation, a practitioner focuses on accumulating merit, as well as on cultivating serenity and gaining the correct view if these have not been accomplished before. The second path, the path of preparation, is attained when the practitioner gains the union of serenity and insight on emptiness. This is a conceptual realization held by a mind in which analysis of emptiness does not disturb single-pointed concentration. When the practitioner has his first direct realization of emptiness, he passes onto the path of seeing. The direct realization of emptiness, in conjunction with other factors such as the collection of merit, will be able to abandon the objects that are to be abandoned by the paths of seeing and meditation. On the path of seeing he abandons the acquired afflictions. And on the path of meditation, he abandons the innate afflictions. *Acquired afflictions* are ones that we have acquired this lifetime from learning incorrect philosophies. *Innate afflictions* are much more ingrained and harder to eliminate because they have been present in our minds beginninglessly. All of these afflictions, their seeds, and the karma that causes samsaric rebirth are called *afflictive obscurations*, and someone who eliminates them is liberated from cyclic existence and becomes an arhat.

Practitioners following the bodhisattva path abandon an additional, subtler level of obscurations, the *cognitive obscurations* that prevent total knowledge of all phenomena. They do this in the latter part of the path of meditation, and they have completely abandoned all afflictive and cognitive obscurations upon attaining the path of no-more learning of the bodhisattva vehicle when they become fully enlightened buddhas.

This is the power of the realization of emptiness, what we are able to accomplish when we realize it directly. The fruit of our present willingness to work hard at attending teachings on emptiness, trying to understand them, meditating on what we have heard, and familiarizing ourselves with them again and again is freedom from everything that obscures our mind. At first it is difficult to figure out what all this talk of emptiness is about, but it will become easier and easier until at last we will realize emptiness. That initial realization will become clearer as we apply ourselves repeatedly in meditation, until finally liberation and enlightenment are attained.

The process for generating the precious bodhichitta in our minds is similar. We first listen to the teachings on bodhichitta and think about them until we clearly understand what they mean. Then we meditate on bodhichitta again and again until this attitude becomes familiar and sinks in to our minds. If we don't do this, we will not arrive at the point at which bodhichitta is natural for us. However, if we meditate on it repeatedly, it will arise easily and remain in our minds, influencing our motivations and actions. This is similar to hearing instructions and reading books about how to drive a car. We may think about what we have heard until we have a correct intellectual grasp of the process, but at some point we have to get behind the wheel and practice driving. We have to learn how to handle the car in diverse circumstances and practice in those situations before driving feels natural. No matter what we learn from books, this repetitive process of training is necessary. Athletes put a lot of energy into training their bodies, and we, as Dharma practitioners, need to put a lot of energy into training our minds. As we do so, we become more and more familiar with the Dharma, and the experience of the Dharma becomes part of us.

In every moment we spend meditating on any aspect of the path, we gather a huge collection of merit. Seeing this, let's be eager to learn and practice these precious teachings.

MORE THAN ONE WAY TO PRACTICE

Sitting in formal meditation posture in the seven-point position of Vairochana is excellent. If we are able to give up everything and just devote our time to meditating on emptiness and bodhichitta, it will be wonderful. But that is not the only way to practice. A practice that combines learning the teachings, reflecting or contemplating on their meanings, and meditating to integrate those meanings with our minds is a complete process. This is the approach of Dromtonpa, the famous emanation of Chenrezig and disciple of Jowo Je Atisha. Dromtonpa would receive teachings on a particular topic then follow up with reflecting and meditating on their meanings. His reflection on a topic was always done on the basis of first having received teachings on it, and his meditation was always done on the basis of having listened to teachings about the topic and reflected on their meaning. Not only did he advise us to practice like this, but also he modeled it himself.

If we think that Dharma practice occurs only when we are sitting in formal meditation posture, we will miss out on many opportunities. The great yogi Milarepa described himself as having attained enlightenment by meditating at all times. We have to properly understand what this means. When he ate, he meditated; when he walked, he meditated; when he sat down, he also meditated. This is an excellent way to make good use of every moment of our lives to cultivate Dharma understanding and realization.

This resembles the advice that the Buddha gave to his disciple, King Bimbisara. Since the king had so many responsibilities to his subjects, he could not give up his kingdom, go to a secluded place, and spend all his time in formal meditation. The Buddha told him nevertheless he could make his life rich and worthwhile by continually meditating on bodhichitta while remaining involved in the activities of the kingdom. In other words, the king should use whatever circumstances he was living in to practice bodhichitta. He did not give up on practice simply because the ideal circumstances were not present.

If we think about it, when will the ideal circumstances for practice ever appear? If we wait for the perfect situation, our lives will go by and no inner transformation will take place. We want to get out of cyclic existence because cyclic existence is not satisfactory. So how can we wait until cyclic existence is satisfactory in order to practice to get out of it? It's impossible. We must practice in whatever situation we find ourselves.

Of course, if we can devote our entire lives to listening, reflecting, and meditating on the Dharma, that is wonderful. If we can assemble all the conditions to go off to an isolated place and do serenity meditation, that is fantastic. But that doesn't mean that if we can't do that, we cannot do anything. We should practice and meditate during the time and in the situations available to us.

Sometimes we might be undisciplined or distracted and not get around to practicing. Those are situations we can do something about. In addition, we can combine our daily activities with Dharma practice, doing more serious practice and formal meditation when we have time. The effect of doing this over the long term will be very good. Our Dharma experience will grow gradually, like a large container is filled drop by drop. A tiny drop may not look like much, but eventually the whole container is full. The point is to do whatever we can without lamenting the lack of perfect conditions and to rejoice and give ourselves credit for whatever we do without berating ourselves.

Confidence

Worldly people are attracted to objects and people they find beautiful and desirable. They feel greatly drawn to them, yearn for them, and think about them a great deal. As Dharma practitioners, we cultivate a similar feeling about emptiness. We want to understand it and think about it as much as we can. When we hear someone say, "the wisdom realizing emptiness," we smile inside and feel so happy, just like a worldly person does when he hears the name of the person he is attached to.

Another attitude we want to cultivate in relation to the understanding of emptiness resembles that of a person with a well-paying job. This person does not give up her job because she sees its benefits. Even if she has to work hard and undergo many difficulties, she does so happily. Similarly, Dharma practitioners feel so happy to learn, think, and meditate on emptiness that they don't want to stop. They are happy to bear any difficulties that might arise in their endeavors because they see the benefits.

We cultivate great confidence by understanding that the realization of emptiness will enable us to uproot ignorance completely and thus cut the root of cyclic existence that has caused us to suffer for beginningless life-times. We feel joy at the idea of forever banishing ignorance, afflictions, and the contaminated karma that causes samsaric rebirth. Our lives have a deep sense of purpose, so that no matter how difficult, we will not give up our efforts to try to understand and realize emptiness.

When we meditate on bodhichitta, we make the strong determination, "I myself am going to lead all beings to enlightenment." Will we actually be able to do this, even after we become a buddha? Probably not, because some sentient beings have stronger karmic connections with other buddhas. But even if we are not able to actually lead all sentient beings to enlightenment by ourselves, there is no disadvantage in cultivating that determination. Having such a determination makes all the activities we do motivated by it—the practices of purification, accumulation of merit, the six perfections, the four ways of gathering followers,[15] and all our virtuous activities—much more powerful.

For example, a medical student may make the strong determination, "I am going to cure all the illness in the world when I become a doctor." Even if she is not able to do this, all her activities of caring for the sick will be more powerful because she has this intention. In the same way a warrior who vows to wipe out all enemies no matter what it takes will put everything he has into the fight due to his powerful intention. Similarly, with strong compassion and bodhichitta for all sentient beings, our ability to progress along the path and work for the benefit of others will increase dramatically.

CHAPTER FOUR

Looking at the Landscape

The Buddha was an extremely skillful teacher who worked with wisdom and compassion to guide sentient beings to enlightenment. He taught a variety of views in order to gradually lead sentient beings to the correct view of reality. The four seals outline four points by which a doctrine is considered Buddhist. While they constitute the basic Buddhist approach, within them we begin to see the diversity of ideas among the tenet systems. Following Aryadeva's advice to doubt inherent existence, let us begin to explore these systems. Doing so not only inspires us to think about how things exist, but it also helps us to appreciate the Buddha's kindness in guiding us on the path in a gradual way.

THE FOUR SEALS

Everything we study and practice on the path—the four noble truths, the twelve links of dependent origination, the two methods to generate bodhichitta—is founded on the principle of dependent arising. That is, meditating on one point acts as a cause to help us to meditate on the next one, its result. The four seals present a good opportunity to examine dependent arising extensively. The four seals are:

1. All conditioned phenomena are impermanent.
2. All contaminated things are unsatisfactory.
3. All phenomena are empty and selfless.
4. Nirvana is peace.

The four seals are accepted by all Buddhist schools—Vaibhashika, Sautrantika, Chittamatra, and Madhyamaka—although each school presents them according to its own tenets.

1. All conditioned phenomena are impermanent.

All conditioned phenomena are impermanent because they depend on the causes and conditions that produce them. That means they are in a state of constant flux, never remaining the same in the next moment.

2. All contaminated things are unsatisfactory.

Everything that is created under the influence of ignorance is unsatisfactory. *Contaminated* mainly refers to the influence of self-grasping mind. Through its influence, afflictions and karma arise, so they are contaminated by ignorance. Due to afflictions and karma, the five aggregates—our present body and mind—as well as the environment, arise, so all these are contaminated by ignorance as well. Everything that is contaminated is in the nature of duhkha, which means that it is unsatisfactory and cannot bring us enduring and secure peace. It is like the situation of a pet dog. He doesn't have any choice about what he does but must follow his owner. Similarly, we don't have much choice about what we do; things happen to us under the control of our afflictions and karma. This is an unsatisfactory situation, don't you agree?

3. All phenomena are empty and selfless.

The third of the four seals is that all phenomena are empty and selfless. This indicates their ultimate nature. When the four seals are explained in a way that is common to all Buddhist schools, *empty* refers to the lack of a permanent, unitary, and independent person that does not depend on causes and conditions and is a different entity from the five aggregates. *Selfless* refers to the absence of a self-sufficient, substantially existent person that is the same entity as the aggregates. All other phenomena are empty or selfless of being objects of use of such false selves.

No Buddhist system asserts the existence of a person that is a totally separate thing or a different entity from its aggregates. Such a thing is only asserted by some non-Buddhist philosophers, who, for example, assert the existence of a creator who is separate from the aggregates; the existence of a universal or cosmic principle out of which everything is formed; and the existence of a permanent, unitary, and independent self or soul.

Je Tsongkhapa says in *Ocean of Reasoning* that the reason that the Buddha did not spend a long time refuting the existence of a person that is a separate entity from the aggregates is because the main audience of the sutras was Buddhist. As Buddhist followers, they did not accept a self that is a different entity from the aggregates to begin with, and thus they didn't need such a refutation.

In distinction from the lower schools, Prasangikas say that both *empty* and *selfless* refer to the lack of inherent existence and that both terms apply to all phenomena, not just to the person. Here we see that the Prasangika view of the ultimate nature of all phenomena differs from that of the lower schools.

4. Nirvana is peace.

When the self-grasping mind is overcome, all mental afflictions and contaminated karma that arise due to it are eliminated, and nirvana, true peace, is attained. As we saw above, *nirvana* means "gone beyond sorrow." When someone realizes that all phenomena are empty and selfless, he or she uses this realization to purify his or her mind of all afflictions and in that way goes beyond the sorrows of the afflictions. That state beyond sorrow is peaceful and free from the torment of the afflictions. The pacification and extinction of the afflictions is true cessation, and that is nirvana.

ARYADEVA'S ADVICE

In his *Four Hundred Stanzas* (verse 190), Aryadeva says:

> First prevent the demeritorious.
> Next prevent [ideas of a coarse] self.
> Later prevent views of all kinds.
> Whoever knows of this is wise.[16]

This verse presents a systematic way to lead our minds to the full realization of the nature of reality. Under the guidance of an experienced teacher, we begin with easier topics and proceed to more difficult ones. This reflects the skillful way in which the Buddha presents selflessness, beginning with coarser levels and progressing to increasingly subtler levels.

In this quotation, "the demeritorious" refers to the view that the law of karma and its results does not exist. If we hold this view, we believe there is no connection between the actions we do now and our later experiences.

We do not believe that our actions bring results that we experience in future lives. Since the law of karma and its results is one way in which dependent arising operates, if we reject it, we will not be receptive to learning the even subtler types of dependent arising that are necessary in order to realize emptiness.

Understanding karma and its effects is preliminary to understanding the dependent arising explained in the twelve links of dependent origination,[17] where the Buddha says, "Depending on this, that arises. Depending on the cessation of this, that ceases." A person who rejects the functioning of karma and its results may still accept causality on a superficial level. For example, he knows that a seed will grow into a plant when the conditions are suitable. However, he will not be able to understand the causality explained in the twelve links of dependent origination. This understanding is preliminary to understanding the subtler types of dependent arising that are used to prove the emptiness of inherent existence. Thus someone who denies the ethical ramifications of our lives as expressed in the law of karma will not be able to comprehend emptiness or selflessness. In addition, this person may carelessly engage in destructive actions and thus obscure his mind and make it more difficult for Dharma understanding to arise.

After a person has gained confidence in the functioning of karma and believes there is a link between our causal actions and resultant experiences, Aryadeva says it is possible to move forward with the explanation of the various levels of selflessness. This commences with learning about coarse selflessness in order to abandon grasping at coarse levels of self, as is expressed in the second line of the verse. The coarse levels of selflessness refer to the person not being permanent, unitary, and independent. Slightly subtler, but still considered coarse, is the fact of the person not being self-sufficient and substantially existent. Understanding these two levels of selflessness will reduce coarser levels of ignorance.

In the third line, Aryadeva advises eliminating all views of the true or inherent existence of persons and phenomena. This refers to the subtlest selflessness of persons and the subtlest selflessness of phenomena. Understanding this level of selflessness will lead to the elimination of the subtle levels of ignorance.

As the fourth line says, this is the correct order in which to proceed, and a person who follows it is wise and will be able to progress well.

An Overview of the Levels of Selflessness

Just as Aryadeva recommends that we gradually refine our understanding, Je Tsongkhapa advises us to begin with an explanation of the coarse level of selflessness of persons and gradually distill our understanding until we reach the subtlest view of the selflessness of persons and phenomena found in the Prasangika system. In presenting a general description of these levels of selflessness, I will use some terminology that may be unfamiliar to you. Don't be concerned. As we continue, these terms will be explained; you will become used to them and will come to know what they mean.

The first level of selflessness is the lack of a permanent, unitary, and independent self. To understand this coarsest level of selflessness, we must listen to an explanation about it, reflect, and then meditate on it. *Permanent* here means it does not change from one moment to the next, *unitary* means one cannot point to its having various components, and *independent* means it does not arise from causes. With respect to the person, no such permanent, unitary, and independent person can be found.

Next, we move to a subtler level, which is still a comparatively coarse selflessness of person compared to the subtlest view of the Prasangika. The second level of selflessness of persons is the lack of a self-sufficient, substantially existent person. Such a person would be independent of the aggregates yet in control of them.

This is followed by investigating the view of reality according to the Chittamatra system, which goes beyond speaking about the selflessness of persons to question how other phenomena exist. According to them, the selflessness of phenomena is the lack of an object of consciousness and the valid mind that apprehends it being unrelated substantial entities. This is because both the object and the subject of a cognizer arise from the same latency, or imprint on the mind. The Chittamatrins also put forth a related selflessness of phenomena: that form, consciousness, and so forth are empty of existing by their own characteristics as the basis for their names and labels, such as "form," "consciousness," and so forth. "Existing by their own characteristics" means existing from their own side without being imputed by conception. Chittamatrins refute the belief that these phenomena are natural bases for the names that we affix to them.

This is followed by the Madhyamaka view, of which there are two divisions: Svatantrika and Prasangika. Svatantrika-Madhyamikas say that the selflessness of phenomena is the emptiness of existing from the side of the object's own uncommon mode of subsistence without being posited by the force of appearing to a nondefective consciousness. "Existing from the side of the object's own uncommon mode of subsistence" means something has its own unique way of being. It has something in it that makes it what it is. "Without being posited by the force of appearing to a nondefective consciousness" means that object exists without appearing to and being labeled by a mind free from superficial errors. The Svatantrikas negate inherent existence on the ultimate level but affirm it conventionally.

The Prasangika-Madhyamikas delve deeper and say that nothing—neither persons nor other phenomena—exists inherently, that is, without being merely designated by name and concept. For them, everything is empty of inherent existence, both ultimately and conventionally.

Contemplating these levels of selflessness is like peeling away the outer layers of an onion in order to get to its center. In future chapters, we will explore them in more depth.

CHART: SELFLESSNESS

Selflessness of persons (from coarse to subtle)
1. Emptiness of a permanent, unitary, and independent person
2. Emptiness of a self-sufficient, substantially existent person
3. Emptiness of an inherently existent person
Selflessness of phenomena
1. Emptiness of existing by its own characteristics as the basis or referent for its name
2. Emptiness of form and so forth and a valid cognizer of it being different substances (different substantial entities)
3. Emptiness of true existence (existing without being posited by the force of appearing to a nondefective consciousness)
4. Emptiness of inherent existence (existing from its own side, existing by its own characteristics, and so on)

The Buddha as a Skillful Teacher

Each of the four Buddhist tenet systems has its own idea about the nature of reality, and the non-Buddhist schools have their ideas as well. Some of these beliefs are completely mistaken. Others are not mistaken, since the reality they describe is factual, but what they claim to be the subtlest form of reality is not. It is only when we learn the Prasangika system that we encounter an explanation of this subtlest level of reality. To say that a view is the subtlest or deepest implies that realizing it removes the ignorance that is the root of cyclic existence. Realizing the Prasangika view does just that.

To understand selflessness according to the Prasangika system, we follow the writings of Nagarjuna, Shantideva, Chandrakirti, and so forth. How do these scholar-practitioners respond to other Buddhist systems' interpretations of the Buddha's teachings? They cannot say that these systems are completely wrong, because these systems were also taught by the Buddha. Rather, they point out that a deeper level of reality exists that the proponents of the other systems do not assert.

The philosophical assertions of all the Buddhist schools were taught by the Buddha. We may ask ourselves, why did the Buddha teach so many different views on the nature of reality? Why not teach only the most profound view, the Prasangika, and leave the others aside? Each time the Buddha taught, he had a particular audience in mind. Depending on the inclinations, abilities, and interests of a certain audience, he taught a particular view of selflessness. His aim was to benefit these sentient beings, and his teachings did just that. Based on the version of reality he taught them, which they believed to be the ultimate view, they were able to practice, create virtue, accumulate merit, purify, and so on. That teaching helped them in their quest for liberation and enlightenment.

A skillful teacher knows that not everybody is suited to receive the same teaching. The people to whom the Buddha gave the teachings on which the Vaibhashika system is based would not be able to accept the subtlest teaching on selflessness. They would misunderstand it, which would be detrimental for their spiritual wellbeing. Instead, the Buddha gave them a teaching that was suitable for their minds, a teaching they could accept that would help them progress along the path to liberation and enlightenment.

For example, in the teachings that form the basis of the Chittamatra system, the Buddha taught that phenomena are of three natures: imputed, dependent, and consummate (or thoroughly established). The first includes permanent phenomena such as unobstructed space, as well as our false projections on phenomena. The second is conditioned things that exist dependent on causes and conditions, and the third is their ultimate, empty nature. Among these, he said that the dependent and consummate phenomena truly exist. Although in reality nothing is truly existent, if the Buddha taught the emptiness of true existence to that particular audience, they would think, "If phenomena don't exist truly, they must be utterly nonexistent." Thinking this would be disastrous for them spiritually, because they would believe that karma and its results, the Three Jewels of refuge, and the path to enlightenment do not exist at all, and thus they would not be able to practice. Instead, the Buddha taught them that dependent phenomena truly exist, and based on that belief, they were able to take refuge and follow the law of karma by adopting virtue and discarding nonvirtue. Thinking that sentient beings have some measure of true existence, Chittamatrins practice compassion toward them and generate bodhichitta.

Of course in general, it would be better to engage in a practice with the belief that things do not inherently exist, but in this case, it was better for the Buddha to provisionally say that phenomena exist truly. This is similar to parents treating their children according to their present stage of development. They don't try to teach their children everything all at once; it might confuse the children and make them lose their eagerness to learn. So parents lead their children gradually. Similarly, when we follow a course of studies at school, our instructors do not teach us the most difficult topics at the beginning. Rather they give us a basic education that is more suitable for our minds. On that basis, as time goes on, they teach us more complex topics. Gradually, we are able to understand more difficult things. In the same way, the Buddha leads his various disciples step by step, teaching them what is helpful at that time. As they mature, he leads them to deeper perspectives and more subtle teachings.

Those of you who want to study and practice these methods extensively should bear in mind the purpose of each topic and teaching, the benefits of learning it, the reasoning behind it, and how to put it into practice correctly. Then you will be able to see how things fit together, and your minds will be comfortable. Otherwise, it could be quite confusing. If you want to study and practice extensively, this is important to remember.

THE VALUE OF REASONING

How do we distinguish the final, correct view among all the views the Buddha taught? How can we know what actually is the deepest level of reality as the Buddha himself understood it? Reasoning is the key. A good teacher will be able to explain the various types of selflessness and differentiate the coarse and the subtle on the basis of reasoning. He or she will say, "This assertion of selflessness is coarse because of this," and "This other assertion is more profound because of that." Based on what we learn, we must analyze and cultivate our own wisdom, which will enable us to meditate with confidence. Otherwise we might say one view is right and the others are wrong without knowing why, or we might feel obliged to accept our teacher's view without understanding it. That can be frustrating. Accepting a view through having understood the reasoning is much more comfortable for our minds, and it will keep us from going astray.

The non-Buddhist philosophers are called *outsiders* in the sense that they are not within the fold of those who have taken refuge in the Three Jewels. They are learned scholars who rely on their own founding teacher and that person's teaching, not on the Buddha and his teaching. They are not uneducated charlatans; each of their schools has reasons for its assertions, and in ancient India there was a great deal of debate between Buddhist and non-Buddhist scholars, all aimed at unearthing the truth about ourselves and the world we inhabit. The discussion would often be heated, and those who lost the debate often became followers of those who won. When we consider the aim and subject matter of these discussions, it is not surprising the participants would be energetic and eager to devote so much time and energy to debate. They seriously wanted to discern the actual meaning of liberation and enlightenment and the correct path to practice to attain it for their own or others' sakes.

When a Buddhist debates with a non-Buddhist, he cannot say, "This is correct because the Buddha said so!" The non-Buddhist would say, "So what! My teacher says otherwise!" Rather, they had to rely upon reasoning until they could come to a conclusion that everybody accepted as true.

His Holiness the Dalai Lama says that quoting scripture is not sufficient. Instead, he emphasizes the importance of employing reasoning. When I first heard him say this, I thought, "This is really useful," so I want to share it with you. If we want to study and practice in depth, using reasoning is very important. Without it, we only have blind faith, which is unstable. The moment someone questions us, our beliefs begin to shake and our confidence tumbles. On the other hand, when we have thought about things thoroughly and have faith that is based on in-depth reflection, our refuge in the Three Jewels is firm.

Emptiness Is an Obscure Phenomenon

There are three types of phenomena: obvious, slightly obscure, and very obscure. *Obvious* or manifest phenomena are those that are immediately evident to us. All the objects perceived by our five sense consciousnesses are obvious phenomena. Nondefective sense consciousnesses know obvious phenomena directly without having to rely on reasoning or logic. For example, we know various colors just by looking at them. Our auditory consciousness hears sounds, and our gustatory consciousness directly knows sweet and sour tastes.

Slightly obscure phenomena, on the other hand, cannot be known straightaway. To understand them, we initially need to use reasoning. Reasoning is in the realm of our mental consciousness. For example, the brahmans who recited the Vedas in ancient India believed that sound was permanent. The impermanence of sound cannot be known by the auditory consciousness of ordinary beings. We must first understand it by applying reasoning, such as the syllogism, "Sound is impermanent because it is a product of causes."

Like impermanence, emptiness is also a slightly obscure phenomenon. Thus we must initially use reasoning to understand it. We cannot just sit still, close our eyes, and expect the emptiness of inherent existence to appear to our minds. This is especially true because inherent existence appears to all consciousnesses of sentient beings, except to an arya's meditative equipoise on emptiness. Because all of our conventional consciousnesses are contaminated in this way, the only way to initially realize emptiness is by reasoning. After we realize it inferentially, by practicing meditation that combines the single-pointed concentration of serenity with the probing awareness of insight, we will gain a direct, nonconceptual realization of emptiness. At this time it is said that the mind and its object are like water mixed with water—there is no perception of subject and object.

Very obscure phenomena are those that we know by depending on the word of a reliable expert on the topic. For example, to know our birth date, we rely on our parents. Similarly, to understand the minute details of the functioning of karma and its effects, we rely on the Buddha and his explanations.

With knowledge of the four seals, the types of selflessness, and the importance of using reasoning to realize slightly obscure phenomena such as emptiness, let's now examine investigate the nature of the person.

CHAPTER FIVE

What Is a Person?

THE PERSON

The wish to be free from the suffering of unfortunate realms and of all of cyclic existence in general, and the confidence in the ability of the Three Jewels to guide us, inspires us to take refuge in the Buddha, Dharma, and Sangha. When we reflect on the kindness of others and the fact that they, too, suffer in cyclic existence, we aspire to become a buddha in order to guide them to enlightenment as well. Now the question is: Who is the person who suffers in cyclic existence, going from one life to the next? Who is the person that attains liberation and enlightenment?

As we've seen, all the unsatisfactory conditions and suffering we face in cyclic existence are rooted in a misapprehension of phenomena and in particular of the person. We believe that we exist in a way that we do not. We must correct an error about the way we perceive the person. To do this, we need to know something about the person that is the focal point of the discussion. If we don't, saying such things as "The person lacks permanent, unitary, and independent existence" or "The person is empty of inherent existence" will not mean very much to us.

What do we mean by "the person"? There are many different types of beings, all of which are included under the label *person*: Hell beings, hungry ghosts, animals, human beings, demigods, and gods are all persons. These are the beings who are continually compelled to take rebirth in cyclic existence under the control of afflictions and karma. Other persons are those on the path to liberation and enlightenment, such as the hearer and solitary-realizer learners and the bodhisattvas. Still other persons are liberated and have gone beyond cyclic existence—the hearer arhats and the solitary-realizer arhats. Buddhas are persons who have attained full enlightenment. All of these beings are included within the word *person*. So when we talk about the selflessness of persons, these are the persons we are talking about.

PERSONS AND PHENOMENA

Before we go any further, it may be helpful to note that the word *self* has different meanings in different contexts. In some contexts *self* is synonymous with person; in other contexts *self* refers to the object of negation, what doesn't exist. Asking "Who is the self that we treasure more than anyone else?" is an instance of the former. The "self" in *self-grasping* and *selflessness* is the latter.

Selflessness is of two types: selflessness of the person and selflessness of phenomena. In general, a *phenomenon* is defined as "that which holds its own nature." Everything that exists is a phenomenon, including the person. This is also the sense when we say, "Buddha's omniscient mind knows all phenomena."

But when talking about self of persons, self of phenomena, selflessness of persons, and selflessness of phenomena, *phenomena* refers to everything except persons. Here, *phenomena* refers to what the person uses, specifically the five psychophysical aggregates that are the basis of designation of the person. In this context, the person is the "user," and phenomena are what are used by the person. Although *phenomena* here principally refers to the five aggregates of a person, it is also inclusive of other things. For example, the food we eat and the clothes we wear are phenomena, and we, as persons, are their users. Similarly, the five aggregates are "used" or "clung to" by the person, and the person is their user and the one that clings to them. Thus in the Prasangika system, the *self of persons* is the inherent existence of persons and the *self of phenomena* is the inherent existence of all other phenomena aside from persons. Similarly, the *selflessness of persons* is the emptiness of inherent existence of persons, and the *selflessness of phenomena* is the emptiness of inherent existence of phenomena other than persons.

In general terms, the person is the experiencer of happiness and suffering, and the suffering and happiness are the feelings or phenomena that are experienced. The person wanders in cyclic existence from the deepest hell to the peak of samsara, experiencing happiness and suffering according to the karma he or she has created. The person is the one who practices the path and attains liberation.

In specific, there are various ideas about how the person is to be identified. While there is some variance among non-Buddhists on this, in general they share the belief that the person does not depend on the aggregates of the person. Instead, the person is identified as being something completely different from the aggregates. It exists from its own side, independent of causes and conditions. Its nature—its entity or identity—is different from that of the aggregates.

In *Ocean of Reasoning*, Je Tsongkhapa states concisely that only non-Buddhist systems assert a person that is a different entity from the aggregates and that remains after the aggregates are gone. No Buddhist system asserts a discrete self or soul. Remembering this is helpful as our investigation of emptiness continues. Another point to keep in mind while studying this topic is that apart from the Prasangika system, all other Buddhist systems assert that the person is found among the aggregates. Only the Prasangikas say the person is not found at all, either as a separate entity from the aggregates or within the aggregates that are its bases of imputation. Nevertheless, they assert a theory of agents, actions, and objects on the basis of everything being mere name and mere imputation.

THE FIVE AGGREGATES

All the Buddhist schools have some way of speaking about the person in relation to the five mental and physical aggregates. It is often said that the aggregates are the basis of designation and the person is what is designated.[18] Although we discussed the five aggregates previously, it is good to review them because they play such a vital role in our existence. In your meditation, you may want to try to identify each of your own five aggregates in order to get a better sense of what they are. The five aggregates are:

1. The form aggregate. *Form* (matter) and *form aggregate* are generally synonymous. When speaking of the five aggregates that are the basis of designation of the person, the form aggregate indicates the physical body.

2. The feeling aggregate. *Feeling* here does not mean emotion but refers to the pleasant, painful, and neutral quality of whatever we experience physically or mentally.

3. The aggregate of discrimination. This is the mental factor that discerns or identifies objects and their attributes.

4. The aggregate of volitional factors. This consists of a variety of mental factors that work together. Emotions, attitudes, and

views are part of this aggregate, as are abstract composites—impermanent phenomena that are neither matter nor consciousness, such as karmic latencies—that are related to an individual.

5. The consciousness aggregate. This consists of the six primary minds: visual, auditory, olfactory, gustatory, tactile, and mental. Each primary mind cognizes a specific kind of object: colors and shapes, sounds, odors, tastes, tactile sensations, and phenomena respectively. The mental consciousness is especially important because it is what thinks and conceptualizes. The mental consciousness is also what can be transformed into yogic direct perceivers, such as the minds directly realizing impermanence and the minds directly realizing emptiness.

While feeling and discrimination are themselves mental factors, the Buddha separated them from the other mental factors in the fourth aggregate and made them distinct in order to show their importance. Feelings are important for the role they play in the generation of afflictions. Attachment arises when we have pleasant feelings, anger is the reaction to unpleasant feelings, and confusion is generated in response to neutral feelings. Thus, due to feelings, the three poisons—attachment, anger, and confusion—easily arise.

Discrimination is considered a separate aggregate because it performs the important function of identifying objects and their attributes. Discrimination, or discernment, forms the basis for either afflicted opinions or analytical wisdom.

Aggregate means a heap, collection, or group. The form aggregate is a collection of all things that are composed of matter. The definition of *form* in the philosophical texts is "that which is suitable to be called form." The feeling aggregate is not a single thing but is a collection of all the various nuanced feelings of pleasant, painful, and neutral.

Fifty-one mental factors are important to understand in terms of attaining liberation. Aside from feeling and discrimination, which are their own aggregates, the remaining forty-nine mental factors are included in the fourth aggregate, volitional factors. Impermanence, birth, aging, and karmic seeds are examples of abstract composites that are also included in the fourth aggregate. In short, the fourth aggregate includes everything that is impermanent, part of a person's basis of designation, and not included in the other four aggregates.

Each aggregate is not a single item but a collection of things. For example, the body, which is the form aggregate, is made of parts. The feeling aggregate consists of many different feelings. All beings in the desire and form realms have these five aggregates. Beings in the formless realm lack a material body and thus have only the four mental aggregates.

Buddhas also have five aggregates—forms, feelings, discriminations, volitional factors, and consciousness. However, unlike our own, a buddha's aggregates are purified and do not arise due to ignorance, afflictions, and karma.

The five aggregates may be presented in another way as well, inclusive of all impermanent phenomena, not just the impermanent phenomena related to a specific individual. All impermanent things are subsumed within the general five aggregates. Trees, cars, bodies, books, and so forth are classified within the form aggregate. The pleasant, unpleasant, and neutral feelings of all beings comprise the feeling aggregate. Similarly the discriminations of all beings are included in the discrimination aggregate. The aggregate of volitional factors includes all the other mental factors of beings except feeling and discrimination. In addition, abstract composites, such as the person, time, words, democracy—things that are impermanent but are neither forms nor consciousness—are included within volitional factors. The six primary minds of beings together constitute the consciousness aggregate.

The five aggregates that form the basis of imputation of the person are a subset of the general five aggregates. Joe's body is his form aggregate. The physical bodies of others are not. His feelings are his feeling aggregate, and so on. A specific person is labeled in dependence on a specific set of aggregates—the aggregates that he appropriates—not on the five aggregates in general. Furthermore, as an abstract composite, the person itself is included in the general fourth aggregate. However, it is not included in *that individual's* fourth aggregate, which is the basis of imputation of that individual. That is, Joe is a person and thus is subsumed within the general aggregate of volitional factors. However, Joe the person is not included in the volitional factors aggregate that is part of his own basis of designation.

The Continuity of Consciousness

Each aggregate is a continuum, a series of similar moments of a similar type of thing. Our bodies are continuities from the fertilized egg to the fetus, the body of the newborn, the toddler, the child, the teenager, the young adult, the middle-aged adult, the senior citizen. Similarly, our mental consciousnesses are continuities. When you think of the continuity of the mental consciousness, don't think of it as being like a long stick. It's not like that. There is continuity in the sense that moment-by-moment change occurs. When a particular moment of the mental consciousness ceases, it gives rise to a new moment of mental consciousness. This is turn gives rise to a further moment of mental consciousness, and so on. In this way there is continuity into the next moment.

The continuity of mental consciousness goes from one life to the next. It is an ever-changing flow of moments. You can begin to counteract the view that the mindstream is self-existent by considering the flow of time. Time continues without ever stopping. Yesterday became today, which will become tomorrow. Time is constantly changing. In the same way, the mental consciousness is continuously changing.

We can see how this works by thinking about the death process. The body, the form aggregate, is left behind, as are the more superficial levels of consciousness, which gradually cease functioning as death approaches. The mental consciousness becomes more and more subtle until the moment of death. At that time, the last moment of mental consciousness of this life ceases, followed by the arising of the first moment of mental consciousness in the intermediate state, the bardo. Thus it is said that the continuity of the mental consciousness goes into the bardo. At the end of the bardo, the last moment of mental consciousness of the bardo is followed by the arising of a new moment of mental consciousness. In a human rebirth, this would be the first moment of mental consciousness in the womb.

When trying to identify the person and examine the relationship between the person and the aggregates by looking for the person within the aggregates, we discover that the person exists through depending on the aggregates. In fact, the person is merely imputed in dependence on the aggregates, but it is not the aggregates themselves. Thus, do not think that when we search for the person in the aggregates—that is, when we try to find something in the aggregates that can be identified as being the person—we find that the continuity of mental consciousness is the person. Rather, when we seek the person, we see that there is no self-existent person at all. An inherently existent person does not exist. There is only a merely labeled person.

WHO IS JOE?

When we say, "Joe is coming," or "I see Joe," what is happening? How do we know Joe is coming? When that person's aggregates appear, we think, "Joe is here." But what exactly is that person? If we say to Joe, "Come over here," he will come here. If we say, "Go over there," he will go there. But what is Joe? Is Joe his body? Is Joe his mind? Who is Joe?

We have to think about this and analyze to find the answer. What is it that we are pointing to as being Joe? Similarly, what do we mean when we say "I"? Who is this person that our entire life centers around? Once we have understood the nature of the person, understanding how karma works will not be difficult. It is easy to see the link between the actions we do and the results we experience.

Before answering these questions, we first have to see what the person isn't. While we may believe that there is a permanent, unitary, independent self, a self-sufficient, substantially existent person, or an inherently existent person, we have to examine if these notions are true. Are we what we think we are? Do we exist in the way we appear to?

NO PERMANENT, UNITARY, AND INDEPENDENT SELF

Let us begin with the coarsest level of selflessness: the lack of permanent, unitary, and independent self. This analysis will help us to refute all three attributes: the person's permanence, the person's being unitary, and the person's independence. *Permanent* refers to not arising and disintegrating; *unitary* means being a single entity without component parts; and *independent* signifies not depending on causes and conditions. No Buddhist system of tenets asserts the existence of such a person.

In Buddhist philosophy, a person that is permanent, unitary, and independent is the coarsest level of self. The mind grasping or believing that the person exists in such a way is the coarsest level of self-grasping. The nonexistence of such a self is the coarsest level of selflessness. Meditation in which we prove to ourselves that the person is empty of being permanent, unitary, and independent is meditation on the coarsest level of selflessness.

To understand there is no such self we need to investigate whether there actually is a person that is permanent, unitary, and independent. Applying this investigation to ourselves is essential. We ask ourselves, "Am I permanent, unitary, and independent?" We investigate, "Am I subject to birth and death? Do I have parts? Do causes and conditions influence me or am I impervious to them?" By exploring this in depth—not just briefly for a few days—we will be able to conclude with confidence, "I am not permanent because I am impermanent. I am impermanent because I change moment by moment and am subject to arising and disintegration. I am not unitary because I have parts. I am not independent because I am a product of causes and conditions." Reflecting and meditating in this way is very useful.

As we have seen, there are two types of self-grasping and two types of afflictions in general—acquired and innate. *Acquired self-grasping* is the self-grasping acquired through learning a system of philosophy or psychology that teaches that a person exists in such-and-such erroneous way. Through coming in contact with this mistaken view in this life, we learn it, believe it, and grasp it as correct. *Innate self-grasping* is the self-grasping that we have had since beginningless time. It travels with us from one life to the next. Even animals and babies have innate self-grasping and the innate afflictions that arise from it. Depending on what a person learns in her present life, she may have both acquired and innate self-grasping and afflictions.

Grasping the existence of a permanent, unitary, and independent self is intellectually acquired; it is not an innate grasping. Thus a person who holds this view is usually considered a "proponent of a tenet," someone who is trained in a system of philosophy or psychology. This person has employed the reasoning taught in that system and has come to a conclusion about what the person is and how the person exists through this reasoning. Otherwise, that person would not have the conscious belief, "The person exists in this way because of this and that reason."[19]

Although the absence of a permanent, unitary, and independent self is the coarsest and most superficial level of selflessness, it is still important to understand it, because this is the first step on our ascent to liberation. This being the case, understanding this coarse selflessness is much more important than almost anything else on this earth. This very understanding, along with the person who possesses such knowledge, is worthy of our homage and respect.

The arguments disproving the existence of a permanent, unitary, independent self can be applied to the notion of a soul and to the idea of an external creator, for both are said to have the attributes of permanence, unitariness, and independence. Looking at each of the three attributes individually, let's continue to explore why the existence of a permanent, unitary, and independent self is not possible.

IMPERMANENCE: COARSE AND SUBTLE

Non-Buddhists who assert a permanent, unitary, and independent self falsely conceive of the self as unchanging, as not arising and ceasing. They believe that the Self or soul is not born and does not die. Eternal and unchanging, it is beyond life and death.

To counteract this wrong idea of the self, we must understand the impermanence of the self, which is the opposite of this wrong view. *Permanent* means something that does not change from one moment to the next. It is unconditioned in that it is not produced by causes and conditions. Examples are unobstructed space, selflessness, and emptiness. *Impermanent* means that something changes under the influence of causes and conditions. Together, impermanent and permanent comprise all existents.

There are two levels of impermanence, coarse and subtle. All things can be understood on both levels. Take a house, for example. Its coarse impermanence is the fact that eventually it will fall into ruins. Change on this coarse level is obvious to our senses; it is an object of direct perception— we can see a house collapse. In general, reasoning is not needed to gain an understanding of coarse impermanence.

The subtle impermanence of the house is the fact that from the moment it comes into existence, the house does not remain static and unchanging for even an instant. This level of change is not visible to our senses; we are unable to see it directly. Instead, reasoning is needed to realize it. How could coarse, visible changes take place without more subtle changes also taking place moment by moment? For example, in the spring we see the growth of a sprout from one day to the next. That change doesn't occur in one big jump. Rather, the sprout is growing and changing in each nanosecond. We only notice the accumulation of moment-by-moment changes after an entire day has gone by. Although we cannot see the continuous small changes that are occurring, we infer them due to the fact that the big changes we can see could not occur without them. This moment-by-moment change—imperceptible to our senses and first known by using reasoning—is subtle impermanence.

The birth and death of a person is another example of coarse impermanence. We see such events with our eyes. But in between birth and death are many small moments in which we are aging. We don't notice these momentary changes with our eyes. Rather we initially know the subtle impermanence of a person by reasoning that without the nonstop, moment-by-moment changes that constitute the aging process, the person would not grow old and die.

Subtle impermanence can also be known through examining the passage of time. One hour has sixty minutes, and each minute has sixty seconds. The seconds, too, can be divided into smaller periods. Think about the time one o'clock. All the minutes preceding one o'clock are the causes for one o'clock to come into existence. What is the cause for one o'clock to end, to stop being, to become nonexistent? If all of the preceding minutes produce one o'clock, what makes it end? Are those preceding minutes also the cause for one o'clock to disintegrate and become 1:01 and then 1:02? Do you think that there three separate stages that constitute one o'clock, that the instant that is one o'clock is first produced, then abides, and finally disintegrates? Or do you think they all happen at the same instant—that they arise, abide, and disintegrate simultaneously?

If arising and disintegrating are not simultaneous, there has to be a period of remaining or abiding in between them. Do you see the logic of that? This means there must be arising, followed by abiding, followed by disintegration. If the three phases of arising, abiding, and disintegrating do not exist, the only other possibility is that arising and disintegrating are simultaneous. Which is it?

If we start counting at noon, one o'clock can't happen without fifty-nine minutes passing. Simultaneous with the beginning of the sixtieth minute, one o'clock occurs. It is in this sense that the previous fifty-nine minutes are the cause of one o'clock because they have to pass in order for one o'clock to happen. The cause of something exists prior to it; the causes of one o'clock must exist prior to one o'clock. Something that exists at the same time as one o'clock cannot be its cause. Certainly something that happens afterward cannot be the cause of one o'clock. The cause definitely has to occur first. That being the case, is the ending of one o'clock also a result of fifty-nine minutes having passed?

At the very same moment that one o'clock comes into existence, the disintegration of one o'clock also happens. It's difficult to establish exactly when one o'clock comes into being, but as soon as we say, "It is now one o'clock," one o'clock has ceased and it is a split-second past one.

This is subtle impermanence. Sometimes when we think about this superficially, it seems clear. But when we start analyzing, it gets to be a little bit complex, doesn't it?

Look at the time that it has taken to make one o'clock come into being. For example, noon has already passed, fifty-nine minutes have gone, and still it is not yet one o'clock. Look at the fifty-ninth minute after noon. During fifty-nine seconds, it is still not one o'clock. Pinning down the precise point at which one o'clock comes into being is actually quite difficult. When we get to one o'clock, the fifty-nine minutes and fifty-nine seconds that began at noon have already gone. When the sixtieth second has occurred, one o'clock has come. But right after the sixtieth second has ticked into being, the very next instant, it is not one o'clock any more. It is past one. When did one o'clock go out of existence? When did it stop?

The point is that a thing's disintegration doesn't require any other cause than the very cause that brought about its production. In other words, arising and disintegration do not result from two separate causes: one that brings about the arising of one o'clock and another cause that makes it cease. Similarly, the causes for a flower to bloom and wilt are the same. There is not another, separate cause that brings about the disintegration of the flower. The very cause that produced it is also the cause of its demise. To paraphrase Dharmakirti's *Commentary on Valid Cognition* (*Pramana-varttika*), "When an object arises, it is certain to perish, because a separate cause for its perishing is not required other than the cause which brings about its arising." If a separate cause were needed for something to perish, that thing would be permanent, because until the further cause occurred, it would remain unchanging.

There is a seventy-six-year-old Tibetan lama. When was he born? If you say, "Seventy-six years ago," then you're saying that this old lama existed seventy-six years ago and that he was born as an old man. If you say he was a baby then, well, that can't be because he was seventy-six years old.

Someone says the seventy-six-year-old lama is born right now. If that is the case, then either his mother must be quite old or he was born after his mother died! If the seventy-six-year-old lama arose today, when did those seventy-six years exist?

Someone who believes there is a person that doesn't rely on arising and disintegrating rejects both the coarse and subtle impermanence of the person. She believes there is an unchanging soul that does not arise at the time of birth and does not change in the least at the time of death. Is it possible for such a permanent, static person to exist? When we examine the person—you, me, or any of us—we see that we change in each split second. The person does not remain for a second moment after arising. The person exists within moment-by-moment arising and disintegration. This is the person's subtle impermanence. The separation of the person's body and mind at the time of death is the person's coarse impermanence.

The Meaning of "Unitary" and "Independent"

Something that is unitary is one seamless whole that has no parts. Of course each of us is an individual—that is not being questioned here. However, if we were a unitary person we would not have prior and later moments. We could not speak of what we were like as children and what we are now like as adults. But since a person does have prior and later moments, the existence of a unitary self is not possible.

In speaking of self and selflessness, we repeatedly come across the word *independent*. This word is used in many contexts. In ordinary language, a person may consider himself to be an independent individual who doesn't depend on other people, but in fact there is no such thing as a person that doesn't rely upon anything or anybody else. Each person is dependent in countless ways. For example, we depended on our parents to receive this body, and we depend on the kindness of other sentient beings to stay alive. In ordinary language, we think of children being dependent when they are small; they have to rely on their parents for everything. But when they grow up, have some education, and can make a living and support themselves, we say they are independent. And among adults, we speak of financial independence, political independence, and so on. There are many usages of the word *independent*.

But here we are talking about independence in terms of how the person actually exists, and in this context, *independent* has different meanings according to the circumstances. One is in the expression "the person is empty of being permanent, unitary, and independent." Another meaning of independent has to do with the meaning of *self-sufficient*, which refers to a subtler level of self-grasping that we will explore below. While both uses of the term involve the idea of independence, what is being negated differs in the two cases. The former refers to independence in the sense of not being affected by or not relying on causes and conditions. The second is the person being independent of the aggregates. *Self-sufficient* means being able to exist independently in a self-supporting manner, without depending on anything else, such as the aggregates.

In the sutras, the Buddha clearly taught that a person that is independent of the aggregates does not and cannot exist. In one sutra, the Buddha compares the aggregates to a burden and the person to the one who carries the burden. This analogy indicates the interdependence of the person and the aggregates. That is, the carrier of the burden can only be posited in relation to the burden he carries.[20] Likewise, the person can only be posited relative to the aggregates. Thus the person is not independent of the aggregates but exists in relation to the aggregates and is imputed in relation to them.

A self-sufficient, substantially existent person would be a person that could be seen without anything else, such as the aggregates, appearing to the mind. In fact, for us to know a person is present, the aggregates have to appear. We cannot identify a person independent of her body-mind complex.

In addition to *independent* meaning not depending on causes and conditions and not depending upon the aggregates, the Prasangika system indicates a third way of being independent. Here Prasangikas speak about the very nature of the object itself—that the object by its very nature is dependent, not independent. They take the meaning of independent to an even deeper level, where it means existing without depending on being merely imputed by name and concept.

The Lack of a Self-Sufficient, Substantially Existent Person

The next level of self-grasping of persons is holding the person to be self-sufficient and substantially existent. The nonexistence of such a person is the selflessness of a self-sufficient, substantially existent person. This is a subtler level of self-grasping and selflessness than those concerning a permanent, unitary, and independent person. For the lower schools—the Vaibhashika, Sautrantika, Chittamatra, and the Svatantrika—the nonexistence of a permanent, unitary, and independent person is the coarse selflessness of the person, and the nonexistence of a person that is self-sufficient and substantially existent is the subtle selflessness of the person.

While many non-Buddhist schools accept the person to be self-sufficient and substantially existent, no Buddhist tenet system asserts this. For the lower Buddhist schools the lack of such a person is subtle selflessness. However, the Prasangika school, which has the most accurate view, considers this coarse selflessness. They say that there is another level of self-grasping and of selflessness that is still deeper.

All Buddhist schools agree that the person is established depending on its basis of imputation, the aggregates. But only Prasangikas says that the person is not findable in the aggregates. Unlike the lower schools, they say that everything exists by imputation, because substantial existence is equivalent to inherent existence.

Everything is either an imputed existent or a substantial existent. In this context, *imputed existent* means that to identify the person, something else—such as the aggregates—has to appear to our mind. Without some portion of the aggregates—the person's voice or her face, for example—appearing to our mind, we would not be able to identify a person being in front of us. If the person were a *substantial existent*, we would be able to know a person was there without the appearance of either his body or mind.

If the person were *self-sufficient*—that is, independent of the aggregates—it could not be imputedly existent, because imputed implies dependent on the aggregates. If the person isn't imputedly existent, it would have to be substantially existent. That is the meaning of the expression "self-sufficient, substantially existent," which we could rephrase, "self-sufficient and therefore substantially existent."

We may wonder, "When negating a person being self-sufficient and substantially existent, do we first negate the person being self-sufficient and then negate the person being substantially existent?" No. When the possibility of the person being self-sufficient is negated, the possibility of it being substantially existent is implicitly negated at the same time. If it exists and is not self-sufficient, it must depend on others; if it depends on others, it cannot be substantially existent.

Unlike grasping at a permanent, unitary, independent self, which only has an acquired form, grasping the person to be self-sufficient and substantially existent has both innate and acquired forms. The *innate* grasping at a self-sufficient, substantially existent person has been with us since beginning-less time; it and its seeds are only eliminated after we realize emptiness. In his *Supplement to the Middle Way* (*Madhyamakavatara*), Chandrakirti says that a bodhisattva on the fourth of the ten grounds becomes completely free of the innate grasping at a self-sufficient, substantially existent person. The *acquired* grasping at a self-sufficient, substantially existent person depends on reasoning and is acquired by studying incorrect philosophies, thinking about the reasoning they present, and agreeing with that reasoning.

The Prasangikas assert that the grasping at a self-sufficient, substantially existent person that the Svatantrikas and the schools below them seek to eliminate is actually the acquired, not the innate, grasping. Je Tsongkhapa says that this is because the way they describe it has a component of reasoning. The proponents of the lower schools use many different reasons to insist that the person exists inherently. Thus a person who grasps a self-sufficient, substantially existent person believes there is an inherently existent person who is self-sufficient and substantially existent. It is from this viewpoint—because it arises from the grasping at inherent existence that is based on many incorrect reasonings—that the Prasangika say the grasping at a person as self-sufficient and substantially existent as asserted by the Svatantrikas is an acquired grasping.

To describe this in a different way, the lower schools say a self-sufficient, substantially existent person would have discordant characteristics from the aggregates—that is, it would be a different entity from the aggregates. Prasangikas say seeing the person as a different entity from the aggregates is an acquired grasping, not an innate one.

In this chapter we have inquired what a person is and seen that a person depends on his or her aggregates—the body and mind. Given this nature of dependence, the person cannot be a permanent, unitary, independent self or a self-sufficient, substantially existent person. Having negated these two alternatives, in the next chapter we'll explore the possibility of the person being inherently existent and will also investigate what the various Buddhist tenet schools assert to be the person that circles in samsara and attains nirvana.

CHAPTER SIX

Searching for the Person

THE BASIS OF DESIGNATION AND THE DESIGNATED OBJECT

When we study emptiness and dependent arising, the terms *basis of designation* and *designated object* appear often. The basis of designation, or basis of imputation, is the basis upon which a label or name is given. It is the basis to which the name of an object refers. The designated object is the object designated in dependence on its basis of designation. For example, in dependence on the collection of car parts arranged in a particular way, we label "car" and the car exists. The designated object is the car, and the car parts arranged in a certain way are the basis of designation. While the basis of designation and the designated object depend on each other, they are not exactly the same. If we try to find what the name "car" refers to within its basis of designation, we cannot find anything that we can isolate and point to as being the car.

In terms of the person, the person is the designated object, and the aggregates are the basis of designation. That is, the aggregates are the basis in dependence on which the name "person" or "I" is imputed. They are what the name "person" refers to. While the various Buddhist tenet systems have different ideas about exactly what "I" refers to, generally speaking they agree that when we say that the aggregates are the basis of designation of the person, it means that by the aggregates appearing to us, we can identify a person. We sometimes recognize the person by hearing his voice or by seeing his face, back, or hands. Without any of the aggregates appearing, there is no way to know a person is there. Thus the aggregates are considered the basis of designation of the person; they are the basis depending on which the person is imputed.

CHART: ILLUSTRATION OF THE PERSON

School	Illustration of the person
Many non-Buddhist schools	Permanent, unitary, and independent person that is separate from the aggregates
Vaibhashika	• Five aggregates • Consciousness aggregate • Inexpressible as either one or separate from aggregates
Sautrantika Following Scripture	Continuum of the aggregates
Sautrantika Following Reasoning	Mental consciousness
Chittamatra Following Scripture	Foundation consciousness
Chittamatra Following Reasoning	Mental consciousness
Sautrantika-Svatantrika-Madhyamaka	Subtle, neutral mental consciousness
Yogachara-Svatantrika-Madhyamaka	Continuum of mental consciousness
Prasangika-Madhyamaka	Mere I

AN INHERENTLY EXISTENT PERSON CAN'T BE FOUND

Previously we mentioned three wrong conceptions or wrong ways of grasping the person: grasping (1) a permanent, unitary, and independent person, (2) a self-sufficient, substantially existent person, and (3) an inherently existent person. Having explored the first two, we now arrive at the third, the subtlest object of negation in relation to the person—a self-existent or inherently existent person that can be found among the aggregates.

While the lower schools all posit a person who is findable when searched for within the aggregates, the Prasangikas alone say this is not possible. What does it mean to say that the person cannot be found when we search for it? After all, there are many people in this room, and if someone asks, "Where is Susan?" we can point to her right over there.

In understanding what inherent existence and its emptiness would be in terms of the person, it is helpful to first do this in terms of a physical object. Let's take a microphone as an example. The microphone exists. It is something we use in various ways: We bring it here, take it there, turn it off and on. But when we inquire what the microphone is and try to pinpoint a microphone within its parts, it is difficult to isolate something that is it. Is the microphone the top part? The bottom part? Is it the plastic or the metal? When we look beyond the superficial appearance of the microphone, we cannot find one part to identify as the real microphone. And there certainly isn't a microphone that exists separate from its parts.

Yet still the microphone can be used to make my voice louder. The microphone exists: We can buy it and sell it; it can break and get fixed. But when we look within its parts and ask, "What is the real microphone?" there is nothing we can point to as being the microphone. We find ourselves having to accept that the microphone is merely labeled in dependence on the assembly of its parts.

Similarly, a person exists. A person is born, dies, experiences happiness and suffering—the person exists in life after life in cyclic existence. But if we ask, "What is the person that does all these activities?" the Prasangikas say that, upon analysis, there is nothing we can point to as being the person. We cannot find anything that is a real person that continues from life to life. We are left with the conclusion that the I is empty of inherent existence.

At the same time the person is empty of inherent existence, the person still exists. What is the person that exists but is empty? It is the mere I. The mere I is the person that exists by being merely imputed by name and concept. It's nothing more or less than that. It exists, and yet when we search with ultimate analysis to find it, we cannot.

Prasangikas assert that when we search within the parts, we won't be able to find anything that exists from the side of the object. We cannot pinpoint a person existing from the side of the five aggregates. There is no person that is the aggregates. There is no person in the aggregates. There is no person that possesses the aggregates. Nor is there a person that is possessed by the aggregates. And there is no person separate from the aggregates either.

When we say that the person can't be found, do not understand it in the conventional sense. In our normal, daily life, we ask, "Where is John?" and someone points to the person on the chair across the room. Conventionally, we find John sitting on the chair. But if we were to say this is what is meant by searching for the person, someone could legitimately think it ridiculous, because anybody can see that there are people here in this room. On the superficial, everyday, nonanalytical level, there are teachers, students, monastics, and laypeople in a room together.

But that is not what is meant here. Here we are looking at the basis of designation—the basis upon which we designate or impute "person"—and inquiring, "What are we pointing to as being the real person? What does the word *person* refer to?" When we look within that basis—the five aggregates—and search for what the label "person" or "I" refers to, we will not find something that is the person. That's what is meant when we say, "You can't find the person."

Because this is a difficult concept to understand, I'll give another example. If I tell you that this clock on the table can't be found if you search for it, you will say, "That is absolute nonsense, because anybody can see that this clock can be found on the table. You can see it there!" That's not the kind of unfindability we are talking about. Here "not findable" means that when we look within the parts, when we search in the basis that we use the name "clock" to refer to, can we pinpoint something that is the clock? No, we cannot identify anything as being the clock. Here "unfindable" means that we cannot find the clock when we look within the basis of designation of the term "clock."

Previously I warned that misunderstanding the meaning of emptiness and selflessness can be dangerous. For example, if we think that since we cannot find the person when we search in its basis of designation, the clock does not exist at all, we fall to the extreme of nihilism. Thinking that the person is totally nonexistent because it cannot be found under analysis is incorrect. In that case, we think emptiness means that nothing exists. If that is so, then karma and its results do not exist, the Three Jewels do not exist, nothing exists. That is a very dangerous way to think. So please be careful and do not misunderstand emptiness to mean total nonexistence. Things exist and function on the level of appearances. It is only when we analyze to try to find what exactly the name of the object refers to that it eludes us.

The Illustration of the Person

Each of the four major Buddhist tenet systems posits a different idea of the nature of the person. They have arrived at these conclusions after a great deal of analysis and investigation. Their conclusions about the nature of the person are not whimsical, offhand statements but well thought-out propositions. Each Buddhist school seeks to eliminate grasping at a hypothetical person that sentient beings erroneously grasp as existent. In doing so, each school arrives at what it considers to be the ultimate nature of the person. Having done that, the question still remains, "What is the person who sometimes engages in destructive actions and as a result experiences suffering, the person who sometimes engages in constructive actions and experiences happiness, the person who goes from birth to birth, who creates karma and experiences the results, the person who renounces cyclic existence, practices the path, and attains liberation?" While all of the Buddhist schools agree that the person is related to the five aggregates, they do not all agree on just what is the person.

In exploring this topic, we encounter the expression the "illustration or example of the person." The use of the term *illustration* is clear in the context of the three: definiendum (the object that is defined), definition, and illustration. For example, impermanence is a definiendum, its definition is "momentary," and an illustration of something that is impermanent is a jug. Similarly, the person is a definiendum, "the (mere) I imputed depending on the four or five aggregates" is its definition, and an illustration would be me, my mother, a teacher, a dog, a monastic, a god, a hell being, and so on. While these are illustrations or examples of a person, here our interest lies in the illustration of the person that cycles in samsara, practices the path, and attains liberation. Each tenet system has its own ideas about what is the illustration of this person that continues from one life to the next and on to liberation.

Among Vaibhashikas, some say the five aggregates are the illustration of the person. Others say the fifth aggregate, consciousness, is the illustration of the person. Some other Vaibhashikas say that the person can't be expressed as permanent or impermanent or as one with the aggregates or separate from the aggregates.

Most Sautrantikas conclude that the mental consciousness is the illustration of the person. However, "Sautrantikas Following Scripture"[21] say that the continuum of the aggregates is the illustration of the person.

"Chittamatrins Following Scripture" have a different idea. They accept eight consciousnesses—the five sense consciousnesses and the mental consciousness accepted by the other systems plus an afflicted consciousness and a foundation consciousness where all the karmic seeds are stored until they ripen. Chittamatrins assert that the foundation consciousness is the illustration of the person.

Within the Madhyamaka system, the Svatantrikas say a subtle, neutral mental consciousness is the illustration of the person. Bhavaviveka states this in his *Blaze of Reasoning* (*Tarkajvala*).

Each school from the Vaibhashikas up to the Svatantrikas finds the person when searching for the person within the five aggregates. In brief, each tenet system except for the Prasangika says that to identify the illustration of the person we must look for it within the five aggregates and that it is found when sought among the five aggregates, which are the basis of designation of the person. However, what the systems find as the person differs. They say, "The mental consciousness, collection of the aggregates, foundation consciousness is the illustration of the person. It is what we find when we look for the person in its basis of designation. This is the person who cycles in cyclic existence, who creates karma and experiences its effects, and who attains liberation." By saying this, they all say that the person exists from its own side.

The Prasangikas have a different idea. They say that when you look for the person in the aggregates, you don't find anything. If you were able to find the person within the aggregates, that would mean that the person would exist from its own side. If it existed from its own side, it would be self-existent. But this mind that thinks the person is self-existent is the root of cyclic existence! It is the ignorance that has kept us trapped in cyclic existence from beginningless time. Therefore, the Prasangikas insist that when you search for the person who cycles in cyclic existence and who attains liberation, you cannot find it. You cannot identify something that definitely is the person.

As we've seen, each tenet system posits that whatever it asserts to be the person is what goes from life to life, accumulates karma, experiences the resultant rebirths, and so forth. To the Vaibhashikas who assert that the five aggregates are the illustration of person, the Prasangikas say, "If that were so, then all five aggregates accumulate virtuous and nonvirtuous karma, experience happiness and suffering as a result. This is because whatever arising or perishing the person experiences, the aggregates must also experience. That is, if the person goes from one life to the next, the body must go to the next life too. That is the consequence of saying that the five aggregates are the person. Likewise, if the body perishes, the self must as well. In that case, there would be no person to continue to the next life and experience the result of his or her karma." These are the contradictions the Prasangikas point out in the Vaibhashika position.

The Prasangikas say that once the person is asserted to be self-existent, many unacceptable consequences inevitably follow, such as the person being independent of any causes and conditions or the person being permanent. By pointing out these faulty consequences that result from identifying the person among the aggregates, they refute a person that is self-existent.

In contrast to each of the lower schools that posit something among the aggregates to be the person, the Prasangikas say *the mere I* is the illustration of the person. That is, the mere I is what creates karma, experiences its results, circles in cyclic existence, and attains liberation. The mere I—the I that exists by being merely labeled by name and concept in dependence on the aggregates—is what does all this. But what kind of I is that? There is nothing to hold on to.

To avoid this seeming nihilism, Svatantrikas say the continuity of the mental consciousness is the person. At first glance, this seems quite convincing, because it is the mental consciousness that goes from life to life. When we talk about the person creating positive karma, leaving that life and that body behind, going on to a new life, taking on a new body, and experiencing the results of the previous actions—the mental consciousness is what is actually doing all that. Therefore the continuity of the mental consciousness, which is the illustration of the person, is what goes from one life to the next. This continuity of the mental consciousness is always present; it is able to "hold everything together" so that the karma created in one life is experienced by the same person in the next life. In other words, faced by the questions, "What carries the karmic latencies from one lifetime to the next so that the person who did the actions experiences the results?" the Svatantrikas reply, "The continuity or stream of the mental consciousness."

The Prasangikas totally disagree with this, saying that if we look for something to point to that is definitely the person, we are not able to find anything. If we insist that there is something that is the person, we are grasping at an inherently existent self, which is precisely what the Buddha said does not exist. For this reason the Prasangikas say that everything is mere name, mere label, and mere imputation by conception.

The Illustration of the Person, the Mere I, and the Continuity of Mental Consciousness

Why do the Prasangikas say the mere I is the illustration of the person? To make the point that the person is not found when searched for in the aggregates. The *mere* in "mere I" negates the same thing that is negated when we say "merely imputed by conception" and "merely labeled"; it negates existing from its own side. Saying that the mere I is the person eliminates any of the aggregates being the person. It gives the idea that the person is not findable among the aggregates. Nevertheless, the mere I and the person are one nature because the mere I is the illustration of person.

The mere I is the I that is merely imputed in dependence on the continuity of the mental consciousness[22] because the mental consciousness is what goes from life to life and to enlightenment. The Prasangikas say that what the mere I *refers to* is the continuity of the mental consciousness. This is very different from the other schools that say that the continuity of the mental consciousness *is* the illustration of the person, because those systems also assert that when you search for the person in the aggregates, you find the continuity of the mental consciousness. It is in the context of searching for the person in the aggregates and finding the continuity of the mental consciousness that they claim the continuity of the mental consciousness to be the illustration of the person. The Prasangikas do not agree; they maintain that when you search for the person in the aggregates, you cannot find anything that is the person. Thus while they say that what the mere I *refers to* is the continuity of the mental consciousness, they do *not* say that the continuity of the mental consciousness *is* the illustration of the person.

The mere I is the illustration of the person, and the basis of imputation of the mere I is the continuity of the mental consciousness, which changes moment by moment. The continuity of the mental consciousness acts as the basis upon which the karmic seeds are deposited. When that continuity of consciousness is purified, it becomes the omniscient mind of a buddha, and the person becomes an arya buddha.

This is very difficult to understand. I myself found it very confusing, but listening to His Holiness the Dalai Lama's teachings many times has made it clearer. I would like to review this point to help you understand. The continuity of the mental consciousness is the basis of designation of the mere I, or to say it in another way, the mere I is labeled in dependence on the continuity of mental consciousness. The mere I is the illustration of the person, and *mere I* refers to the continuity of mental consciousness. However, the continuity of mental consciousness is not the person, although it is the basis of designation of the person.

The continuity of mental consciousness is called the *mere I*. This means that referring to the continuity of the mental consciousness, we can say, "This is the mere I." But someone might object, saying, "Wait a minute! If the continuity of the mental consciousness is the mere I, then you're saying the mere I is findable under analysis; that when you search for the mere I, you find the continuity of the mental consciousness."

No, the mere I is not findable under analysis. When we say, "The continuity of the mental consciousness is the mere I," we are using ordinary speech, not philosophical language. For example, in ordinary speech, a person may say, "*I am* Jennifer." However, to be precise in philosophical language, she would say, "*My name is* Jennifer." Similarly, in everyday conventional language she may say "I am a monastic" and "I am a human being." If someone protests and says, "You can't say you *are* a human being!" then she might respond, "If I'm not a human being, which of the six types of sentient beings am I?" If she couldn't say, "I am a human being," she would be going against Chandrakirti's axiom, "Don't lose worldly conventions."

To give another example: As Buddhist philosophers, we say, "That yellow thing is a flower" in accordance with worldly convention, even though there is nothing in that yellow thing that is a flower. Even though the basis of designation (the yellow thing) and the designated object (the flower) are not the same when we analyze, when we speak according to nonanalytical worldly conventions, we can say that and people will understand what we mean. Otherwise, if we always spoke in philosophical language searching for the imputed object, people would get really fed up with us!

These differences are subtle and we need to think well about them to understand. Initially it may seem to be just semantics, but actually there is deep meaning.

Now we can understand the meaning of the definition of the person as the Prasangikas interpret it. In that definition, the collection of the aggregates is the basis of imputation of the mere I, and the mere I is imputed in dependence on that.[23]

In summary, the person is designated in dependence on the five aggregates in the case of beings in the desire and form realms or on four aggregates in the case of beings in the formless realm. When the aggregates of a particular person appear as an object to the mind, the person is designated in dependence on the aggregates. For example, when we see someone's body approaching, we think, "Susan is coming." When we hear someone's voice, we say, "Fred is talking."

When speaking of the person that goes from one life to another, the continuity of the mental consciousness is the basis of designation of the person. The mental consciousness is what the term *I* refers to. However, the mental consciousness is not the person. Remember, the basis of designation and the designated object are not the same thing, so the basis of designation of the person is not the person. If it were, when we searched for the person in the aggregates that were its basis of designation, we would find something that could be identified as the real person. However, no person is found when searched for in the aggregates.

The General I and the Specific I

When we speak of a person, we talk about the general I and the specific I. When we say, "The person is what goes from life to life," we are referring to the general person or the general I. This is the person that is merely imputed in dependence on the aggregates in general. This general I does indeed go from life to life, but not all instances or specific examples of the person go from one life to the next. For example, the person of the past life did not carry on to this life. It ceased at the end of that life. And the person of this life will not go on to the next life. It will cease at the end of this life. But the continuity of the "person that pervades all our lives, past, present, and future" does go on to the next life and to enlightenment, even though there is nothing that can be identified either in the aggregates or separate from them as being this person.

If the person goes from one life to the next, why can't we say the person of the previous life goes to this life? Let's say someone was reborn as a human being named John who lived in England in his previous life. John died and that person's next life is Margaret who lives in the United States. We can't say that John is Margaret, can we? The person called John ceased when he died in England, and a new person, Margaret, was born in the U.S. While not being the same, these two persons are not totally unrelated. They exist in the same continuity. That continuity is the general I that goes from life to life. John and Margaret and all the other lives that general I has ever lived and will ever live are instances of the general I.

Thus the continuity of the person carries on from the past life to this life, although the specific person of the past life ceased and does not carry on to this life. This means that the person of the past life finished at the end of the past life. But the person at the very last moment of the previous life was the main cause for the first moment of the intermediate state being that followed. After the intermediate state being ceased, the person of this life was born.

Normally we would say, "I died, I entered the intermediate state, and then I was reborn." The I that we refer to in this case is the general I. The Buddha himself said, "In a previous life, I was King So-and-so." It is correct to say this. Similarly, since we have been born with precious human lives, we can validly say, "In a past life I must have engaged in virtue, and that is why I have a precious human life in this rebirth." In both cases, we are speaking about the general I.

However, it would not be correct to say, "That animal is now a human being," because the specific I that was an animal ceased at the end of the previous life and a specific I that is a human being is born this life. These two specific I's are different even though they belong to the same continuum and are instances of the same general I.

From the Prasangika viewpoint, the conventional I, the mere I, and the aggregates that are its basis of designation are one entity, although the aggregates are not the self, and the self is not findable within the aggregates. The aggregates of this life and the self of this life are one entity, but the aggregates of this life and the general I are not one entity, because if they were, when the aggregates of this life ceased when the body died, the self would also cease. However, this is not the case. The mere I—which is empty of inherent existence—continues to the next life.

CHAPTER SEVEN

Investigating the I

IGNORANCE AND WISDOM

Wisdom is the antidote for overcoming our mental afflictions. To overcome the afflictions, we must understand their nature and functions, as well as the nature and functions of wisdom. We need to know how things appear to ignorance and how they appear to wisdom—how ignorance grasps things to exist and how wisdom apprehends them to exist. This is vital in order to conclude that ignorance is mistaken and that nothing exists in the way ignorance believes it does.

In *Engaging in the Bodhisattva's Conduct*, Shantideva says that when it comes to meditating on emptiness, if we don't understand precisely what to negate, we will make mistakes. Our meditation on emptiness might take the form of negating something that in fact exists. We have to have an idea of how ignorance grasps the person so that we will know what to look for or all this analysis will not make sense and could lead us astray.

To avoid this fault, let's now determine exactly how ignorance and the wisdom realizing emptiness apprehend phenomena. Both of them refer to the same object; the focal object of those two minds is the same. However, the way they grasp or apprehend that object is different. Ignorance grasps it as truly existent while wisdom apprehends it as empty of true existence.

The person that is referred to by both ignorance and wisdom—the person who is the focal object of both these minds—is the self, the person, the I, and the being. These four terms are synonymous and indicate the conventionally existent person.

The Valid I-Apprehending Mind
and the Erroneous I-Grasping Mind

As in English, many Tibetan words have multiple meanings. This is true of the word *dzin* (*'dzin*). In relation to cognition, it can mean "to apprehend" or "to grasp." In terms of our discussion about the nature of the person, we will use these two English words to distinguish between a valid mind *apprehending* the I and a mind erroneously *grasping* the I as inherently existent. The valid conventional mind that apprehends the conventionally existing I is the mind that thinks, "I'm coming, I'm going. I'm eating. I'm practicing Dharma." The erroneous mind that incorrectly grasps the I as inherently existent keeps us bound in cyclic existence and is therefore extremely harmful. It has both innate and acquired forms; the innate I-grasping has been in our mindstream since beginningless time, while the acquired I-grasping is learned by studying erroneous ideas in this life.

The valid I-apprehending mind is not erroneous. It is a valid mind because there is an I that is the agent of actions; there is an I that comes here and goes there, an I that is reborn in this realm and goes to that realm after death. This I-apprehending mind apprehends the I that exists, whereas the innate I-grasping mind grasps a truly existent I that does not exist at all. The former is a valid mind, the latter is erroneous and distorted.

In what order do the valid I-apprehending mind and the erroneous I-grasping mind arise? Before answering this, I'd like to clarify that when I say "arise" or "occur" here, I mean "become manifest." Both of these minds can exist in the mind in a dormant state without being manifest in the mind. Therefore, the question actually is: Does the manifest I-apprehending mind or the manifest I-grasping mind arise first?

Here is the sequence of how the I-apprehending and the I-grasping manifest according to the Prasangika system. First the aggregates, which are the basis of designation of I, appear to our minds. The aggregates are a valid basis of designation of I, and in dependence on them we impute I. As soon as the I is imputed, the I-apprehending mind arises; its object is the mere I that exists by being merely labeled in dependence on the continuity of the aggregates or in dependence on the aggregates. It is a valid mind. After that, in some but not all cases, the I-grasping mind will arise.

To both the valid I-apprehending mind and the erroneous I-grasping mind, the I appears to exist from its own side. But the valid mind does not think the I is inherently existent, even though that is how it appears. It does not assent to or agree with that appearance, although it does not disagree with or refute it either. However, in the case of the I-grasping mind, not only does the I appear as if it exists from its own side and exists inherently, but that mind also thinks there is an inherently existing I. It believes that the appearance of an inherently existent I is true; it assents to and agrees with that appearance, and thus it grasps at an inherently existing I.

In the case of us ordinary sentient beings, sometimes it seems that the afflictive I-grasping mind leads to anger without the valid I-apprehending mind arising first. This is a false impression. In this case, the valid I-apprehending mind lasts only a moment, and the innate I-grasping follows very quickly afterward. For example, while Jim is sitting in a relaxing place and reading a book, he thinks simply, "I'm reading." At this time, the valid I-apprehending mind is manifest, as it often is due to habit or latencies. The afflictive I-grasping mind has not arisen.

Then suddenly something happens—someone walks in and insults him or strikes him. Initially, there is a moment of the valid I-apprehending mind, but it is followed very quickly by the innate I-grasping. Now the I not only appears inherently existent, but Jim also grasps it as inherently existent. Then, due to habit and latencies, he gets angry.

Due to beginningless obscurations, everything that appears to us sentient beings always appears as inherently existent. There is not one occasion—except for an arya's meditative equipoise on emptiness—in which something appears to a sentient being's mind in any other way. All these minds are mistaken because, although inherent existence appears to them, inherent existence does not exist. In addition, we often assent to this appearance of inherent existence and grasp the object to exist inherently. We have both the appearance of inherent existence as well as the grasping at inherent existence.

To the arya's meditative equipoise on emptiness that knows emptiness nonconceptually, there is no appearance of inherent existence, and that mind does not grasp inherent existence. In fact, that mind actively negates inherent existence and thus directly sees the emptiness of inherent existence. When aryas arise from their meditative equipoise on emptiness, the things they see in their daily lives still appear inherently existent to them, but because they have perceived the emptiness of inherent existence directly, they don't believe that appearance. They know it is false. Therefore,

I-grasping seldom manifests in their minds, and by the eighth ground, when they have abandoned the last of the afflicted obscurations, it has been totally eliminated.

Let's take the example of a reflection of a face in a mirror. When small children and adults look in the mirror, there is the appearance of a face. Small children believe that appearance to be true. They think there is another child in the mirror, and they reach out to touch her and play with her. Although a face appears to an adult in a similar way, we don't believe that appearance. We don't think another person is really there.

Similarly, sentient beings who have not realized emptiness have both the appearance of inherent existence and the grasping at inherent existence. They accept that appearance as true, just like the small children accept the appearance of another child in the mirror as true. However, when aryas encounter objects in their daily lives while they are not in meditative equipoise on emptiness, although those things appear inherently existent they do not believe that appearance. They know it is false and that things do not exist from their own side. Thus they do not grasp at inherent existence and instead see things as existing like illusions in that they appear one way (i.e., as inherently existent) but exist in another way (i.e., as empty of inherent existence). While aryas are in meditative equipoise on emptiness, there is neither the appearance of inherent existence nor the grasping at inherent existence.

Realizing emptiness does not immediately eradicate the grasping at inherent existence from an arya's mindstream. This takes time. Thus until bodhisattvas reach the eighth ground and have abandoned the last of the afflictive obscurations, the I-grasping mind is in their continuum, even though it seldom manifests due to the speed at which they apply the antidote to it by reflecting on emptiness.

The bodhisattvas on the eighth, ninth, and tenth grounds no longer have the afflictive obscurations and thus no longer grasp phenomena as inherently existent. Nevertheless, in their daily lives, things still appear inherently existent to them. That is because they still have cognitive obscurations, of which the appearance of inherent existence is one. Nevertheless, these high bodhisattvas effortlessly recognize the appearance to be false and see things to be like illusions. For them, all appearances are like reflections in a mirror.

In summary, the focal object of both the valid I-apprehending mind and the erroneous I-grasping mind is the conventional I. This I appears as inherently existent to both of those minds. Although I-grasping is not always manifest in the mindstreams of ordinary beings, when it does arise, it follows the appearance of the continuity of the aggregates that is the basis of designation of the mere I. Depending upon that appearance, the valid I-apprehending mind arises. The I appears to that mind as if it were inherently existent, although it is not. But the valid I-apprehending mind does not grasp the I as inherently existent. Later, when triggered by an external or internal event, the mind grasping an inherently existent I manifests. This I-grasping thinks the I exists inherently, just as it appears. This is analogous to a child thinking that the face in the mirror is a real face and trying to touch it.

However, in the minds of those who haven't realized emptiness, I-grasping does not immediately follow all perceptions. In many of our daily perceptions, the valid I-apprehending mind is manifest, but the I-grasping mind only follows when it is triggered.

Valid and Mistaken, but Not Erroneous

To proceed in our discussion, it will be helpful for you to understand the different types of objects a consciousness may have. Every consciousness has a *focal object*, which is the main object that the consciousness is concerned with. The *appearing object* (*snang yul*) is the object appearing to that consciousness, and the *apprehended object* (*'dzin btangs kyi yul*) is the object the mind apprehends or grasps.

While the I-apprehending mind does indeed apprehend an I that appears inherently existent, this does not prevent it from being a valid mind. This is because the I that it apprehends does in fact exist. Being a valid mind, it is incontrovertible or infallible with respect to its *apprehended object*, which in this case is the conventional I. However, it is *mistaken* with respect to its *appearing object*. That is, its focal object—the I—appears inherently existent even though it is not. Because the conventional I (the focal object and the apprehended object) appears to exist inherently (the appearing object) although it does not exist inherently, this valid I-apprehending mind is mistaken. However, the valid I-apprehending mind does not *grasp* the I as inherently existent, and therefore it is incontrovertible. It knows a person is there. Thus we say the I-apprehending mind is "mistaken with respect to its appearing object" because the I appears inherently existent although it is not. But it is "valid with respect to its apprehended object"—the I—because it apprehends it without grasping it to be inherently existent.

In other words, even though the valid mind does not grasp the I as inherently existent, the I that is the focal object of that mind appears as if it were inherently existent. That appearance is mistaken, and for that reason, that mind is said to be mistaken, even though it is not *erroneous* in the sense of grasping the I to exist in the wrong way.

Mistaken and *erroneous* have different meanings and are determined in terms of different objects of a mind. A mind is mistaken with respect to its appearing object because that object appears inherently existent. However, it is not erroneous, because it can still know a person or a flower is there. A mind is erroneous with respect to its apprehended object when it apprehends that object in a wrong manner. A coarse example is apprehending a mannequin to be a person; a subtler example is grasping something that is not inherently existent as inherently existent.

The valid I-apprehending mind is incontrovertible with respect to its apprehended object because even though the conventionally existent I appears inherently existent, it does not believe or grasp at the I as existing inherently. It just apprehends the I, without assenting to that appearance of it being truly existent. However, it is mistaken with respect to the appearing object because that mere I appears inherently existent.

The I-grasping mind, on the other hand, is both mistaken and erroneous. Let's say the innate I-grasping mind is activated. It is *mistaken* with respect to its appearing object because the I appears to be inherently existent although it is not. It is also *erroneous* with respect to its apprehended object because it grasps the I to be inherently existent. Due to its grasping the I as inherently existent, other afflictions arise, karma is created, and we wander in cyclic existence without end. The valid I-apprehending mind does not have those undesirable effects.

To a person who has realized emptiness by means of a valid inference, things still appear inherently existent, but in general she does not grasp them as existing as they appear.[24] In other words, she does not believe that appearance. She does not think and grasp that things are inherently existent as they appear to be. Thus her mind is mistaken with respect to the appearing object, because things still appear inherently existent. But it is incontrovertible with respect to the apprehended object because she does not grasp it to be inherently existent.

Remember the example of the reflection in the mirror. We know that even though a face appears to be in the mirror, there isn't a face in the mirror. We know that it is just a reflection of our face, not a real face. It is a false appearance. Likewise, those people who have a valid inferential realization of emptiness have the appearance of inherent existence, but they don't believe that appearance. They know it is false and do not assent to it. They do not grasp things to inherently exist as they appear.

In summary, there are three different sorts of minds, with respect to the I:

1. The valid I-apprehending mind that is incontrovertible with respect to its apprehended object but is mistaken with respect to its appearing object. The I appears inherently existent to this mind, but it does not grasp the I to be inherently existent. However, it does not know the appearance of inherent existence is false.

2. The innate I-grasping mind that is erroneous with respect to its apprehended object and is mistaken with respect to its appearing object. An inherently existent I appears to this mind, and it grasps that appearance to be true: it grasps inherent existence.

3. The daily-life perceptions of someone who has realized emptiness. This mind is mistaken with respect to its appearing object because the I appears inherently existent. However, it is incontrovertible with respect to its apprehended object because it apprehends the I without grasping it as inherently existent. In addition, it knows the appearance of inherent existence to be false and does not believe it.

Above, the focal object is I, but it could be any phenomenon. These three different possibilities of cognition occur for anything.

THE SELF THAT EXISTS AND THE SELF THAT DOESN'T

According to Prasangikas, "to exist" means "to exist conventionally," "to exist nominally," and "to exist as mere imputation." This is the only type of existence possible. Something that exists is not findable under ultimate analysis, because if it were findable, it would exist from its own side, exist ultimately, exist truly, and exist inherently, and it is not possible for anything

CHART: I-APPREHENDING AND I-GRASPING MINDS AND THEIR OBJECTS

	Focal object	In relation to the appearing object	In relation to the apprehended object
I-apprehending mind	I	The mind is mistaken because the I appears inherently existent.	I; this mind is valid but does not know the appearance of inherent existence is false.
I-grasping mind	I	The mind is mistaken because the I appears inherently existent.	This mind is erroneous because it grasps the I to exist inherently.
I-apprehending mind in continuum of someone who has realized emptiness	I	The mind is mistaken because the I appears inherently existent.	I; this mind is valid and knows the appearance of inherent existence is false.

to exist in those ways. Therefore all phenomena exist conventionally and nothing exists ultimately. For this reason, the self that exists is the conventional self.

The self that does exist is the focal object for both the true-grasping mind (grasping at true existence) and the wisdom realizing selflessness. The self that does not exist is the one referred to when we say, "There is no self." The Sanskrit term *anatman* means "no self" or "selfless." It is a term that negates the existence of a false self that has never existed. The self whose existence is being denied is not the conventionally existent one; it is a truly existing self. Such a self is believed to exist by the true-grasping mind, whereas in fact it does not exist. This is the object of negation in our analysis.

The mere I—the conventionally existing I—is the one that exists. This I walks, talks, eats, takes rebirth in samsara, practices the path, and attains enlightenment.

This I contrasts with the I that does not exist, a truly existent self. The self that does not exist is sometimes referred to as "the aspect I" or the "I that is the aspect of the mode of apprehension of the self-grasping mind." This means that the self-grasping mind refers to the person that exists but grasps it as truly existent.

The distinction between the I that is the focal object and exists and the I that is the aspect object and does not exist applies in all three levels of the self of persons. For example, if we apply this to the coarsest level of self, a permanent, unitary, and independent self, the self-grasping mind focuses on the conventional I and believes it to be permanent, unitary, and independent. Such a permanent, unitary, and independent person doesn't exist at all. That is the aspect I, the person that is the aspect of the mode of apprehension of the self-grasping mind grasping a permanent, unitary, and independent self. We can't say it is the focal object of that mind or the apprehended object (also called the object of the mode of apprehension) of that mind because such a self does not exist.[25] An object of mind has to exist, but because this one doesn't, it is called "the aspect of the mode of apprehension of that mind."

In your experience, try to distinguish between the person that is the focal object—the one that exists conventionally—and the person that is the aspect of the mode of apprehension of ignorance, which does not exist. For example, observe the sense of I when you are sitting peacefully. Then observe it when someone criticizes you unfairly. There is a difference in the way you experience the I. Try to keep the difference between the two in mind as we continue, because it is an important distinction: One is valid and the other is the object to be negated.

INDEPENDENCE AND IMPUTATION

Let's return once more to the meaning of *independence* since this word occurs frequently when we speak of the object of negation in the meditation on selflessness. Three levels of independence have been negated in the three types of selflessness mentioned so far:

1. The lack of a permanent, unitary, and independent person. Here *independence* means "independent of causes and conditions." To negate this type of independence, we realize that the person depends on and is a product of causes and conditions. When the causes and conditions are present, the person comes into being; when the causes and conditions cease or do not exist, the person ceases or does not exist.

2. The lack of a self-sufficient, substantially existent person. In this context *self-sufficient* means "independent from the aggregates."

To refute this, we realize not just that the person is dependent on causes and conditions but that the person depends on the aggregates that are its basis of designation.

3. The lack of an inherently existent person. In this context *inherent existence* means "independent of all other factors," including name and concept.[26]

A difference exists in subtlety between depending on causes and conditions in general and depending on the aggregates in particular. These are the two kinds of dependence that are the opposite of the first two kinds of independence. There is also a difference in subtlety between those two on the one hand and dependence on name and concept on the other.

What does it mean for the person to depend on the aggregates? Most Buddhist philosophical systems say not only that the person depends upon the aggregates but also that it is findable within the aggregates. They refute the existence of a person who is independent of the aggregates. The Chittamatrins specifically assert that the person depends on the foundation consciousness, and they identify the foundation consciousness as the illustration of the person. That is what the person is, according to them. Those who assert that the continuity of consciousness is the illustration of the person say that the person depends on the continuity of consciousness.

All Buddhist systems say the person is an imputed existent. However, in the eyes of those who say that the mental consciousness is the person, saying that the person is imputedly existent does not conflict with their assertion that the mental consciousness itself is substantially existent. That is because they define an object being imputedly existent as not being recognizable without the appearance of something else—such as the parts—to the mind. This is the case with the person: We can only recognize a person when his or her aggregates appear to us. The mind, on the other hand, is considered substantially existent because it can be known without something else appearing.

The Prasangikas disagree and say that nothing is substantially existent. They accept that the person depends upon the aggregates, but they do not take that further step and say it is findable within the aggregates. In fact, they emphatically insist that the person cannot be found within the aggregates. They say instead that the person is merely imputed or designated in dependence on the aggregates. Following the appearance of the aggregates, "person" is merely designated without analyzing. That is, the person is not posited by searching for the imputed object in its basis of designation; the person is not posited after being found in the aggregates.

This does not mean that everything that appears to us necessarily exists, just that conventionally existing objects are posited without analyzing to see if they are findable in their bases of designation. In other words, things exist on the level of appearance without analyzing or searching for them in the basis of designation. This doesn't mean that no analysis whatsoever is done, because Prasangikas would still investigate to see if the figure over there is a person or a mannequin.

We've already discussed that just because something is not findable under analysis, it doesn't mean that it doesn't exist. We know very well that we have friends and acquaintances. They exist. If you speak to them, they will answer. They come and go. However, if we analyze, looking for just exactly who or what is Catherine in her body and mind, we cannot find something to isolate and say, "For sure, this is Catherine."

When we look for a person, or any object for that matter, searching within its basis of designation to find it, we cannot. When we seek what exactly the name refers to, we won't find anything. For that reason the Prasangikas say that nothing is findable under ultimate analysis. According to them, that lack of findability when searched for within the basis of designation is the meaning of emptiness and is the ultimate nature of reality. However, when we don't analyze, we can still posit things, use them, relate to them. That is the meaning of existing by being imputed through mere appearance without analysis, and it is the conventional nature according to the Prasangikas.

CHAPTER EIGHT

Exploring Selflessness

SELFLESSNESS IN THE FOUR SCHOOLS

We may wonder: "If the Prasangika system explains the deepest level of the actual mode of existence, why bother studying the other systems? Isn't it hard, time-consuming, and a waste of energy for both teacher and student to learn all these assertions that we then refute?"

Studying the various tenet systems has a purpose. It is done in order to lead our mind gradually to a deeper understanding of selflessness. Instead of beginning with the Prasangika, the tenet system that is most profound and difficult to understand and is the most unlike our ordinary, habitual way of looking at things, we begin with the lower schools, which are easier to understand and whose assertions are more acceptable to us beginners. Then we slowly progress to higher tenet systems. The previous highly realized masters have discerned that the Prasangika-Madhyamaka system contains the most accurate explanation of the nature of reality. We learn the others systems first in order to understand the unique qualities of the Prasangika more clearly.

A thorough grounding in the lower tenet schools will, in the long run, yield a far deeper understanding of the Prasangika system. By seeing the flaws and insufficiencies of the lower tenets for ourselves, our confidence in the Prasangika system will increase. Having said that, I will not present the beliefs of the other systems exhaustively but will explain only the central points of each one's view of reality. Knowing these, we will be able to compare them and discern which one is most accurate.

Of the four Buddhist tenet systems, two are Fundamental Vehicle schools and two are Mahayana schools. The Fundamental Vehicles schools—Vaibhashikas and Sautrantikas—are so called because their tenets mainly outline the basis, path, and result for the practitioners of the Fundamental Vehicle, who seek to become arhats. These schools assert a coarse and a subtle selflessness of the person, but they do not assert a selflessness of phenomena, because they say that there *is* a self of phenomena. Nevertheless, they accept the teaching of the four seals that all phenomena are empty and selfless. They do this by agreeing that all phenomena are selfless because they are empty of being objects of use of a self-sufficient, substantially existent person. In other words, the selflessness of the person is an attribute of everything that exists, not just the person.

The two Mahayana schools are the Chittamatra and Madhyamaka. The latter has two branches: Svatantrika and Prasangika. All of these accept a coarse and a subtle selflessness of the person. In addition they assert a selflessness of phenomena.

For Chittamatrins, the selflessness of phenomena is form (and so forth) and the valid cognizer apprehending form (and so forth) being empty of a different substance. That is, both the subject—the valid cognizer apprehending form—and the object—form—arise from the same latency on the foundation consciousness. When activated, this latency gives rise to the form and to the valid cognizer apprehending it. For example, when we perceive blue, both the blue and the mind perceiving it are produced by a latency of the foundation consciousness. When Chittamatrins say subject and object are empty of being different substances, this is what they mean. Thus Chittamatrins say there are no external objects because everything arises from latencies on the foundation consciousness.

The Chittamatrins also assert that phenomena are not naturally the basis or referent of their names; they do not exist by their own characteristics as the referent of their labels. In other words, there is nothing intrinsic to make an apple the referent of the word *apple*. It can also be called *manzana*, as it is in Spanish. If objects were naturally the basis or referent of their names, it would be impossible for one object to have many names or for one word to apply to several objects. This absence of existing by their own characteristics as the referent for their name is also the selflessness of phenomena.

All Buddhist schools except the Prasangika assert that the coarse selflessness of person is the lack of a permanent, unitary, and independent person and the subtle selflessness is the absence of a self-sufficient, substantially existent person. For the Svatantrikas, the emptiness of true existence of the person is not considered the selflessness of the person. Rather, it is the selflessness of phenomena of the person (or the selflessness of phenomena based on the person)—that is, the person's selflessness of phenomena. In other words, they say the person has both a selflessness of the person and a selflessness of phenomena.

Or to put it slightly differently, the Svatantrikas and the Prasangikas both assert the selflessness of person and the selflessness of phenomena, but the way they assert them is different. For the Svatantrikas the lack of self-sufficient, substantial existence of the person is the person's selflessness of person, and the lack of true existence of the person is the person's selflessness of phenomena. Thus there is both a selflessness of person and a selflessness of phenomena based on the person. Grasping the person as self-sufficient and substantially existent is self-grasping of person, and grasping the person as truly existent is self-grasping of phenomena. Grasping the person to exist from its own side or to exist inherently is a valid mind according to the Svatantrikas because they think that everything, including the person, exists from its own side and exists inherently. They don't see grasping at the inherent existence of persons or phenomena to be an erroneous mind; for them it is a valid cognizer.

For the Prasangikas, however, the selflessness of persons applies only to the person, and the emptiness of inherent existence of the person is the subtle selflessness of the person. Similarly, selflessness of phenomena applies only to phenomena other than persons, and it is the emptiness of inherent existence of phenomena.

The point is that for the Prasangikas the difference between the two selflessnesses is in terms of the object on which inherent existence is negated—either the person or phenomena. For the Svatantrika the difference between the two selflessnesses is in terms of the self that is negated—self-sufficient and substantially existent or truly existent. The absence of the coarser object of negation is the selflessness of persons, and the absence of the subtler object of negation is the selflessness of phenomena, whereas in Prasangika the subtlety of the object of negation in both the selflessness of persons and of phenomena is the same.

THE TWO MIDDLE WAY SCHOOLS

The Madhyamaka or Middle Way school is so called because it takes a position "in the middle," avoiding the two extremes of absolutism and nihilism. It is considered the highest philosophical system within Buddhism. It

Chart: Self—The Object of Negation

School	Coarse self of persons	Subtle self of persons	Coarse self of phenomena	Subtle self of phenomena
Vaibhashika	Permanent, unitary, and independent self	Self-sufficient, substantially existent person	—	—
Sautrantika	Permanent, unitary, and independent self	Self-sufficient, substantially existent person	—	—
Chittamatra	Permanent, unitary, and independent self	Self-sufficient, substantially existent person	—	1. Phenomena existing by their own characteristics as the referent of their names 2. Form (and so forth) and the valid cognizer apprehending form (and so forth) being different substances
Sautrantika-Svatantrika-Madhyamaka	Permanent, unitary, and independent self	Self-sufficient, substantially existent person	—	Truly existent persons and phenomena
Yogachara-Svatantrika-Madhyamaka	Permanent, unitary, and independent self	Self-sufficient, substantially existent person	Form and the valid cognizer apprehending form being different substances	Truly existent persons and phenomena
Prasangika-Madhyamaka	Self-sufficient, substantially existent person	Inherently existent person	—	Inherently existent phenomena

has two branches, the Svatantrika and the Prasangika, which disagree on some important points. Although both of them avoid the coarse extremes of absolutism and nihilism and thus avoid the gravest of errors, still they disagree on the meaning of the Middle Way.

The nature of the person in the Prasangika system, like everything else that exists, is mere name, mere designation, mere imputation by conception. Things are merely labeled from the side of the conceptual mind, without there being anything existing from the side of the object. The object does not exist by its own power at all.

The Svatantrika system, however, does not agree. Svatantrikas do not accept that phenomena are completely empty of self-existence. While they refute some levels of self-existence, they say phenomena have some self-existence in that they exist inherently on the conventional level. In other words, something is findable when we search for the imputed object within the basis of designation. For that reason, they say that the object has to exist from its own side, because finding the object when you look within the basis is the meaning of *existing from its own side*. Although they say that things lack true existence, they distinguish true existence and inherent existence, negating the former while affirming the latter on the conventional level.

While both Svatantrikas and Prasangikas say things are merely labeled, what *mere* negates in the two cases differs. For Svatantrikas *mere* negates true existence, which they define as existence without being posited by the force of appearing to a nondefective mind. For Prasangikas *mere* negates "existence from its own side," or something findable on the side of the object.

Up until now, you may have heard that only Prasangikas assert that things are mere name, mere designation, and mere imputation. That is correct if you understand that it means that the Svatantrikas do not accept that things are mere name in the same way that the Prasangikas do. When it is said that only the Prasangikas say everything is mere name, it means they are the only ones who understand *mere* as negating inherent existence and existence from its own side. However, if you don't define *mere* in that way, then it can be said that both systems assert that things are mere name or mere imputation. In this case, *mere* has a more general meaning, with the Svatantrikas explaining that *mere* eliminates true existence, while the Prasangikas say it eliminates existence from its own side.

Both the Svatantrika and Prasangika schools accept that we designate certain names onto objects. Both say that there has to be a valid basis for the designation, something that can perform the function associated with the designated name. But the Prasangikas say that valid base for designation doesn't exist from its own side and isn't findable, whereas the Svatantrikas assert that a valid base has to be found from its own side. Although the Prasangikas say that there must be a valid basis of imputation, according to them, it is wrong to say that *from the side of the object* there has to be a valid basis. That is because they say nothing in the slightest—not even a tiny atom—exists from the side of the object. If there were a valid basis of designation from the side of the object, it would be findable, and that is impossible!

In the example of desire arising for another person, the Svatantrikas say there has to be something beautiful from the side of the person. Since we don't feel desire toward everyone, there must be some attractive quality in the other person that makes us desire that one. If something is beautiful it is inherently beautiful, and its beauty can definitely be found when searched for. However, while Prasangikas agree that when "beautiful" is imputed on another person, there should be a valid basis for imputing "beautiful," they do not say there is beauty on the side of the other person, because if there were, then he or she would be inherently beautiful, and everyone would see that person as beautiful.

In fact, things do not exist from their own side. Let's take a camera as an example. If we look at each piece that makes up the camera—the lens, the knobs, the battery, and so forth—we can't find one of them that is the camera. What we talk about when we say "camera," what the word "camera" refers to, is something that can perform the function of a camera. "Camera" is merely designated in dependence on that, without there being anything findable in the basis that the word "camera" refers to.

When we don't analyze—that is, when we don't look in the basis to find what the name refers to—something is there. There is a camera that we can buy, sell, move from here to there, and use to take photos. All this can happen without there being a findable camera, without there being something in the basis that we can point to as the camera. But when we search the basis of designation, we cannot find the object. Nothing exists upon analysis. Things are empty of existing from their own side; they lack ultimate existence. But the fact that they appear and function when not analyzed indicates that they exist conventionally. These two facts are not contradictory.

In the process of negating inherent existence, it is helpful to contemplate, "What would happen if phenomena were inherently existent?" Then it becomes clear that everything would get stuck and nobody could do anything because everything would be independent of all other factors. In our lives we know that change occurs, events happen, objects are produced and destroyed, people are born and die, our social status goes up and down—in all these cases, the interaction of many factors are required. This interaction could not occur if things were independent of each other. In short, if things existed inherently, they would be permanent, static, and unable to interact and change. Clearly things are impermanent, which means they depend on causes and conditions. Since they are dependent, they cannot be independent because those two are opposite.

Both the Svatantrikas and the Prasangikas accept that what we refer to as a camera has to be a valid basis; it has to be able to perform the function of a camera. Calling a piece of wood a camera wouldn't work because that piece of wood cannot take photographs. It is not a valid basis to be labeled "camera." The Svatantrikas say that since there needs to be a valid basis from the side of the object, the camera exists from its own side. The Prasangikas, however, assert that while a valid basis for the name is required, it doesn't follow that the object exists from its own side, because *exists from its own side* means that we can find the object when we search within the basis, and that is impossible.

MERE IMPUTATION WITHOUT THE SLIGHTEST EXISTENCE FROM ITS OWN SIDE

The Svatantrikas and Prasangikas are both Madhyamikas, but when we look more deeply into their assertions, they differ considerably. The Svatantrikas say that everything exists by its own characteristics and is naturally existent, exists from its own side, and inherently exists. However, they deny true existence, ultimate existence, and existence as its own reality. The Prasangika system refutes all six of these, saying they all come down to the same point.

Svatantrikas posit that phenomena must inherently exist and exist from their own side, because otherwise they would not exist at all. They insist, for example, that there has to be something within the aggregates of a human being that we can point to as being a human being, otherwise we could point to the aggregates of a dog and call it a human being and it would be one. But that isn't possible. Why not? The Svatantrikas say because the dog doesn't have that something from its own side that qualifies it to be a human being. A human being, on the other hand, does have something from its own side that makes it a human being. For that reason, when we see the aggregates of a human being and say it is a human being, it works.

All of the Buddhist systems except the Prasangika agree that things exist from their own side. What does it mean for something "to exist from its own side"? The Svatantrikas' argument about another person being inherently attractive is pretty convincing, isn't it? When we examine our experience, we find that we don't feel attracted to just anyone. There are certain people we are attracted to and certain people we are not. This implies that those we are attracted to must have some kind of beauty, some appealing and attractive qualities from their own side, otherwise we wouldn't be attracted to them at all. There must be something wonderful from the side of the other person. Otherwise attachment would not arise.

But according to the Prasangikas, there doesn't have to be anything existing from the side of the other person at all. In fact, if we search for the beauty in the other person, we won't be able to find it. There doesn't have to be any beauty or attractive quality from the side of the other person in order for our attachment to arise toward that one. That sounds outrageous, doesn't it? On the other hand, if the attractiveness existed from the side of the other person, why doesn't everyone perceive that person in the same way? Why do some people see defects in the person who we think is so marvelous? If those fantastic qualities existed from the side of the person, everyone should see them, but they don't.

The Prasangikas respond that if even the slightest thing existed from the side of the object, the object would have to be truly existent. True existence, inherent existence, and existence from its own side are all equally subtle. For the Prasangikas, no distinction is drawn between inherent existence and true existence, while for the Svatantrikas they are different. Svatantrikas say everything exists *inherently* on the conventional level because it is findable when we look for it within its basis of designation, but nothing exists *truly* because to be truly existent for them means existing without appearing to the mind. They say everything exists through the force of appearing to the mind. True existence and ultimate existence both imply existing without having to appear to the mind, and for the Svatantrikas that is the object of negation.

For something to exist for the Svatantrikas, two factors are necessary: It must have some inherent existence that appears to a nondefective mind and it must be labeled. Why are both qualities needed? For them, if phenomena were only inherently existent, totally independent of appearing to and being labeled by mind, they would be truly existent. But if they existed only by being labeled, then anything could be labeled anything. This is the essential difference between the two systems. The Svatantrikas say that if everything were completely empty of inherent existence and merely labeled by the mind as the Prasangikas assert, there would be no difference between imputing a snake on the aggregates of a snake and imputing a snake on a coiled, striped rope. Anything could be labeled as anything because everything is merely labeled.

For Prasangikas, mere name or mere imputation does not mean that calling a rope a snake makes it one. *Mere* negates existing from its own side; it denies being findable when the basis is analyzed. A valid basis is still needed.

In his *Essence of Good Explanations Discriminating the Definitive and Provisional Meanings*, Je Tsongkhapa summarizes the Svatantrika assertion that things exist by being posited through the force of appearing to a nondefective mind. *Nondefective* means that there is not a superficial cause of error such as having bad eyesight or being influenced by incorrect philosophical tenets; in this case, that mind is nondefective with respect to its inherently existent appearing object and nondefective with respect to its inherently existent conceived object. It is valid to label "snake" on the aggregates of a snake, but it is not valid to impute "snake" on a coiled rope. In the first case, the basis on which we impute "snake" exists from its own side, inherently, as a snake. When we look within the basis, we will be able to find a snake. But the coiled rope doesn't exist inherently, from its own side, as a snake. If we look within that basis, we cannot find anything to point to as being the snake. That is, we won't find something that is a snake from its own side in the coiled rope, but we will find something that is a snake within the actual aggregates of the snake. For that reason, Svatantrikas assert inherent existence and existence from its own side.

The Prasangikas agree that the aggregates of the snake are a valid basis for imputing "snake" and the coiled rope is not, but they don't agree with the Svatantrikas on the reason why it is a valid basis. According to the Prasangikas, there has to be a valid basis for imputing "snake," but it doesn't have to be valid from the side of the basis. In other words, we cannot say, "From the side of the object or basis on which we impute 'snake' there has to be a valid basis." If we were to say that, it would imply that the object or basis of designation were findable when analyzed; that is, a valid basis for designation would inherently exist because it could be found upon ultimate analysis.

This is tricky. When we hear the Prasangikas say, "There has to be a valid basis. The coiled, striped rope isn't a valid basis, but the aggregates of a snake are a valid basis," we think, "Fine, so there *does* have to be something from the side of the object that makes it a valid basis!" But for the Prasangikas, the fact that there has to be a valid basis does not imply that something exists from the side of the object that makes it a valid basis, because that would imply findability under ultimate analysis. When they say there has to be a valid basis of imputation, it simply means the basis in dependence on which we impute "snake" has to be able to function as a snake.

Let's use another example. Whether we label "airplane" on a paper airplane or in dependence on a collection of parts with an engine, wings, fuselage, and so forth that can fly in the sky, both are cases of labeling. The difference is that one is a valid basis of imputation while the other is not. A paper airplane will never become a valid basis of imputation for "airplane," while an assemblage of airplane parts is a valid basis of imputation for "airplane." Labeling "airplane" on a nonvalid basis of imputation—for example, the paper airplane—is the same as labeling "snake" on a rope. Why isn't it a valid basis of imputation for an airplane? Because it cannot perform that function. Why not? The conditions are not complete. Svatantrikas say the incomplete condition is that the assemblage of airplane parts is not inherently an airplane. Prasangikas, on the other hand, say that to perform the function of an airplane, dependently related conditions are necessary. In other words, for Svatantrikas and the lower schools, what is missing is inherent existence; to exist, it must be inherently existent. For Prasangikas, even the fact that a paper airplane cannot perform the function of an airplane is because it is a dependently arisen phenomenon; it is not inherently existent.

It is comfortable for us to think, "If there has to be a valid basis, then it has to exist from its own side," because since beginningless lifetimes we have been grasping at things as existing from their own side. From beginningless time, we have believed there is something findable from the side of the object. This habitual way of thinking is very strong. So it is understandable that when we hear about a valid basis, we think, "Yes, of course, it must inherently exist."

But we also have the sense, as the Prasangikas state, that everything exists by depending upon something else; everything exists through relying upon other things. To exist from its own side or to exist inherently would mean it does not depend on other things. But this valid basis does depend on other factors, and in that case, it can't exist from its own side. Think about it—if that basis were inherently existent, it would have to be independent of everything else. Contemplating this for a while will help dislodge the sense of it existing from its own side.

You may wonder, "When a clock is broken, is it still a clock? It can't function as one." It is probably a valid basis for imputing the name "broken clock." When something is broken, your feeling about it changes. If someone steals your broken clock, you don't get so upset, saying, "Someone stole my clock!" However, sometimes we continue to impute the name on a basis even when the basis has stopped functioning in that way. For example, when someone dies, we say, "Martha was buried yesterday," when actually it was her body that was buried; the person Martha ceased at the time of her death. Or referring to the broken clock, we say to a friend, "I'm taking the clock to the repair shop," and our friend understands what we mean. This illustrates the unfindability of an object within the basis and the fact that things exist nominally.

The question also arises, "If the clock is merely labeled, when we start to take away its parts one at a time, at what point does it stop being a clock?" This is precisely why the Prasangikas say that things exist by mere name and cannot be found when searched for in their basis of designation. When we remove the parts one by one, eventually nothing is left. If it existed from its own side as a clock, when we took its parts away, there would be something left. But when we remove the parts one by one, there is nothing left that we can point to as being a clock, and none of the individual parts we remove is the clock. This demonstrates that it doesn't exist from its own side as a clock.

In the same way, not everyone can be called "president of the country." That wouldn't work, because the person we label "president" has to be able to function as the president. He or she has to be properly elected and must be able to do the job of the president. In other words, there needs to be a valid mind imputing "president" and the basis on which "president" is imputed has to be a valid basis. In this case, a valid basis would be someone who has been elected president and sworn into office, someone who has been invested with the power of that office and can do the work of the president. When he visits other countries, he is greeted as the head of the state; he is recognized as having been voted into office by the citizens of that country. He signs bills, bringing them into law. If somebody else were to sign the bills, it wouldn't work. Imagine what would happen if someone thought that just by labeling himself "president" he had the power to negotiate trade agreements for the country!

To use another example, space is the mere lack of obstruction and tangibility; it is a permanent phenomenon that does not change moment by moment. If we impute "impermanent" onto that, it does not work. It is not a valid basis for being called "impermanent." In the same way labeling "permanent" on a jug would not be suitable because a jug changes moment by moment. It doesn't have the characteristic of being static and permanent. It is not a valid basis on which to impute "permanent."

The point is that when we say things are merely imputed, it doesn't mean that it is enough to simply label something. The basis on which we give something a certain label has to be able to function in accordance with the commonly recognized meaning of that label.

Thus when the Svatantrikas say there would be no difference in labeling "snake" on a snake's aggregates and on a striped rope, we disagree and say, "The striped rope isn't merely labeled as a snake, because 'mere' negates its inherent existence. In order to be merely labeled as a snake, that thing has to be able to function as a snake, and it can't."

The Prasangika explanation that all phenomena are mere name, mere label, and mere imputation by conception has profound meaning. We will see this more as we delve deeper into exploring this mode of existence.

Mere Name

Although all phenomena cannot be found under ultimate analysis, they still exist on the conventional level. How do they exist? By being merely labeled in dependence on their basis of designation. According to the Prasangika system, everything is mere name. Does that mean that only names exist? Does that mean that when I touch the wall, I'm touching a name? The answer is no in both cases. Thinking that apart from the name nothing else exists is the extreme of nihilism. Following this wrong view, we could think that karma is just a word and there is no such thing as karma, and thus conclude that therefore there is no need to observe the law of karma and its effects.

Saying that everything is mere name means that everything is named on its basis of designation. *Mere* negates its inherent existence; it negates phenomena existing from their own side. Things exist by being merely named, imputed, designated, or labeled in dependence on their respective bases of imputation; they do not exist inherently; they come into existence by being merely labeled by name and concept.

Thus, saying that things exist by mere name is not negating their conventional existence. Things do exist conventionally. *Mere* only negates the possibility of existing inherently and existing from their own side, without needing to be labeled, independent of name and concept.

In general, all phenomena exist, and within that context it is possible to stop the process of rebirth in cyclic existence. Within everything existing conventionally but not being findable when searched for with ultimate analysis, it is possible to practice the path and attain liberation and enlightenment. Although everything exists by being merely labeled, everything functions. Individuals create virtuous and nonvirtuous causes for rebirth in cyclic existence and take birth in the various realms. They study, contemplate, and meditate on the path; they realize renunciation, bodhichitta, and the wisdom realizing emptiness, and attain enlightenment. All of this happens even though there is no findable existence. Things exist in mere name, not inherently, and in that context they interact and function.

If things did not exist by mere name, they would be inherently existent. If something were inherently existent, it would be independent of all other factors, including causes and conditions. Something that does not depend on causes and conditions cannot function; it is permanent. Here we see that if things—you, me, the clock, virtue and nonvirtue—did not exist by mere name, they could not function at all. Thus the only choice is to say that they exist by mere name but do not exist inherently.

Take the example of a cup. It exists; we use it to drink from, we can move it here and there, we can give it as a gift; we can break it and repair it. But when we look for that cup within all of the different pieces that go to make it up, we can't find the cup. It doesn't exist as something that is findable under analysis. It isn't found when searched for within its basis of designation. Yet it still exists. Everything functions perfectly despite the fact that it cannot be found when we look for it within its basis of designation.

It is helpful to look into the way in which things appear to us, to examine our perceptions, and to observe to what extent we believe things to exist just as they appear. Similarly, it is useful to inquire and examine whether the way they appear is indeed the way in which they exist. If we do this earnestly and intelligently, we will discover a great disparity between the two.

CHAPTER NINE

Imputed and Empty

What Is This Fluid?

To aid in our efforts in understanding the view of the Madhyamaka school, let us examine the traditional example of a god, a human being, and a hungry ghost looking at a glass filled with fluid.

Each of these beings in the past has accumulated a certain type of powerful karma leading to his present rebirth. Due to this, the god will see the fluid as ambrosia, the hungry ghost will see it as pus and blood, and the human being will see it as water. The three different appearances to those three different beings are all valid. There doesn't have to be something from the side of the object that makes it ambrosia, pus and blood, or water. If the fluid were ambrosia from its own side, the human and hungry ghost would also see it that way. If it were pus and blood from the side of the object, all three beings would be equally disgusted by it. If it were water from its own side, the god, the human, and the hungry ghost would all experience it as such. Since they don't, there is no ambrosia, no pus and blood, and no water from the side of the fluid.[27]

This is an example that those of us who have not realized emptiness can understand in order to understand the Prasangika view. Due to his karma, that glass of fluid appears as ambrosia to that god, the god imputes "ambrosia" on it, and it exists and functions as ambrosia for that god. That same glass of fluid appears as pus and blood to the hungry ghost, is labeled "pus and blood" by that being, and functions as pus and blood for the hungry ghost. Similarly, for us human beings, due to our karma, it appears to us as water, we calls it "water," and it functions as water for us.

A similar example could be three women looking at a man or three men looking at a woman. To one, he appears ugly, to another he appears okay, and to the third he is handsome. These qualities do not come from the man's side but are imputed by each woman.

We may wonder, "When we impute different things onto an object, does it actually change the object? That is, by the god, hungry ghost, and human being each imputing something different onto the fluid, does the object change and become whatever was imputed?" This depends on whether the function of the object changes according to the label given it. In some cases, it does not; we may impute "nourishing fruit juice" on a bottle of poison, but that won't make the poison become juice. It will still make us sick if we drink it, no matter what we label it. In other cases, the function of the object changes when the label is given to it; when someone is imputed "president," she assumes a new role with new responsibilities and powers.

In the case of the gods imputing "ambrosia" on the liquid, because the gods have accumulated very powerful karma in the past, a facet of the liquid appears as ambrosia to those gods, they think of it as ambrosia, and they enjoy and experience ambrosia when they drink it. The same process occurs with the hungry ghosts and the human beings, only what appears, what they label, and what they enjoy are pus and blood and water, respectively.

The water itself can be said to have three facets—one facet appears as ambrosia to the gods, but that facet doesn't appear to the hungry ghost and human; the second facet appears as pus and blood to hungry ghosts, but it doesn't appear to the gods and humans; the third facet appears as water to the human beings, but it doesn't appear to the others. But this does not mean that after the human has drunk the water, the glass will still be two-thirds full: one-third being ambrosia and one-third being pus and blood.[28]

Due to the strong karma of the gods, that facet of the liquid is a valid basis for imputing ambrosia if you're a god. It is not the gods' minds thinking "This is ambrosia" that makes it become ambrosia. It's not that the water we human beings see changes into ambrosia or into pus and blood.

Is the glass of liquid a valid basis for imputing all three—ambrosia, pus and blood, and water? The facet of the liquid that appears as ambrosia to a god is a valid basis for imputing ambrosia. The facet that appears as water is a valid base for a human being imputing water, and the facet that appears as pus and blood is a valid basis to impute pus and blood for a hungry ghost.[29] These facets are not mixed; that is, a god enjoys a full glass of ambrosia and no pus, blood, or water is mixed into it. When the god finishes drinking, the entire glass is empty, not just one-third.

Not Findable, but Existent

Bhikkhuni Vajira says in a sutta in the Pali Canon:

Why now do you assume "a being"?
Mara, is that your speculative view?
This is a heap of empty formations.
There is no living being in them.

Just as one designates a cart
in dependence on a collection of parts,
so we assert the convention "living being"
in dependence on the aggregates.[30]

Vajira tells Mara, the personification of wrong views and hindrances, that a person cannot be found amid the collection of aggregates but is designated in dependence on them. She gives the analogy of a cart that is designated in dependence on its parts but cannot be found in or among the collection of parts. Just as a cart is established in dependence on the mere collection of the parts, so too is the person established in dependence on the aggregates. However, if we look for the person in the collection of the aggregates, we cannot find the person as being one of the aggregates in particular or the collection of aggregates in general. Rather the person is a mere convention; it is merely labeled in dependence on the aggregates.

One of the common analyses we use to search for the object in the basis of designation is the four essential points. When we search for an inherently existent person these are: (1) identifying the object of negation, an inherently existent person, (2) establishing that if it existed, such a person would be findable either in the aggregates or as totally separate from them, (3) searching in the aggregates and concluding such a person is not findable there, (4) searching things other than the aggregates and concluding that such a person is not findable there either. The four essential points will be described in more depth in a future chapter.

If the person were inherently existent, we should be able to find it in the aggregates. The fact that we cannot indicates that the person lacks inherent existence. The "not finding" of the person when searched for within the basis of designation is finding the ultimate nature of the person, the emptiness of inherent existence of the person.

This doesn't mean the person doesn't exist. The fact that we cannot find the person when searched for within the basis doesn't mean we should conclude that the person doesn't exist. In other words, not finding an inherently existent person when we search for it in the basis of imputation does not negate the existence of the conventional person that exists to a conventional, nonanalytical mind.

The way that the I or the person appears to the innate I-grasping mind is as if it were existing from its own side. We look for such a person within the aggregates, examining, "Is it the form aggregate? The feeling aggregate? The discrimination aggregate? The aggregate of volitional factors? The consciousness aggregate? Is it the collection of the aggregates?" If we look even in the tiniest subatomic particles that make up the body or in the smallest moment of mind, we won't be able to find the person.

But to then conclude that the person in general doesn't exist would be a big mistake, one that is falling to the extreme of nihilism. Such an error is very dangerous, because we would then run the risk of thinking nothing— even the law of karma and its effects, the Three Jewels, the path to enlightenment, and so on—exists. It is said that when the person who does not understand the important points contemplates emptiness in the wrong way, this brings about his downfall. For that reason, it is important to learn about emptiness first so that our meditation on emptiness will be done correctly and will lead us to enlightenment. Even to have the doubt, "Because the person is not findable when searched for, maybe it doesn't exist," is a big obstacle. Just as a positive doubt inclined toward the emptiness of inherent existence is a very powerful threat to cyclic existence, doubt inclined toward nihilism is a strong obstacle to liberation.

Due to everything existing by being merely imputed in dependence on its basis of designation, everything exists. The person, karma, the Three Jewels, rebirth, liberation, the path—everything exists although it is not findable under analysis in its basis of designation. Causes bring results; practicing the path leads to liberation. All of these things exist nominally, conventionally, but not inherently, truly, or from their own side.

Everything exists by being merely labeled, even atoms, which are the basic units out of which larger objects such as the body are composed. The body is merely labeled, the parts of the body such as the arms and legs are merely labeled, and even the subatomic particles that compose the arms and legs exist by being merely labeled. None of them is findable in its respective basis of designation, but they exist conventionally.

If we take the fact that we can't find the object existing from its own side to mean that nothing exists at all, it means our analysis did not go well; we did not understand the correct point. On the other hand, if we think that even though the person is not findable when we analyze the aggregates, the person still exists conventionally and the entire matrix of agents, actions, and objects still work, then our analysis has gone well and we have understood the correct point. Someone who falls to the extreme of nihilism finds it difficult to practice the Dharma, because he thinks exerting himself is useless. For this reason, it is important to be able to establish conventional existence, even in the face of its ultimate unfindability.

SEARCHING FOR THE CART

While everything is mere imputation, a valid basis for the name is necessary. The imputed object, cart, exists in dependence on the basis of designation, which emphasizes that it does not exist *in* the basis of designation or *as* the basis of designation. A valid basis for the imputation "cart" is necessary, but we cannot find the cart in that valid basis. In addition, when we search for the valid basis with ultimate analysis, we discover that it, too, is mere name. In other words, not only does the object not exist from its own side, but also the valid basis of designation does not exist from its own side.

One well-known reasoning attributed to Chandrakirti examines the relationship between the imputed object and the basis of imputation, showing that they are not inherently one and the same, inherently different, and so on.[31] When we analyze using Chandrakirti's sevenfold reasoning to search for the cart in its parts, we cannot find the cart because none of the parts alone can function as a cart. Yet it seems that the collection of the parts should be the cart because they function as a cart.

How does Chandrakirti respond to this argument? He says that if the collection of the parts were the cart, then if we took the cart apart and piled up the pieces, the cart would still be there. But that surely isn't the case, is it? A pile of parts cannot function as a cart, and no one would call it a cart.

You might say, "Any random collection of the parts cannot be the cart. But if the parts are assembled in the proper order, that arrangement of parts is the cart." But if you say that, more questions arise. Does that arrangement have parts or not? If it doesn't have parts, the parts can't be collected to form an arrangement. If it does have parts, then which of the parts of the arrangement is the cart? In addition, the same parts are present whether they have been arranged in a correct or incorrect way and nothing new has been added to the collection of parts, so it should be the cart no matter how the parts are arranged. Therefore, even before they are assembled, we should see a cart and the parts should be able to function as a cart. Since the arrangement of the parts is a collection of parts, we are still left with the fact of the unfindability of the cart within the parts.

We may think that the parts have the potential to become a cart when put together and that therefore the cart that they have the potential to become is already present. Saying this unavoidably implies the following absurdity. Suppose there is an ant on the tip of a blade of grass, and this ant has the karma to be born as an elephant one hundred times in the future. It would absurdly follow that a hundred elephants on the tip of the blade of grass are already present because, later on, when all the causes and conditions come together, there will be a hundred elephants.

Or we may think, "When we search for the cart, we find the basis of designation. So that is the cart!" However, the basis of designation is not the cart, because if it were, the basis of designation and the designated object would be the same. But they must be different. If they were inherently the same, there would be no need to impute an object, because it would already be present in the basis of designation.

This is similar to someone thinking, "Since there has to be a valid basis, that is what we find when we search for the object." But if the valid basis is the cart, the name and what it refers to would be the same thing. On the conventional level, that doesn't work; the system of naming things would break down because the basis of designation and the designated object would be one and the same. We wouldn't be able to differentiate between them.

An example will help us see that the basis of designation and the designated object are not the same. An old lamp is designated "antique" and seen as valuable by one person, while it is designated "garbage" and tossed away by another. One basis having two different designations could not happen if the basis of designation were the designated object.

The Svatantrikas say that if we search the basis of designation we will find the unique ability to perform the function of a cart, which cannot be found in anything else. The ability to function as a cart cannot be found in a table, a grapefruit, and so on. We cannot put things in a mountain, for example, and transport them to a different location. This unique ability to function as a cart is what we find, and it is the cart.

The Prasangikas reply, "Show me where this ability to perform the function is. Is it in the wheels of the cart? The bottom of the cart? The axle?" If we look for the ability to perform a function, we cannot find it in any of the parts. This proves that neither the ability to function as a cart nor the cart exists from its own side.

APPEARING WHEN NOT ANALYZED, UNFINDABLE WHEN ANALYZED

When we don't analyze, we see that things exist and function. But when we analyze, nothing exists. Saying "nothing exists" doesn't mean absolutely nothing exists. It's not nihilistic. It means that when we don't look for the thing within the basis, we can say it exists. It can be used and we can do this and that with it. But when we analyze, we can't find the object. In other words, to that mind analyzing the ultimate nature of the object, the object doesn't exist. But conventionally, the object still exists; we know this very well. While ultimately hunger, cold, and thirst do not exist, conventionally they do; we experience them.

The example of a reflection of the moon in water illustrates this point. The reflection of the moon in a still lake is present, and it is quite beautiful and serene. But thinking there is a real moon in the lake is not correct. That is the mistake. When we don't analyze, there is the appearance of the moon in the lake, but when we look for the moon in the lake, we won't find a moon there. The appearance of the moon exists, but it is false. It appears to be a real moon, but it isn't. The appearance is mistaken. Likewise, although people and things in our daily life appear to be inherently existent, no inherently existent things are present. That appearance is mistaken. Nonetheless, they exist conventionally on the level of appearance, yet they are unfindable when analyzed.

In the same way, the five aggregates exist conventionally but not ultimately. When the *Heart Sutra* says, "There is no form, no feeling, no discrimination, no volitional factors, no consciousness," it indicates that none of these ultimately or inherently exists. It also says, "Emptiness is not other than form; form also is not other than emptiness," indicating that a conventionality and its emptiness are the same nature and they both exist. Conventional existence and emptiness of ultimate existence go hand in hand. The emptiness of ultimate existence means that when we look for something within its basis, we cannot find it. Conventional existence means that when we don't analyze, things appear and exist.

In the same way that cups, cars, and people exist conventionally but not inherently, so do virtuous and nonvirtuous actions. When we analyze and see that nonvirtue is not findable in its basis of designation, we may start to think that maybe nonvirtue doesn't exist at all. This is incorrect, and thinking like this is very dangerous. In this case, we need to go back and reflect that virtuous and nonvirtuous actions do exist. How do they exist? By depending on various factors, such as the motivation, the method of doing the action, its result, and so on.

Conventionally, the mind is clarity and awareness. Svatantrikas say that when we search in the basis of designation of the mind, we will find the ability to cognize objects, which is the function of mind. That shows that the mind exists from its own side. However, Prasangikas assert that while that basis of designation must be able to perform the function of knowing objects in order to be a valid basis for the label "mind," that doesn't mean the mind exists from its own side. Why? Because if it existed from its own side, we would be able to find it within its basis.

How to Learn about Emptiness

These are the kind of topics we debate in the monasteries. The monastics don't wait until they have a profound question to start a debate. Rather, if something seems a bit odd to them and they don't see how two statements fit together, they just put it out there and see how people respond. In that way they hear many new ideas that help them clarify their own understanding. So if you have a question come up in your mind, ask it—start a discussion—and in that way you will learn.

In one way, the meaning of emptiness is quite simple and straightforward. We need to apply the reasoning and the analysis to just one object, and when we have understood how it works with respect to that object, we can then apply it to everything else. In this way understanding emptiness is not too difficult, compared to understanding the vast variety of conventional truths and their definitions, relationships, classifications, and so on, which is very complicated. On the other hand, emptiness is quite profound because through our analysis, we will find the ultimate nature of reality.

Various lines of reasoning can be used to establish that phenomena do not exist from their own side. There is the reasoning of dependent arising, the reasoning of one and many, the reasoning of diamond slivers, and so on. Several of these are explained later in this book. All of these lines of reasoning come back to the same point, which is that phenomena cannot exist from their own side. Perhaps the most convincing and straightforward reasoning that the Prasangikas use to refute existence from its own side is the one we have just completed—that is, that we should be able to find the object when we search within the basis to which the name refers. However, if at the beginning we don't have a clear idea of what existence from its own side means, then using those lines of reasoning doesn't have much impact on our minds.

The reasoning of dependent arising is quite straightforward. Things exist dependently: They depend on causes and conditions, on parts, and on the mind that conceives and labels them. Something that exists from its own side could not depend on other things. It would be independent of causes and conditions, of parts, and so on. As soon as we recognize that something exists dependent on causes and conditions, we know that it cannot exist from its own side. Existence from its own side and dependent existence are contradictory.

To realize the Prasangika view we must walk a tightrope between the two extremes of absolutism (believing things exist inherently) and nihilism (believing they do not exist at all). Not finding our hand when we search for it does not mean our hand is totally nonexistent. It doesn't negate its conventional existence. Thus even though persons cannot be found under analysis, they exist, and having compassion for them is important. While our own and others' suffering cannot be found in its basis of designation, it still exists and we should try to eliminate it. A valid basis for persons exists, and so do valid bases for suffering and for compassion. Saying that something is mere name or mere imputation implies the existence of a valid basis. Ultimate unfindability and conventional existence are mutually compatible, so everything fits together and works.

CHAPTER TEN

Enlightenment Is Possible

ALL SENTIENT BEINGS CAN ATTAIN ENLIGHTENMENT

Since sentient beings are limitless in number, is there an end to cyclic existence? When this is examined in terms of each individual being, we say, "Yes, there is an end to the cyclic existence of each sentient being." This is because each and every sentient being has buddha nature—the potential to attain full enlightenment. This potential is of two types: (1) the naturally abiding buddha nature, which is the empty nature of the mind, and (2) the transforming buddha nature, which is all the impermanent qualities of the mind that can be further developed, becoming the omniscient mind of the Buddha. When this potential is nourished by listening, reflecting, and meditating on the Dharma, it will progress and each being will attain enlightenment.

We cannot point out any sentient being who is unable to attain enlightenment because there is no sentient being who lacks this potential. If someone argues that there are sentient beings who are unable to attain enlightenment, we should ask them, "Does that mean there is no way for them to abandon mental afflictions? Is there no antidote to their afflictions? If they generated the wisdom realizing emptiness, would that wisdom be unable to eradicate their afflictions?" In addition, we should ask, "If some sentient beings cannot go beyond cyclic existence, then who is it that determines who can and who cannot?"

While there is no beginning to each sentient being's cyclic existence, there is an end. While there is no beginning to the afflictions, there is an end to them because the antidote that can eradicate them exists and each sentient being is able to cultivate that antidote.

ADVENTITIOUS STAINS CAN BE ELIMINATED

We may wonder, "Can the self-grasping ignorance be removed from the mind?" Yes, it can. It is an adventitious stain on the mind, not a natural one. Being a type of consciousness, ignorance also has the nature of being clear and aware. It is called *ignorance* from the point of view of its not knowing the actual way of existence of phenomenon, and its being *adventitious* means that it has not entered the nature of the mind. If it had entered the nature of the mind, then when ignorance was eliminated, the mind would also be eliminated. Inversely, since the mind cannot be eliminated, neither could ignorance. However, while the continuum of mind can never cease, ignorance can be eradicated because the antidote to ignorance exists: It is the wisdom directly realizing the emptiness of true existence.

That is, the self-grasping mind that focuses on the conventionally existing person and thinks it exists from its own side—that mind is an adventitious stain. It cannot be a natural stain—something that is an intrinsic part of the mind—because the person has never existed from its own side. If it were a natural stain, the person would have always existed from its own side and self-grasping would be a valid mind. In fact the person has never existed from its own side, even though the self-grasping mind erroneously believes it does.

If self-grasping ignorance were a natural stain, then grasping at self-existence would reflect the object's actual nature. Then, if we meditated on the opposite of that—noninherent existence—we would negate the object itself. In that case, nothing would be left, and the meditation would have annihilated the object itself.

The self-grasping ignorance—which includes the view of the perishing aggregates—is an innate affliction: It has been present within us since beginningless time; we did not acquire it in this life by coming into contact with erroneous philosophies. Nevertheless, it is adventitious and can be removed from the mind. Why? Because it grasps things as existing in the opposite way than they actually do. Phenomena do not exist from their own side and never have. The self-grasping ignorance can be eliminated by seeing the actual way in which phenomena exist—their emptiness of existing from their own side. Thus the wisdom realizing emptiness has the power to eliminate self-grasping.

For example, let's say someone has a visual aberration that makes her see what is in fact a white snow mountain as blue. This is an adventitious, temporary mistaken mind that came about due to an error. It doesn't reflect the actual nature of the snow on that mountain, which is white, not blue. This error can be remedied because in fact the mountain is not blue and there is a correct mind that apprehends the white snow mountain as white.

Similarly, the afflictions have not entered the nature of the mind and are adventitious. If attachment had entered the nature of the mind, since the mind is always manifest, attachment would always be manifest. However, we know that attachment is not always manifest. It is the same with anger. If it had entered the nature of the mind, anger and the mind would be inseparable and anger would always be manifest in us. However, this is not the case, thank goodness!

The emptiness of inherent existence of our minds is our buddha nature. Since it is the ultimate nature of our minds, it cannot be removed from our minds. As we meditate on the antidotes to the mental afflictions and the other adventitious faults of the mind, they are purified, and we gradually become free of them. When we become completely free from all those adventitious stains and faults, our minds become the wisdom truth body of a buddha, and the emptiness of inherent existence of our minds becomes the nature body of a buddha.

The Perfection of Wisdom sutras state that the nature of all phenomena is clear light and the stains are adventitious. The meaning of *clear light* varies according to the context. Here it means that all phenomena are empty of existing from their own side. The ignorant mind that grasps phenomena to exist from their own side arises depending on certain conditions. When those conditions cease, that self-grasping mind also ceases. Thus ignorance can be eliminated through meditating on the antidote, the wisdom realizing the emptiness of inherent existence. This wisdom and ignorance have opposite and contradictory ways of apprehending the same object. If phenomena were inherently existent, grasping them to exist in that way would be an accurate mind. In that case, ignorance could never be eliminated. But because phenomena don't exist inherently, wisdom can cut this erroneous grasping from its root.

In short, because (1) self-grasping is an adventitious stain that obscures the actual nature of the object, and (2) the object does not exist from its own side, meditation on the antidote—the direct realization of the emptiness of the sixteen aspects of the four noble truths—eradicates this obscuration by seeing the actual nature of the object. The object itself will remain, but now we will be able to see its actual nature.

INCONCEIVABLE AND INEXPRESSIBLE

The following verse is found at the beginning of the Perfection of Wisdom sutras, and we often recite it before listening to teachings:

> Inconceivable and inexpressible is the wisdom gone beyond,
> not arising, not ceasing, the nature of space,
> the object of experience of the discerning exalted wisdom
> . awareness itself,
> to the Mother of the Conquerors of the three times, I bow.

The perfection of wisdom alluded to in the first line as "the wisdom gone beyond" is the natural perfection of wisdom—emptiness itself. The nature of everything that exists is clear light, in the sense of it being empty of inherent existence. That empty nature is "inconceivable and inexpressible," which means words and concepts cannot convey the actual experience of directly realizing the ultimate nature.

This doesn't mean we cannot talk about emptiness or teach or listen to teachings on emptiness. Emptiness can be explained, but no matter how precise the words used to describe emptiness may be, they cannot capture the true experience of emptiness. Likewise, even if we ordinary beings have an accurate inferential realization of emptiness—which is a conceptual understanding—we are still unable to experience emptiness in the way a directly perceiving mind does. Because neither words nor the conceptual mind can apprehend emptiness like a direct perceiver does, emptiness is said to be inconceivable and inexpressible.

For example, if someone who has never tasted molasses before asks us what it tastes like, we could say, "It's sweet," or use an analogy to something else. But we couldn't say more than that, really. Saying "It's really sweet" or "It's delicious" does convey something about the molasses, but the words cannot convey the actual experience. The other person must taste the molasses in order to really understand and know what it is like.

The meaning of "not arising, not ceasing" in the second line is the same as the meaning of the expression of worship in Nagarjuna's *Treatise on the*

Middle Way, where he speaks of "no coming, no going, no arising, no cessation..." This means there is no inherently existing arising or cessation of things. It does not refer to the fact that emptiness itself is unborn and unceasing, which are qualities applicable to all permanent phenomena.[32]

"The nature of space" means that the nature of the perfection of wisdom resembles the nature of space in being a nonaffirming negative. When we cognize space, the only appearance is the lack of obstruction. Similarly, when realizing emptiness directly, there is only the appearance of the emptiness of inherent existence; nothing else appears to that mind.

The third line explains that the natural perfection of wisdom (emptiness) is the object of the discerning exalted wisdom itself. That is, it is the object of the aryas' exalted wisdom of meditative equipoise directly realizing emptiness. That wisdom is nonconceptual and is completely free from conceptual images or conceptual appearances. Ordinary beings who lack this nonconceptual perception of emptiness cannot experience it as the aryas do. It is inconceivable and inexpressible to their minds.

In the last line, this precious wisdom is likened to the mother of all the buddhas of the past, present, and future. Wisdom is like a mother in that it gives rises to all the buddhas, as well as to all the hearer and solitary realizer arhats. Just as children are born from their mother, the buddhas and arhats are born from the wisdom realizing emptiness. Renunciation, compassion, bodhichitta, and the other virtuous activities that constitute the method aspect of the path are said to be the father.

COMBINING BODHICHITTA AND WISDOM

Bodhichitta is an essential element of the path, so it is important to do all we can to protect it from degenerating and to enhance it so it becomes stronger and more stable. Thus, energy put into generating bodhichitta does not go to waste but creates the cause for happiness for ourselves and others. In addition, joining whatever virtuous activity we do with insight into the emptiness of the three spheres—agent, action, and object—protects our virtue and deepens our wisdom. We do this by meditating that ourselves (the agent), the virtuous activities (the action), and the person or thing we are engaged with (the object) are empty of inherent existence yet arise dependently.

Contemplate the dependent arising and emptiness of true existence of the agent, action, and object at the conclusion of any virtuous action. In the case of the practice of bodhichitta, the three spheres are: yourself, the one who is meditating (the agent); the generation of bodhichitta (the action); and sentient beings, for whom you want to attain enlightenment (the object). After meditating on one of the two methods to generate bodhichitta outlined in chapter 2, meditate on the emptiness of the three spheres in this way. In the context of the practice of generosity, they are: yourself, the person who is giving (the agent); the object you are giving (the action); and the person who is the recipient of your gift (the object). By meditating on the three interrelated spheres as empty, you deepen your understanding of the compatibility of emptiness and dependent existence.

CHAPTER ELEVEN

Easing into Emptiness

A Review: How Ignorance Arises and Produces Afflictions

Keeping in mind our reason for learning about, contemplating, and meditating on emptiness is important. It puts our study into context and makes our actions meaningful. For this reason, I will now summarize the major points we have covered so far, expand upon a few of them, and introduce some new ones.

Cyclic existence is an unsatisfactory, insecure, and unstable situation. The causes of this undesirable situation are afflictions and karma. *Karma* means "work" or "action." Whether we do nonvirtuous karma or contaminated virtuous karma, both are considered "bad" actions in that they cause us to be born in cyclic existence. More precisely, these "bad actions" are throwing karma—karma that causes us to take another set of aggregates in cyclic existence. In the case of nonvirtuous karma, our actions are motivated by afflictions; in the case of virtuous karma, they are motivated by constructive attitudes. But as long as we are in cyclic existence, ignorance lies at the root of both of these types of actions and therefore keeps us bound in the cycle of misery.

Who exists in cyclic existence? The person, the I. We want to be happy and avoid misery, and to do this, we must examine this state of cyclic existence, its causes, its cessation, and the path to that cessation. Rebirth is due to karma, which arises due to afflictions. Afflictions are rooted in self-grasping ignorance, especially the ignorance that misapprehends the I, the person.

The person cycles in cyclic existence and the person is misapprehended by the self-grasping ignorance that is the root of cyclic existence. Who or what is that person? Among non-Buddhist and Buddhist philosophical tenet systems, there are a variety of ideas about the nature of the person.

Within the Buddhist systems, four main schools exist, and we have examined their notions of what is and is not the person. None of the Buddhist systems accept a permanent, unitary, and independent person or a self-sufficient, substantially existent person. Within the Madhyamaka or Middle Way school, the Svatantrikas negate a truly existent person but accept an inherently existent person. The Prasangikas refute both. The Prasangika view is said to be the highest and most refined view.

The focal object of the self-grasping of persons is the mere I, the person that exists by being merely labeled. For Prasangikas the mere I is also the illustration of the person. In a sutra the Buddha said that the *mere I* principally refers to or depends on the continuity of the mental consciousness.

It is the mere I that creates virtuous and nonvirtuous karma, that goes from one life to the next, that practices the path and becomes enlightened. The mere I depends on the mental consciousness to do these things. While we are alive all six of our consciousnesses—visual, auditory, olfactory, gustatory, tactile, and mental—function while we are awake, and the mental consciousness is present when we sleep. When we are actively dying and approaching death, all the coarse consciousnesses dissolve into the subtle mental consciousness. At a certain point, there is the mind of white appearance, followed by the mind of red increase and then the mind of black near attainment. This gives way to the mind of clear light, the most subtle level of consciousness, which is the consciousness that is present at the time of death. All of these are instances of the mental consciousness, so from normal life with the coarse consciousnesses up to the point of death, we see the continuity of the mental consciousness carrying on. When entering the bardo after the clear light of death, the process occurs in reverse. Again, it is the continuity of mental consciousness that undergoes this process.

Some people misunderstand this explanation of the death and rebirth process and think that the continuum of the mental consciousness is a soul or permanent self. This is not correct. Just by saying "*continuity* of mental consciousness," there is the sense that the mental consciousness is impermanent, arising and passing away in every moment. Neither the mental consciousness nor the continuity of the mental consciousness is permanent, or self-sufficient and substantially existent, or existing from its own side.

What is meant by the *mere I*? When we think, "I'm coming, I'm going, I'm sleeping, I'm practicing, I'm thinking," and so on, the focal object of the mind is the mere I. These minds are valid minds apprehending the mere I. They are not instances of the I-grasping or true-grasping mind. Although the I appears truly existent to them, those valid minds do not grasp the I as being truly existent.

Every instance of consciousness in every sentient being—except for an arya in meditative equipoise directly realizing emptiness—has the appearance of true existence. However, although the things *appear* truly existent to these minds, they do not necessarily *grasp* them as being truly existent. When we are sitting undisturbed, reading a book, we think, "I am reading." This is the valid I-apprehending mind. But when a trigger occurs— someone criticizes us, for example—then just after this valid I-apprehending mind, the I-grasping mind arises. This innate I-grasping mind believes the appearance of true existence; it assents to that appearance and thinks the I exists as it appears. This mind is the root of cyclic existence.

Aryas who have not yet become a buddha, on the other hand, have the appearance of true existence in the time called *subsequent attainment*, after they emerge from meditative equipoise on emptiness. However, they do not grasp things as truly existent due to their practice of seeing them as like illusions. Here we see that not all minds of sentient beings apprehending conventionalities grasp true existence even though true existence appears to them.

The ignorance that is the root of cyclic existence includes the self-grasping of persons and the self-grasping of phenomena. One type of self-grasping of persons is grasping ourselves, our own I, as truly existent. This is the *view of the perishing aggregates*, which, in turn, has two types: grasping an inherently existent I and grasping at an inherently existent mine. Grasping other persons as truly existent is not the view of the perishing aggregates; it is the self-grasping of persons. Grasping the aggregates of the person as truly existent is the self-grasping of phenomena.

All these types of grasping are included within the ignorance that does not understand how phenomena actually exist. This ignorance doesn't just obscure us from knowing the ultimate nature, it also grasps objects as existing in the exact opposite way to how they actually exist. That is, ignorance superimposes true existence onto its objects that lack true existence.

The true-grasping mind, the self-grasping ignorance, the view of the perishing aggregates, the ignorance grasping inherent existence, the self-grasping of persons, the self-grasping of phenomena—all of these are the root of cyclic existence, the ultimate foundation upon which the rest of cyclic existence—the root afflictions, auxiliary afflictions, karma that causes rebirth, and duhkha—is constructed. All of these minds are summarized into two types in terms of the objects that they refer to: the *self-grasping of the person*, which refers to the person, and the *self-grasping of phenomena*, which refers to any phenomenon other than the person. The root of cyclic existence is an innate mind—it is not learned. While ignorance is of two types—innate and acquired—only innate self-grasping ignorance is the root of cyclic existence.

How does it come about that first the self-grasping of phenomena arises and then the self-grasping of person? First we see the aggregates of the person. Actually, we don't necessarily have to see the aggregates with our eyes; we may know one of their aggregates in another way such as hearing someone's voice, feeling his hand on our shoulder, thinking about his kindness, and so forth. Depending on and following this appearance of one or more of the aggregates, grasping the aggregates as truly existent arises. This is self-grasping of phenomena. Due to the appearance of that person's aggregates, we think, "This is Tenzin." Following that arises the grasping of Tenzin as being truly existent, which is the self-grasping of person. That is how, in our continuum, the self-grasping of phenomena arises followed by the self-grasping of the person. Based on this, attachment, anger, jealousy, or a host of other afflicted attitudes or emotions may arise and we create karma that keeps us bound in cyclic existence.

The self-grasping of phenomena followed by self-grasping of persons does not arise every time we apprehend someone's aggregates. However, when we ask, "How did my anger or attachment toward someone come about?" this is the sequence.

THE SEQUENCE FOR MEDITATING ON SELFLESSNESS

As we have discussed, the self-grasping of phenomena precedes the self-grasping of persons; that is, grasping at the inherent existence of the aggregates (phenomena) arises prior to grasping at the inherent existence of the I (persons). In his *Precious Garland*, Nagarjuna says (1:35):

> As long as there is grasping at the aggregates,
> so long the grasping at I will exist.

When we meditate in order to realize selflessness, the sequence is reversed. The Buddha and the great masters advise that first we meditate on the lack of true existence with regard to ourselves and then apply the same reasoning to understand the lack of true existence of our physical and mental aggregates. Having done that, we then apply it to all other phenomena in order to realize their emptiness of true existence.

The reason for reversing the sequence is twofold. In our spiritual search, we first grapple with the question of our own and others' duhkha in cyclic existence. Because it is the person who comes from past lives to this life and goes from this life to future lives, understanding the ultimate nature of the person is most important. Thus our contemplation leads us to inquire into the self-grasping of the person first and meditate on the selflessness of the person first.

Secondly, it is easier to realize the emptiness of persons than to realize the emptiness of phenomena. This is because of the relationship between the I and the aggregates—the I is imputed in dependence on the aggregates. The analogy of the child of a barren women will help us understand this. If we understand that the child of a barren woman does not exist, we easily understand that the child's nose doesn't exist either. In the same way, by first understanding the lack of self-existence with regard to the person, we will find it easy to understand that the aggregates that are the basis of designation of the person also are not self-existent.

By understanding emptiness with regard to ourselves (the selflessness of persons), we know there is not a truly existent user or enjoyer of phenomena. Then it is not too difficult to understand that there are no self-existing phenomena to be enjoyed by such a person. This leads to meditation on the selflessness of phenomena, the chief of which are our own aggregates which are the basis of designation for the I.

Once we have realized the selflessness of one thing, it will be easy to realize the selflessness of other things using the same reasoning. In the beginning, we may have to work hard to understand the reasoning correctly and negate inherent existence on the person. Then, because we are already familiar with the correct reasoning, when we think about the selflessness of other phenomena, we will not have to make great effort. A scriptural passage says, "Just as for oneself, so it is exactly the same for all other sentient beings. Just as with all sentient beings, also all phenomena." It means that the same reasoning used to prove the emptiness of our self can be used to prove the emptiness of other sentient beings and the emptiness of all phenomena.

Another way to look at this is: First the meditator observes how the ignorance that is the root of cyclic existence apprehends everything in a way that is completely incorrect. Although the meditator reflects to some extent on the nature of the aggregates, mainly he is concerned with understanding the process of wandering in cyclic existence—the way that he as a person is reborn in cyclic existence. He then refutes the inherent existence of his own I in order to dispel the ignorance that binds him to cyclic existence. Here the initial contemplation is focused on his own I. Having reflected that there is no self-existing I, he then applies that insight to other phenomena, beginning with his aggregates.

In summary, while self-grasping is not always manifest in our mind, when it does arise, first self-grasping of phenomena arises, followed by self-grasping of persons. This is because first a person's aggregates appear to our mind and then we identify the person. However, when meditating to realize selflessness, first we contemplate the emptiness of the person followed by the emptiness of phenomena. That is because (1) understanding the nature of the person who suffers in samsara is most important and (2) it is easier to realize the selflessness of persons.

With this in mind, in future chapters we will explore the reasonings that prove there are no inherently existent persons and phenomena, the reasonings that establish the selflessness of persons and phenomena.

THREE MODES OF APPREHENDING PHENOMENA

The mind can apprehend phenomena in three ways:
1. As existing from their own side
2. As merely labeled
3. As neither merely labeled nor as existing from their own side

While these three can apply to all phenomena, let's explore these in more depth using the example of the I.

Apprehending the I as existing from its own side.

This mind grasps at the I by distinguishing it as existing from its own side. To this mind, the I appears to exist from its own side, and this mind also grasps the I as existing from its own side. This I-grasping mind is the ignorant mind that keeps us trapped in cyclic existence. Sentient beings who have not realized emptiness directly have this mind, and it is present in the continua of aryas who have realized emptiness directly but have not yet eliminated all afflictive obscurations and become arhats.

Apprehending the I as merely labeled.
This mind apprehends the I as being merely imputed by conception, as being non–truly existent. Such a mind only occurs in someone who has realized emptiness, because only such a person realizes that the I is merely labeled. When this person emerges from meditation on emptiness, although the I still appears inherently existent to her, she knows this appearance is false. She sees the I as being like an illusion in that it does not exist inherently although it appears to. This is a valid mind apprehending the I.

Apprehending the I as neither merely labeled
nor as existing from its own side.
This mind apprehends the I, distinguishing it neither as self-existent nor as merely labeled. This is the valid I-apprehending mind that we spoke of before: It arises prior to the innate I-grasping mind. The conventionally existent I is labeled depending on its basis of designation—the aggregates. Although this I appears truly existent, the mind does not grasp it as such. This is the valid mind thinking, "I'm eating, I'm sleeping, I'm meditating," and so forth. It is valid because there is a nominally existing, conventionally existing I that eats, meditates, and does all the other activities. The fact that the I appears to this mind as self-existent, even though it is not, does not prevent this mind from being valid, because it does not assent to that appearance by grasping the I as existing in that way.

This mind apprehending phenomena as neither inherently existent nor noninherently existent has the appearance of inherent existence but does not assent to it. But neither does it recognize that appearance as false. We have many of these minds each day, for example when we disinterestedly look at a table or casually think, "I'm sitting." This is the valid mind, possessed by ordinary beings and aryas, that apprehends the I or other objects. It is not the case that every cognizer of a sentient being grasps inherent existence or that aryas always perceive phenomena as like illusions.

Dependent Arising Contradicts Inherent Existence

Motivated by great compassion, the Buddha explained emptiness employing hundreds of reasonings. Some of the principal reasonings to guide us to understanding emptiness are (1) dependent arising, (2) the four essential points, (3) not being findable as one or many, (4) the seven-point reasoning, (5) the four extremes of arising,[33] and (6) the four extremes.[34]

Previously we distinguished the self that is the focal object (the conventional object that exists) and the aspect object (what does not exist) of the grasping at inherent existence. This view focuses on the conventional object and erroneously believes it to exist from its own side. It is erroneous with respect to its apprehended object, which in this case is called "the self that is the aspect of the mode of apprehension." This is what must be negated in our meditation on emptiness. How do we negate it? By proving to ourselves that it is impossible for anything to exist inherently. To do so, we employ reasoning, such as one of the reasonings mentioned above.

Among all the reasonings that establish emptiness, Je Tsongkhapa emphasized dependent arising as the most excellent. This reasoning states that phenomena are empty of independent existence because they arise dependently. The Buddha himself taught emptiness in terms of dependent arising, as did Nagarjuna in his five treatises on the Middle Way,[35] which present the explicit meaning of the three mother Perfection of Wisdom sutras. Nagarjuna's spiritual son Aryadeva, as well as Chandrakirti and others, also explained emptiness in terms of dependent arising.

However, after the time of Nagarjuna and the other great Indian masters, this mode of reasoning was relied upon less frequently. Je Tsongkhapa revitalized this presentation and placed great emphasis on it in his works. He considered it tremendously important, so much so that after he composed five major treatises on the subject of emptiness, he also wrote a shorter text called *Praise to Dependent Arising*, in which he praised the Buddha for having taught emptiness in terms of dependent arising. It is amazing to think that after composing five seminal treatises on the Middle Way, Je Tsongkhapa was motivated to write yet another text in praise of dependent arising.

His Holiness the Dalai Lama says that if we study these five great treatises by Je Tsongkhapa as well as *Praise to Dependent Arising*, which summarizes the main points in those treatises, it will be almost impossible not to have a clear understanding of emptiness. Those five texts are huge, and it is difficult to have the time and the opportunity to go into them in depth. But *Praise to Dependent Arising* is short, so try to find the opportunity to study, reflect, and meditate on it, because it contains the essence of the main points of the longer treatises.

All Buddhist tenet systems accept and teach that things are dependent and related, while the non-Buddhist systems do not. We might wonder, "Dependent arising includes cause and effect, such as a plant growing from a seed. Surely the non-Buddhists accept that!" In fact they do, but understanding that very coarse level of depending on causes and conditions does not mean they have a full appreciation for the meaning of dependent arising. Accepting that a plant grows from a seed does not indicate that someone has accepted or understood this concept in terms of one thing arising by depending on another. While all Buddhist systems accept dependent arising, only the Prasangika system accepts it as meaning existing by depending on mere imputation. Just as a person who has realized only coarse impermanence is not said to have realized impermanence, so too a person who has realized only coarse dependent arising has not realized dependent arising. He or she has yet to understand subtle dependent arising in terms of mere imputation by name and concept. Only the Prasangikas accept the most subtle level of dependent arising—that everything exists by dependence on mere imputation.

Using dependent arising to refute self-existence works very nicely, because dependence is the opposite of independence, and independence is the same as self-existence. When we consider that things exist through depending upon causes and conditions and so on, we understand they do not exist independent of other factors, because these two are completely opposite. It is in this sense that we say "empty and dependent arising" or "empty and dependent" are synonyms. That is, everything that exists does so dependent on other factors. Everything that is dependent is empty of inherent existence, and everything that is empty of inherent existence is dependent. Empty and dependent are like two sides of one hand; they always go together.

This is very different from saying that everything is emptiness. Emptiness is a mere absence, a nonaffirmative negation. It is the absence of the object of negation, which is self-existence or independent existence. But all phenomena are not mere negations, even though their ultimate nature, emptiness, is a mere negation. If we realize that something, let's say an apple, is empty, it means we have realized its emptiness of inherent existence. The apple is empty, but it is not emptiness. The apple is empty because it is dependent, but it is not the mere lack of independent existence itself.

In the *Treatise on the Middle Way* (24:18–19), Nagarjuna states:

> Whatever is dependently arising
> is explained to be emptiness.
> That, being a dependent designation,
> this indeed is the middle way.
>
> There does not exist anything
> that is not dependently arisen.
> Therefore there does not exist anything
> that is not empty.[36]

Everything is a dependent arising—there is nothing that exists without depending on other factors—therefore everything is empty of independent existence. Thinking that phenomena are dependent and using that to understand that they are empty, even if we don't realize emptiness right away, makes some conceptual understanding of emptiness arise in our mind. Having even a conceptual understanding of emptiness severely damages the self-grasping ignorance that is the root of cyclic existence. For this reason meditating on dependent arising is powerful purification, for even understanding emptiness by means of a conceptual appearance harms the true-grasping mind, the root of cyclic existence.

When we understand that things are dependent, it is impossible to simultaneously think they are independent, because the two are opposite. Similarly, the way the wisdom realizing emptiness apprehends an object and the way ignorance apprehends the same object are totally opposite. Thus they cannot be manifest in the mind at the same time. Wisdom eventually triumphs over ignorance because wisdom perceives things as they are while ignorance is erroneous. It is not possible for an erroneous mind to conquer wisdom because that erroneous mind does not have any valid base. Wisdom, on the other hand, rests on the valid base of knowing the ultimate mode of existence of all phenomena.

Understanding this gives us confidence that we can gain this wisdom, use it as an antidote to ignorance and the other afflictions, and thereby attain liberation and enlightenment. It also illustrates that every sentient being has the possibility of becoming a buddha because, after learning the way to cultivate the wisdom realizing emptiness, everyone can develop this wisdom.

CHAPTER TWELVE

Dependent Arising

NAGARJUNA'S VIEW

Nagarjuna begins the *Treatise on the Middle Way* by praising the Buddha:

> I prostrate to the perfect Buddha,
> the best of all teachers, who taught that
> whatever is dependently arisen is
> without cessation, without arising,
> without annihilation, without permanence,
> without coming, without going,
> without distinction, without identity,
> and peaceful—free from fabrications.[37]

Here Nagarjuna speaks of freedom from eight kinds of extremes—inherently existent cessation, arising, annihilation, permanence, coming, going, distinction, and identity. "Peaceful—free from fabrications" indicates liberation, the ultimate purpose of realizing emptiness. Here he discusses emptiness in relation to conditioned phenomena, explaining that they do not arise without cause but arise due to causes and conditions. They do not arise depending on just one cause but on many causes. They do not arise due to discordant causes but due to causes that have the ability to produce that result. Cold does not produce heat, nor does heat produce cold.

Furthermore, conditioned phenomena do not arise from self, other, both self and other, or without causes. Arising itself is not self-existent. If things do not arise in any of these four ways, how do they arise? They arise from causes and conditions that are concordant with the result. By showing their dependence, their emptiness is explained. Self-existent production would be the arising of a result completely independent of causes and conditions. But we see that things arise depending on various causes and conditions.

While there is no self-existent arising, there is arising on a conventional level; agent, action, and object function.

THE KING OF REASONINGS

In our meditation on emptiness, what is to be negated is the self—that is, inherent existence, true existence, existence from its own side—of the person and phenomena. This can be approached in many ways, and many different lines of reasoning can be used to understand that such a self does not exist. For people who have studied a great deal, understanding these reasonings is not a problem, while those who lack sufficient background in the material could find it challenging. To understand emptiness, we do not need to understand all the reasons proving that phenomena are empty. As long as we understand dependent arising—even if this is the only line of reasoning we understand—if we keep deepening our comprehension of it, we will eventually understand emptiness.

Dependent arising is called the "king of reasonings" because it not only refutes inherent existence but also establishes conventional, nominal existence. This line of reasoning is a straightforward and simple approach, "The person does not inherently exist because it is a dependent arising." Because the person arises and exists in dependence on other factors, it cannot be truly existent. To understand the import of this reasoning, we must understand the types and meaning of dependent arising.

The reasoning of dependent arising is the simplest and most powerful to undermine both the appearance of self-existence and the self-grasping mind that believes that appearance is true. This reasoning is so powerful because dependent arising is diametrically opposed to self-existence. If we know that something is dependent, we can easily understand that it is not independent. If something is not independent, it is not self-existent either, because the two are synonyms. There's no way something can be both dependent and independent, so by eliminating one, the other is established.

To put it another way, if something were self-existent, it would necessarily be independent of all other factors. However, nothing can exist in that way because everything is dependent on other factors. For example, in relation to our self, we reflect, "If such a self-existent I existed, it would be independent. But I am born due to afflictions and karma. I also depend on the five aggregates, and I am merely labeled by name and concept. Thus the I cannot be independent. It cannot exist inherently as it appears. A self-existent I does not exist."

This reasoning is also powerful because it applies to all phenomena, not just conditioned things. If *dependent arising* meant "to come into being dependent on causes and conditions," then only conditioned phenomena would be dependent arisings. However, it means "to exist in dependence on other factors," and thus all phenomena—both impermanent and permanent—are dependent arisings.

A person trained in science is well equipped to understand the concept of dependent arising, and even those of us who aren't do not find it difficult to see that things come into existence through depending on a multitude of factors.

The words *related*, *reliant*, and *dependent* express the same thought in different ways, and they pertain not only to causal relationships but also to other kinds of relationships. There are different ways to speak about the various types of dependence. In one, phenomena in general are dependent in three ways. From the coarsest level of dependence to the most subtle, these are:

1. Dependence on causes and conditions
2. Dependence on parts
3. Dependence on imputation by name and concept

From another perspective, two types of dependent arising are spoken of:

1. Causal dependence, which is the same as dependence on causes and conditions
2. Dependent designation, which applies to all phenomena, both permanent and impermanent

Whichever way we classify dependent arising, the central principle remains the same: All existents depend on factors that are not themselves. Thus, nothing is self-existent.

DEPENDENCE ON CAUSES AND CONDITIONS

Dependence on causes and conditions, or causal dependence, is the first level of dependent arising. All conditioned phenomena, and therefore all impermanent phenomena, are dependent on the causes and conditions that produce them. Anything produced through depending on causes and conditions is a conditioned phenomenon—food, drinks, houses, clothes, education, families, persons, pets, social status, political parties, happiness, anger, love, opinions, and so on. This is the coarsest level of dependent arising, and it is accepted by all Buddhist tenet systems.

Spend some time looking around at the people and things in your environment and reflect on the long history of causes and conditions that led to their existence. Think about mental qualities as well—love, compassion, anger, jealousy, moods, pleasure, pain, and so on—and contemplate their unique causes and conditions. Abstract things—democracy, an hour, speed, and so forth—also depend on causes and conditions. None of these arise from their own power. They all exist only because their causes exist and the conditions for their production came together.

Causal dependence refers to the way an effect arises by depending on the causes and conditions that produced it. Dependent on prior causes, effects arise; for example, in dependence on a seed, a plant will grow. The Buddha teaches this type of dependent arising extensively using many examples. In the twelve links of dependent origination, the Buddha describes the causal dependence of cyclic existence in detail, emphasizing that our situation does not come about haphazardly, by accident, due to unrelated causes, due to permanent causes, and so on. In *Praise of the World Transcendent* (*Lokatitastava*, verse 19), Nagarjuna praises the Buddha, who, unlike non-Buddhist logicians, teaches that suffering and happiness arise dependently:

> Dialecticians assert that suffering is created by itself,
> created by another, by both self and another,
> or that it has no cause [at all].
> You have stated it to be dependent arising.[38]

This teaching on dependent arising is magnificent, because it makes clear that each cause is itself a result of a previous cause and that it, in turn, produces future effects. The Buddha also clarified that all miserable results can be ceased by stopping their causes, and that if we do not create the causes for happiness, it will not come. Since the path to enlightenment relies upon causal dependence, the Buddha instructs us on the entire spectrum of causes to create in order to experience the enduring happiness and joy that we seek.

DEPENDENCE ON PARTS

The Vaibhashikas and Sautrantikas assert dependent arising only in terms of conditioned phenomena and thus discuss only dependence on causes and conditions. However, there is a more subtle level of dependent arising that applies also to permanent, unconditioned phenomena, and that is dependence on parts.

A few simple examples will give you the idea of the way a whole depends on its parts. By "whole" here we mean anything that has parts—a house, for example. A house is made of many rooms, which are its parts, and the house depends upon those rooms to exist. Each room, in turn, consists of the walls, floor, and ceiling, which are its parts. The existence of a room depends upon the existence of those parts; it cannot exist without them. On a more refined level, the Abhidharma explains that smaller particles of earth, water, fire, and air assemble, forming these coarser objects. These tiny particles are also dependent on their parts—the part in the north, the part in the south, and so on.

Using these simple examples, we can understand how everything depends on parts in one way or another. Even empty space has parts: the empty space in the north, the empty space in the south, and so on. Our body has parts, and it depends on those parts.

Consciousness does not have directional parts, because it is not a physical object. But it does have temporal parts, the various moments of mind that compose it. Yesterday's mind and today's mind are parts of our mind of this life. No matter how short the duration of a consciousness, it still has parts. Therefore there is no such thing as a partless moment of consciousness.

In another approach, one consciousness—for example a visual consciousness apprehending blue—depends on parts: the primary visual consciousness and the five omnipresent mental factors that accompany it. The person also has parts: yesterday's I, today's I, tomorrow's I, and so on. Time, too, is dependent on parts. For example, a year is composed of twelve months, and a month is made of thirty days, more or less. Each day consists of twenty-four hours, each hour is a compilation of sixty minutes.

NO PARTLESS PARTICLES

According to the ancient Indian formulation of the form aggregate, all matter is a mass comprised of the four elements—earth, water, fire, and air—and its derivatives. The four derivatives of the elements are visual form, smell, taste, and tactile objects—the five sense objects excluding sound.

The Vaibhashikas and Sautrantikas argue that the tiniest particles of matter are partless in that they lack directional parts. This means that they do not have a north, south, east, or west side, a top or a bottom. The Chittamatrins and Madhyamikas refute this. Imagine a tiny particle surrounded by ten other tiny particles in the ten directions.[39] Do any of the particles in any of the directions touch the central particle? If we say yes, then we have to accept that where the particle in the north touches the central particle is different from where the particle in the south touches it. Therefore, there is a part of the central particle that the northern particle touches and a part that it does not. So the central particle obviously has parts. If it didn't have parts, the surrounding particles would touch it in the same place, all these particles would collapse into the central particle, and there would never be anything large enough to appear to our coarse sense consciousnesses.

If we instead assert that the particles do not touch each other, we must accept that they couldn't join together to form a larger mass. But since we know this is not the case, we must conclude that even the smallest particles must at least have directional parts. They cannot be totally partless. Thus all physical objects and everything that is considered form, however small, is made up of parts. All forms depend on parts and therefore are not partless, because partless and having parts are a direct contradiction. This reasoning is found in *A Dose of Emptiness*, by Khedrup Je, one of Je Tsongkhapa's chief disciples.

Dependent Designation

Any action that is done involves an agent doing the action and an object of that action. For example, the seed is the agent of the action, the action is arising, and the object that arises is the sprout. The agent—the seed— produces the result—the sprout. In this way the agent of that action depends on the object, because the seed becomes the agent in relation to the sprout it produces, and the sprout becomes the object of the action in dependence on the seed that produces it. Similarly a woman becomes a mother only because she has given birth to a child, and the infant becomes a child in relation to—and thus in dependence on—the mother. The agent depends on the action and the object, and the object depends on the agent and the action. They each exist in reliance on the other. This is the import of what Nagarjuna said in *Treatise on the Middle Way* (8:12):

> Agent depends upon action.
> Action depends upon the agent as well.
> Apart from dependent arising
> one cannot see any cause for their existence.

Everything that exists can be seen in the same way: as coming into existence in dependence on other factors. The factors become factors in dependence on the object, and the object becomes an object in dependence on the factors that make it come into being. They exist in mutual dependence upon each other. One does not exist without the others.

Since everything that exists depends on something else to come into existence, nothing can be self-existent. Nothing exists without relying on or being in relationship with other factors. For this reason, all phenomena are not independent and are thus empty of inherent existence. When our minds become very familiar with this, when we see that everything depends on other factors, we will see that phenomena are empty of self-existence. They are not self-existent because they are dependent.

Furthermore, everything that exists is a knowable, an object of knowledge; there is some mind that knows it. Being a knowable depends on there being a knower; being a knower depends on the knowable. Although these two do not cause each other, they are mutually dependent.

Dependent designation is of two types: (1) mutual or relational dependence, and (2) dependence on being labeled by name and concept. We will explore these below.

MUTUAL OR RELATIONAL DEPENDENCE

Mutual dependence involves phenomena being posited and attaining their conventional identity in relation to other factors, as the examples of seed and sprout and mother and child demonstrate. Mutual dependence also pertains to, for example, long and short; young and old; self and other; and friend, enemy, and stranger. Something is long only in relation to another thing that is considered short. What is long in relation to one object becomes short in relation to another. Likewise big and small, hot and cold, good and bad, right view and wrong view, sentient beings and buddhas are all distinguished in dependence on each other. Thinking along these lines, we can come to understand the way this type of dependence operates.

Two things that are mutually dependent may also have causal relationship in the sense that one of the pair is the cause of the other. For example, the seed is the cause of the sprout and the mother is the cause of the child. But the sprout is not the cause of the seed, and the child is not the cause of the mother. While they do not mutually produce each other, they are mutually dependent because the mother is a mother only in relation to the child and the child becomes a child only in relation to the mother. Likewise, the seed becomes a cause only because there is a sprout that can potentially grow from it, and the sprout becomes a result only because there is a seed that caused it.

It is the same regarding a former moment and a later moment. We can talk about one being the earlier moment only by depending upon the later moment. The later moment becomes a later moment only in reference to the earlier moment. While these two moments clearly depend on each other, they do not mutually produce each other.

The same is true for blue and the consciousness perceiving blue. Blue is the object known by that consciousness; the consciousness is the agent knowing the object, blue. The existence of that object, blue, can only be established by depending on the valid cognizer that apprehends it, and the visual consciousness apprehending blue becomes a valid cognizer only by depending on the valid object, blue, that it apprehends. While these two are mutually reliant upon each other, they do not mutually produce each other. Blue is the cause of the visual consciousness perceiving blue but not vice versa.

Similarly, the parts of a syllogism exist in mutual dependence with each other. Let us look at the example "Sound is impermanent because it is a product of causes." What is being proven is that sound is impermanent; what is doing the proving is "product of causes." The fact that sound is a product makes it impermanent. Each part of the syllogism—the subject (sound), the predicate (is impermanent), and the reason (product of causes)—depends on each other. Without the predicate and the reason, sound would still be sound, but it wouldn't be the subject of the syllogism. It is similar with the predicate and the reason.

Generally speaking, reasoning involves using something we already know to understand something new. If we use the reasoning, "This bread is not old because it was baked this morning," the fact that it was baked this morning helps us to understand that the bread is not old. Here, what is being proved (the bread not being old) and the reason proving it (it was baked this morning) are mutually reliant, but they not do not cause each other.

If we can clearly understand that all existents are dependent, related, reliant—these three terms have the same meaning—then we can easily understand that everything that exists is empty. Nothing can be self-existent without relying or depending on something else. Through examining in this way, we come to understand that every phenomenon is merely imputed by the conceptual mind. They are all imputed in relation to other phenomena.

DEPENDENCE ON IMPUTATION BY NAME AND CONCEPT

This is the subtlest type of dependence. Dependence on imputation means that things exist by being merely dependent on name and concept. Names are imputed or designated in dependence on something that is able to fulfill a unique or specific function that corresponds with the meaning of the name. For example, we designate the name "stove" on something that can be used to heat food. We use the word "fork" to indicate a utensil that can be used to put food in our mouths.

As explained before, there needs to be a valid mind imputing a name onto a valid basis. If we were to call a box of tissue a "microphone," it wouldn't work because the tissues cannot perform the function of a microphone. Thus it is not a valid basis for the name "microphone." But when a valid mind imputes a name in dependence on a valid basis of designation—one that is able to perform the particular function that accords with the name designated in dependence on it—that object becomes known by that name.

Something exists as that object only when we give it a name. Before the name has been given, we can't say that particular object exists. But once that object with four legs and a flat top is labeled "table," then table exists and we can say, "Please put this on the table," or "Let's move the table over there."

Consider how people are given their names. Before someone's parents decide to give him the name Tashi, that baby is not Tashi. Before his parents name him, if someone said, "Tashi is hungry," no one would know who he was referring to. But once his parents call him Tashi, from then onward, throughout his life, when someone says "Tashi" he will respond and other people will know who Tashi is. He functions as Tashi only after being given the name Tashi. Meanwhile, someone who hasn't been given the name Tashi cannot function as Tashi. If someone says, "Tashi come here," but the people nearby are not named Tashi, no one will respond.

Saying that things are "mere name" or "mere imputation" in no way annihilates objects. It just negates inherent existence, existence from its own side. This is the most subtle level of dependent arising and it applies to all phenomena—conditioned and unconditioned phenomena alike. Everything exists as mere imputation from the side of the conceptual mind, by the mind imputing the name on the basis, without there being the slightest existence from the side of the object. This type of dependent arising is accepted only by the Prasangikas.

The Svatantrikas are not able to grasp this. They say there must be both inherent existence from the side of the object and imputation from the side of the mind. While they do accept that things are imputed—and even say they are "merely imputed"—they are adamant that something from the object's side is also required. The object also exists from its own side, they say, because if it didn't, anything could be labeled anything. Therefore, they are not able to understand this level of dependent arising in which all phenomena are merely imputed from the side of the conceptual mind.

While both Madhyamaka schools say that all existents are mere imputation, for Svatantrikas, the *mere* eliminates the object existing *only* from its own side without depending on the mind at all, while for the Prasangikas *mere* eliminates all existence from its own side. From one viewpoint, we could say the Svatantrikas accept that phenomena are imputed, because the conceptual mind imputes names on objects. But they do not accept things being "mere imputation from the side of the conceptual mind" as the Prasangikas do.

ALL PHENOMENA DEPEND ON MERE IMPUTATION

The Essence of Dependent Arising mantra is a powerful mantra that many people recite each day. In Sanskrit it is:

Om ye dharma hetu prabhava hetun teshan tathagato hye vadat
teshan cha yo nirodha evam vadi maha shramana ye svaha

When translated into English, it reads:

All phenomena arise from causes; the Tathagata explains their
causes and that which is their cessation. Such is the doctrine of
the great renunciant.

"All phenomenon arise from causes; the Tathagata explains their causes."
Do you agree that everything that exists arises from causes? What about
permanent phenomena, which do not arise from causes? If we said that "to
arise from causes" means to be produced from causes, applying dependent
arising to all phenomena would not work because permanent phenomenon
are not produced from causes. Therefore, this line cannot mean that all
phenomena arise from causes that produce them.

From what do all phenomena arise? Since all phenomena are merely
imputed by conception, everything that exists arises from the conceptual
mind that imputes it. While that does not mean that a conceptual mind
causes or produces it, it is true that all phenomena depend on, rely on, and
arise from the conceptual mind that imputes them. In that sense, it would
be correct to say that they arise from a "cause," which is the conceptual mind
that imputes them. Here the imputing mind is called *cause*, although *cause*
is not being used in the strictest sense.

Even emptiness is dependent. What does it depend on? It depends on the
object that is empty. We cannot speak of emptiness without speaking of the
object that is the basis of that emptiness, such as the person, the table, and
so forth. Furthermore, emptiness depends on the mind that conceives and
labels it, and it depends on the valid cognizer that directly perceives it.

Because everything is dependent arising and relies on something
else to come into existence, nothing is autonomous, independent, self-
determining, or self-governing. Everything depends on or is governed by
other factors. That means it is not self-existent, does not exist in and of
itself, and only exists in dependence on other phenomena.

Emptiness and Dependent Arising

All of this should prove to us that phenomena cannot be independent. To be self-existent means to be independent. If something is not independent, it cannot be self-existent. In this way, we understand that everything is empty of self-existence, and that dependent, empty, and the middle way are synonymous. The middle way is free of the two extremes: the extreme of absolutism and the extreme of nihilism. All phenomena are the middle way between these two; they are dependent and empty of inherent existence.

Je Tsongkhapa had a direct realization of emptiness after reading Buddhapalita's commentary on Nagarjuna, the *Buddhapalita-mulamadhyamaka-vritti*. His Holiness the Dalai Lama refers to a quotation in this text that he finds particularly useful in understanding emptiness:

> If (phenomena) existed with their own identity, it would be sufficient to posit just that. What would be the point of saying they exist through reliance?

In other words, if phenomena were self-existent, there would be no point in describing them in terms of the various factors in dependence upon which they came into existence. However, the Buddha described dependently arising phenomena in one sutra after another, indicating that they cannot be self-existent.

If something were self-existent, it would be able to exist in and of itself without depending on anything else. That clearly would be impossible. Let's say my rosary existed in and of itself, independent of anything else. If I held it up in the air and let go, it would stay there. But when I do this, it falls down. Its being in the air when I hold it up is not independent of everything else. Reflecting on this simple example can be quite insightful.

To understand that something is empty of self-existence, we meditate that it is dependent. With this in mind, the Prasangika school states that *empty* and *dependent arising* are synonyms. To experience the impact of saying that these two are synonyms, the study of Buddhist dialectics is useful. Here it says that for two things to be synonymous they must meet eight requirements:

1. If it is A, it is B.
2. If it is B, it is A.

3. If it is not A, it is not B.
4. If it is not B, it is not A.
5. If there is A, there is B.
6. If there is B, there is A.
7. If there is no A, there is no B.
8. If there is no B, there is no A.

This expresses the relation between empty and dependent arising. Everything that is empty of independent existence necessarily arises dependently. Everything arises dependently because everything depends on parts, and arising dependently and being independent are mutually exclusive. *Mutually exclusive* means that if something is not one, it must be the other. If phenomena are not self-existent, they must arise dependently. If we realize something arises dependently in the Prasangikas' sense of the word, we realize that is not self-existent. It is in this sense that empty and dependently arising are synonyms.

However, while *empty* and *dependently arising* are synonyms, *emptiness* and *dependent arising* are not. Emptiness is a nonaffirming negation, which is a mere lack or absence of the object of negation—in this case self-existence. If we said that emptiness and dependent arising were synonyms, we would have to say that a jug, for example, would be an emptiness because it is a dependent arising. If a jug were emptiness, it would be the lack of the object of negation, but it is not; we are not negating the jug. Furthermore, since emptiness is permanent, if a jug were emptiness, it would be permanent, and that, too, is not right. So while the jug is *empty*, it is not *emptiness*.

Furthermore, if emptiness and dependent arising were synonyms, it would mean that all dependent arisings would be emptiness. Since emptiness is synonymous with ultimate truth, it would mean that everything would be an ultimate truth. However, ultimate truth is the direct object of the aryas' meditative equipoise directly perceiving reality, and everything that exists is certainly not the direct object of an arya's wisdom of meditative equipoise.

Confusion could arise when we read in the *Heart Sutra* that "Form is empty; emptiness is form." That form is empty is understandable—it is empty of self-existence. But understanding "Emptiness is form" requires more thought. It would not be right to literally say that emptiness is form.

Emptiness is permanent, and form is a functioning thing that is impermanent and produced by causes and conditions. "Emptiness is form" means that the emptiness of form does not have a separate identity from form itself. It is form itself that is empty of inherent existence. This illustrates that the two truths—conventional and ultimate truths—are not separate and unrelated to each other. We'll explore this topic more in later chapters.

THE COMPATIBILITY OF BEING DEPENDENT AND EMPTY

In the glance meditation found in the *Guru Puja*, Lobsang Chokyi Gyaltsen says:

> Samsara and nirvana lack even an atom of inherent nature, while cause and effect and dependent arising are infallible. Inspire me to realize Nagarjuna's thought that these are non-contradictory and mutually supportive.

Nagarjuna is known to have perfectly understood and explained the true intention of the Buddha by teaching that emptiness and dependent arising are complementary, not contradictory. This verse captures Nagarjuna's meaning succinctly by saying that (1) nothing inherently exists, and (2) dependent arising functions without error. We need to make an effort to fathom this insight of Nagarjuna. We consider Nagarjuna's teachings to be a reliable source for our study and practice because the Buddha himself predicted that after his passing, when the understanding of the Perfection of Wisdom sutras had degenerated, Nagarjuna would come into the world to clarify and restore them.

If you study Nagarjuna's teachings and use them to help you study the Perfection of Wisdom sutras, you will be able to understand those sutras well and will discover that he explained their precise meaning very clearly. Nagarjuna composed many treatises, and many of his disciples became outstanding masters through relying on his teachings. Most amazing of all of them was Buddhapalita, who clearly understood Nagarjuna's intention. His commentary comprehensively explains the meaning of Nagarjuna's teachings.

Both Madhyamaka systems, the Svatantrika and the Prasangika, trace their explanations to the teaching of Nagarjuna. Each claims to correctly interpret his explanations. But the system that actually represents Nagarjuna's view is the Prasangika, which conveys Buddhapalita's understanding of Nagarjuna. Chandrakirti and Shantideva were other great Prasangika masters. Shantideva understood the meaning of emptiness through personal instructions he received from Manjushri, and with this wisdom he composed two great texts, *Engaging in the Bodhisattva's Conduct* and the *Compendium of Training* (*Shikshasamucchaya*). All of these magnificent sages explained the explicit meaning of the Perfection of Wisdom sutras—emptiness—according to the Prasangika view.

The verse above describes Nagarjuna's insight into the nature of reality. Saying that all phenomena of cyclic existence and nirvana do not have even the slightest bit of inherent existence expresses the empty aspect of phenomena. Since everything is completely empty of even the slightest inherent existence, we may wonder, "In that case, how do they exist?" They exist by mere name and mere imputation. This refers to the dependent aspect of phenomena, which is expressed by, "cause and effect and dependent arising are infallible." Here causal dependent arising, which applies to impermanent phenomena—those produced dependent on causes and conditions—is specifically mentioned. Other types of dependent arising are implied. In short, things lack inherent existence because they are dependent.

The phrase "these are non-contradictory and mutually supportive" explains that *empty* and *dependent arising* are entirely compatible and not at all contradictory. In fact, dependent arising is the very reason things are empty of inherent existence. Conversely, the fact that something is empty of independent existence is essential for it to exist dependently.

This "non-contradictory and mutually supportive" nature of emptiness and dependent arising is Nagarjuna's ultimate view. The verse ends with a request for help to understand and gain insight into his ultimate intention.

IS THERE CHOICE?

We may wonder, "Since everything arises dependently, is there any true choice? Or is everything completely determined by what occurred before it?" While it is true that we cannot evade previous causes and conditions—we are under the control of our afflictions and our past actions—within that there is a measure of freedom. Freedom here is not the capacity to do anything we wish or to act in a way completely divorced from previous actions and conditions. Nevertheless some choice exists in each situation. Say you are in a heated conflict and your anger is beginning to arise. If you have some experience of watching your mind, you can choose to follow your anger or not follow it. You have the choice between acting in a beneficial way or causing harm to yourself and others. You can choose what to do and how to approach the situation. But when your mind is overpowered by afflictions, you have much less choice. You are pushed in one direction due to the force of specific causes and conditions, in this case the intensity of your anger. Similarly, when you have trained your body, speech, and mind in virtuous acts, you will be inclined toward what is constructive. Your past generosity and self-discipline make those behaviors more easy to choose in the present.

Many different causes and conditions affect how we behave in a situation. One set of causes and conditions makes us lean in one direction; another set inclines us in another. So we are not completely autonomous and independent in our choice. Since our present choices are conditioned by our past actions, it is essential to steer our mind in a constructive direction when we are able to do so.

Here is an example. Say someone has the opportunity to visit India next year. To go there, certain conditions need to be assembled—her passport, visa, air ticket, and so forth. Only if all those preparations are made will it be possible to go. Her visit depends upon those conditions, and she needs to exert effort to arrange them. Likewise, we must assemble the proper conditions to penetrate the meaning of emptiness and dependent arising—we must choose now to study, meditate, and practice virtue.

CHAPTER THIRTEEN

The Four Essential Points

MEDITATION ON THE FOUR ESSENTIAL POINTS

While the fact of the I being a dependent arising is sufficient to negate its self-existence, here we examine another method to achieve the same aim. Approaching emptiness via various reasonings deepens our understanding and later will enable us to teach others from a variety of viewpoints.

In his *Medium* and *Great Expositions of the Stages of the Path*, Je Tsong-khapa explains how to meditate on emptiness by using the reasoning of being free of one and many, which may also be translated as "freedom from one and different." This analyzes the nature or entity of phenomena by asking, "Are the self and the aggregates one nature or different natures?" This reasoning has four essential points:

1. Ascertaining the object of negation
2. Ascertaining the pervasion
3. Ascertaining freedom from being one
4. Ascertaining freedom from being many

Of the many ways to meditate on emptiness, this one is especially effective because it offers us, who have not had a chance to study emptiness in great depth, a relatively straightforward and simple route.

Before going into more detail, I would like to discuss the word *many* in "freedom from being one or many." *Many* usually means "more than one." If there is more than one thing, then there are different things. In the four essential points *many* means "different," "separate," or "distinct." We investigate whether the I and the aggregates are inherently one and the same or inherently distinct and unrelated to each other.

However, sometimes "one and many" is used in the sense of quantity. For example, an apple is either singular or multiple. In this case, we investigate if there is one self or multiple selves, one aggregate or multiple aggregates.[40]

The First Essential Point:
Identifying the Object of Negation

Chandrakirti says in his *Supplement to the Middle Way* (6:120):

> Having seen with intelligence that afflictions and faults
> without exception arise from the view of the perishing aggregates,
> and having realized that the self is the object of that,
> yogis refute the self.

Identifying the object of negation at the beginning of our meditation is crucial. Ascertaining the object of negation is extremely important, because if we haven't understood well what is to be negated, we won't be able to ascertain its nonexistence with precision. For example, suppose somebody robs us, and we don't know anything about the robber. When we look for him in a group of people, we will not be able to say decisively whether he is there or not. Similarly, if all we knew about the robber is that he is bald, we will not be able to identify him definitively. We risk searching for the robber in the east when he has run to the west because we aren't quite sure where to look.

However, if we can identify the thief clearly, when we go to look among a group of people, we will be able to say, "Yes, the person is here" or "No, he is not here." It is similar when we think, "I am or am not truly existent," but we don't know the meaning of true existence.

Since the object of negation does not in fact exist, it cannot actually be ascertained, because ascertainment implies a valid mind realizing an object that exists. What, then, does ascertaining the object of negation mean? It means gaining certainty about the way in which the object of negation would exist, if it did exist. In other words, what would things be like if they were inherently existent, if they existed from their own side?

Our understanding of the object of negation must not be just on the level of words. It is not so useful in itself to say, "A truly existent I doesn't exist." We may even be able to recite all the reasons why something cannot inherently exist, but if we haven't analyzed the meaning ourselves, there is not much effect on our minds. To derive the greatest possible benefit from meditation on emptiness, we need to have a clear image of what a thing would be like if it were truly existent, and we need to have searched for a truly existent I and not found it.

Although inherent existence does not exist, it appears to us. Normally we do not question how objects appear to us and how we grasp or apprehend them to exist. Now we must begin to observe and recognize the way in which things appear to the true-grasping mind and the way that mind apprehends or grasps them. Then, through various lines of reasoning, we explore if inherent existence could possibly exist.

In the meditation on emptiness, the first essential point involves ascertaining the inherently existent I that appears to and is grasped by the innate I-grasping mind as existing from its own side. It is called the *aspect I* because it is the I that is the aspect of the mode of apprehension of the innate I-grasping mind. This mind grasps the conventionally existent I—the I that does exist—in the aspect of inherent existence. The aspect I is also the apprehended object of the self-grasping mind. It is the I that is the object of negation when meditating on the selflessness of persons. Again, we are not refuting the existence of the conventionally existing I.

While the various philosophical terms and ideas above give us a sense of the object of negation, we should not think that the object of negation is some strange phenomenon with a horn growing out of its head that we have to search for in a faraway place. Self-existence appears to us right now. Things appear truly existent to us in this very moment. When we become angry, upset, jealous, or excited, or when we crave for or cling to something, the grasping at inherent existence is present. We need to look at the way the I appears to us at those times. Skill is required to recognize in our own experience how the I appears to the innate I-grasping mind to exist from its own side, completely independent of causes and conditions, independent of parts, and independent of being labeled by name and concept.

It is easier to ascertain the object of negation, an inherently existent I, when it appears vividly to the mind. For example, suppose someone comes along and accuses you of having caused some great harm when in fact you are entirely blameless. At that time you are likely to have a very vivid and strong sense of I. You may think to yourself, "*I* didn't do that. Why are they blaming *me*?" During such times, there is a very vivid appearance of *me* existing from its own side, completely independent of causes and conditions, completely independent of anything else.

Here is another situation in which the inherently existent I appears vividly. Suppose you have helped someone many times in many different ways, but he repays your kindness by insulting you to your face, stealing something valuable from you, and spreading lies about you behind your back. At this time, too, you have a strong sense of I, thinking, "*I* have done so much for this person, and now look at how he treats *me*. He has been taking advantage of *me!*" At this time you can clearly observe the inherently existing I appearing to the innate I-grasping mind. You can also clearly observe that mind grasping the appearance as inherently existent.

In these situations you are usually too caught up in your emotions to pay attention to how the I appears. However, in meditation, you can recall such a situation and allow the emotion to arise. Then with one corner of your mind, observe how the I seems to exist. This I is the object of negation. With practice in meditation, you can then try to apply the same technique in the moment such a situation is happening.

Here is another exercise. Imagine walking along a very narrow precipice. On one side, imagine a huge drop into icy water; on the other, an equally steep fall into a fire. As you walk, a very strong sense of the inherently existent I that is in danger of falling appears to the mind. With one corner of your mind, observe that I and how it appears to exist. It seems as if it exists independently, having nothing to do with its causes and conditions, its parts, or the mind that conceives and labels it. By repeatedly doing this kind of exercise, you will become aware of how the I appears to the innate I-grasping mind.

The innate I-grasping mind grasps the I as if it existed "on" (or more literally "above") the mere collection of the aggregates—not on or above any one of the five aggregates individually—and as if it were not merely imputed by conception. In other words, it grasps the I as existing as it appears.

Once it is clear to us what the object of negation would be like if it existed, it is relatively easy to see that such a thing couldn't exist. But if we are not clear regarding the first essential point, we run the risk of negating the wrong thing. In *Engaging in the Bodhisattva's Conduct* (9:139), Shantideva cautioned us that when the fantasized thing (the object of negation) hasn't been properly identified, its nonexistence cannot be grasped:

> Without having identified the object [of negation], which is imputation,
> the absence of the object cannot be apprehended.

"The object [of negation], which is imputation" refers to the conceptual appearance of the object of negation. "Having identified" it means thinking, "If the object of negation existed, this is what it would be like." In other words, we need to have a clear conceptual picture of what inherent existence would be like if it existed. Without being able to identify the object of negation or without clearly understanding what it means to be self-existent, we will not be able to realized its absence, its emptiness.

We know when we have understood the first essential point and ascertained the object of negation when we have meditated and gained certainty through our own experience—not simply thinking "It is so" because we've heard others say it—that the way the I appears to the innate I-grasping mind is as if it inherently existed on the mere collection of the five aggregates.

When we have ascertained the object of negation on one object, it is easy to ascertain it on all objects. However, having identified the coarse object of negation on one particular object does not mean we have identified the subtle object of negation on another object. Identifying what a self-sufficient, substantially existent person would be like is not the same as identifying what an inherently existent person would be like. Recognizing the coarse object of negation on one object makes it easy to recognize the coarse object of negation on other objects. It is the same with recognizing the subtle object of negation.

THE SECOND ESSENTIAL POINT: THE PERVASION

The second essential point is ascertaining the pervasion. That is, it pervades that if the I exists inherently, it must be either inherently one or inherently different from the aggregates. There is no third possibility. The I would have to be either inherently one nature with the aggregates or inherently different natures from the aggregates. There are only these two choices. We must be very clear that there is no third option for the relationship between an inherently existent I and its aggregates. If the I does not exist in either of these ways, it cannot inherently exist.

For example, if a thief stole something and is still here on the property and we wanted to look for him, we know he must be either indoors or outdoors. There is no other possibility. When we ascertain that there are only these two options, then if the thief isn't in either place, we will know he isn't here at all.

Let's now examine more closely the meanings of "the same and different" and "one nature and different nature."

ONE AND DIFFERENT

First we must understand what *one* and *different* mean and how that is distinct from being inherently one and inherently different. For two things to be one, they must be the same both in name and in meaning, for example, pen and pen. Two things that are not the same in both name and meaning are different, for example car and automobile. Although these two have the same meaning, they are different because they have different names. Table and cup are different in both name and meaning.

Conventionally existent objects that are one do not have to be inseparably one, and those that are different do not have to be totally unrelated. Only in the context of inherent existence must any two things be either inherently one or inherently different.

If things were inherently existent, they wouldn't depend on any other factors and would exist in isolation from other things. In the context of inherent existence, any two things would have to be either inherently one and the same without any possibility of ever being differentiated, or they would have to be entirely different and unrelated. Being inherently one would mean those two things had exactly the same meaning and performed exactly the same function.

In this case, if the I were inherently one with the aggregates, it would have to be inseparably one with them. That is, the I and the aggregates could not be differentiated at all. Saying "I" or "me" would be the same as saying "aggregates" and vice versa; the two words would be interchangeable. Also the I and the aggregates could do the exact same things because they would be inseparably one and the same. If the I were inherently one with the body, for example, then when we said, "I'm thinking," it would mean the body was thinking. If the I were inherently one with the mind, then the mind would be walking when we say, "I'm walking." These absurdities would follow if the I and the aggregates were inherently one and the same.

Conventionally speaking, *different* doesn't mean two things are totally unrelated. Two countries are different, and one state is different from the country it is in. Impermanent and product are different. *Impermanent* refers to something that changes moment by moment and *product* refers to something that is a result of causes and conditions. Product and impermanent are synonyms, but they are not exactly the same thing because they appear differently to the minds that perceive them. They are different because they have two different names, but they are not completely unrelated to each other. But if two things were inherently different, they would be totally different and unrelated. They would not be simply different in the sense of not being exactly the same thing but would be totally unrelated like a tiger and a cow. A tiger and a cow are different and unrelated; they are not synonyms, and one is not an attribute of the other or a subgroup of the other. One doesn't depend on the other, and they are not one nature. This is an important point and without understanding it, we won't be able to understand this reasoning.

Thus in terms of things being inherently existent, they must be either inherently one and the same, which means they would be exactly the same thing, or they must be inherently different, which means they would be totally unrelated and distinct. Do the I and the aggregates exist in this way?

One Nature and Different Natures

The topic of one nature and different natures comes in *Collected Topics*, one of the first texts studied in the philosophy curriculum in the monastery. To understand this, we must first understand the topic of relationships—the way in which two things may be related. Two types of relationships are delineated:

1. Causal relationship. If two things have a causal relationship, one is the cause of the other.
2. Relationship of the same nature or same entity. This means that if this thing exists, the other exists at the same time. This could be a relationship in which two things are synonymous, such as product and impermanent. It could also be a relationship in which one thing is an instance of the other, which is a generality. For example, jug is a particular of the generality impermanent.

A tiger and a cow do not have a causal relationship, nor do they have the relationship of being the same nature. A tiger and cow do not cause each other. Also, tiger isn't a universal category (generality) to which the cow belongs, nor is cow a universal category to which the tiger belongs. Furthermore, they are not synonyms. So neither of these two types of relationship apply to the tiger and cow.

You might say, "Aren't tiger and cow related because they are both animals?" No, this is not the meaning of related in this context. Although the tiger is one nature with the generality animal and the cow is as well, that does not mean they are one nature with each other. A tiger can exist without a cow existing. Similarly, impermanent is one nature with phenomena and permanent is one nature with phenomena, but impermanent and permanent are not one nature with each other; they are contradictory because whatever is impermanent is not permanent and vice versa.

Someone might ask, "Aren't two tigers one nature?" or "Aren't this blue cup and that identical-looking blue cup one nature?" Again, the answer is no. Tiger A and tiger B do not have a causal relationship (assuming they are not parent and cub), nor are they one nature. The same is true for two different cups.

Different and *different nature* do not have the same meaning. Two things may be different without being different natures. Impermanent and product are different because they have different names but they are not different natures. They have the same nature because they are synonyms. Tiger and cow, on the other hand, are both different and different natures; they are unrelated. Similarly, the earlier and later moments of one tiger are not the same thing, they are different and different natures, but they have a causal relationship. The earlier moment of the tiger is the cause of the later moment of the tiger in the same continuity.

However, two things that exist inherently and are different must be totally unrelated. It is impossible for them to be related in either of the two ways because inherent existence means existing independent of all other factors. If they do not depend on other factors, then they cannot be cause and effect. If they do not depend on other factors, they cannot be one nature, because that also involves things depending on each other. When two things are inherently different, they are not just different but totally unrelated, just like the tiger and the table.

Conventionally, if two things are one nature, they don't have to be completely inseparable. The cow and product are not inseparably one, although they are one nature. But if two things are inherently one nature, they would have to be completely inseparable and indistinguishable, so that everything we say about one is also applicable to the other. If the I were inherently one or inherently one nature with the aggregates, the I and the aggregates would have to be completely inseparable and indistinguishable in every way. Everything we said about the person would also apply to the aggregates and vice versa.

Likewise, conventionally, two things that are different or that are different natures don't have to be entirely unrelated. A cause and its effect are different natures, but they are not totally unrelated; they have a causal relationship. If cause and effect were totally unrelated, anything could be produced from anything, and in that case darkness could be produced from a light. In the context of inherent existence, two things that are different and two things that are different natures would have to be totally unrelated. If the I and the aggregates were inherently different or had inherently different natures, they would be totally unrelated, just like hot and cold or light and darkness.

The Third Essential Point: Are I and the Aggregates Inseparably One and the Same?

After ascertaining the second point—that there are only two options for the relationship between the I and its aggregates in the context of inherent existence—we investigate to determine if the I exists in either of those ways in relation to the aggregates. In the third essential point we investigate if the I and the aggregates are inherently one and the same, and in the fourth essential point we examine if they are inherently different.

When the Prasangikas refute the object of negation—an inherently existent I—using the reasoning of freedom from one and different, they establish the nonexistence of a person that is one with the aggregates. This harms the assertions of the other Buddhist philosophical systems, which say that an I can be found within the aggregates. That is, the argument that the person is not one with the aggregates is mainly directed toward the non-Prasangika Buddhist schools.

Apart from the Sammitiyas, a subbranch of the Vaibhashika school, who assert a self that is inexpressible as permanent or impermanent or as one with the aggregates or separate from the aggregates, all other Buddhist philosophical systems aside from the Prasangikas identify the illustration of the person as something "above" the aggregates. Some say it is a foundation consciousness, some that it is the consciousness aggregate, others that it is the mental consciousness. They all say that it is possible to find what came from the past life to this life and what will go from this to the next life among the aggregates. Therefore, they all assert a self-existent person.

The Prasangikas also establish the nonexistence of a person separate from the aggregates. The arguments proving this are mainly aimed at the positions of the non-Buddhists who say there is a person separate from the aggregates. Both those who assert a permanent, unitary, and independent self and those who assert a self-sufficient, substantially existent person accept that the person is inherently separate and different from the aggregates. Therefore all of the arguments against a person being inherently different from the aggregates apply to them.

How do we know that only non-Buddhist systems assert a self that has a separate nature from the aggregates? One sutra[41] enumerates twenty false views of a real self. These number twenty because there are five aggregates and four false views associated with each.[42] If a false view regarding the self and aggregates being different entities were described, there would be twenty-five false views of a real self. Since the particular false view of the self and aggregates being different entities is not described in the sutras, there must be no need to teach it because the audience does not have that view. Because the audience of the sutras consisted uniquely of Buddhists, we can infer that the I and the aggregates being different entities or different natures is not a view held by any of the Buddhists. Because such a view in general exists, it must be a view held only by non-Buddhist systems.[43]

In his *Treatise on the Middle Way*, Nagarjuna added a fifth false view in relation to each aggregate—viewing the self as a different entity from form and so forth. He added this because his refutations were aimed at non-Buddhist as well as Buddhist systems.

Since all of the Buddhist systems apart from the Prasangikas believe that a self-existent person can be found within the aggregates, this third point—if the I existed inherently, it would have to be totally inseparable from the aggregates—is directed specifically at them. The Prasangikas refute the ideas of the other Buddhist systems by saying, "If you assert the existence of a self-existing person that has the same nature as the aggregates or is the same entity as the aggregates, you will have to accept that this person is not just one nature with the aggregates but is inseparably one with the aggregates. The I and the aggregates would be totally indistinguishable."

In the third essential point, we search for the person in the aggregates in order to conclude that it cannot be found as inherently one and the same as the aggregates, either individually or collectively. Here we examine, "Is the body the self? Are the feelings the self? Are discriminations the self? Are volitional factors the self? Are any of the six consciousnesses the self? Is the self one of the aggregates? A part of the aggregates? The collection of the aggregates? The continuity of one of the aggregates? The continuity of all the aggregates?"

If the person were inherently one with the aggregates, three faults would follow:

1. Just as there are five aggregates, there would be five persons or five "me's," or just as there is one person, there would be only one aggregate.

2. It would be pointless to assert an I. If the I and the aggregates were inseparably one, they could not have the relationship of the aggregates being what is appropriated and I being what appropriates them. The agent and action[44] would be the same.

3. Everything that could be said of the aggregates would also apply to self.

Let's look at each of these points in more detail.

1. Just as there are five aggregates, there would be five persons or "me's," or just as there is one person, there would be only one aggregate.

If the I were inherently one with the aggregates, it would be indistinguishable from them. If the I and the aggregates were undifferentiably one, then each aggregate would be a person. In that case, since there are five aggregates at any given moment, there would also have to be five I's simultaneously. The body would be a self; so would the feeling aggregate. The discrimination aggregate would be a third self, the volitional factors aggregate would be a fourth self, and the consciousness aggregate would be a fifth self.

At any given moment we have five aggregates. At any given moment do we have five I's? No. Of course, we can talk about the I of today, the I of yesterday, the I of the day before that. We can talk about an I for each day if we want, an I for each month, an I for each year, an I for each moment, and so on. Talking about these various I's of different time periods is no problem. However, saying that there are five separate I's that exist at the same time flies in the face of the facts.

Alternatively, because there is one self, there would have to be just one aggregate. In that case, we couldn't discern the various aggregates because they all would be completely merged into one aggregate and that aggregate would be inseparable from the I. This clearly is not the case: We have five aggregates. In addition, if the parts (aggregates) were inherently the person, then when any one part was indicated, it would be the entire person. For example, my body would be everything I am as a person. Since I can think, my body would be able to think.

In brief, the person would have to be one with the aggregates in every way. In that case, since there are five aggregates, there would be five I's, or if there were one I, there would be just one aggregate. Neither of these is possible.

2. It would be pointless to assert an I. If the I and the aggregates were inseparably one, they could not have the relationship of the aggregates being what is appropriated and I being their appropriator. The agent and action would be the same.

Conventionally, the relationship between the person and the aggregates can be described as the aggregates being the objects that are appropriated and the person being the one that appropriates them. If the I and the aggregates were one, it would be meaningless to accept the existence of a person who appropriates the aggregates as something distinct from the aggregates themselves.

If the person were inherently one with the aggregates, the appropriator (the agent) and the appropriated (the object acted upon) would be one and the same. In that case, positing them as separate, as we usually do, would be meaningless. They would be inseparably one, and a distinction could not be made between them. In that case, both the I and the aggregates would be the appropriator, and both the I and aggregates would be the appropriated. This makes no sense at all.

3. Everything that can be said of the aggregates would also apply to the self.

If the I and the aggregates were inherently one, whatever is true of the aggregates would have to be true for the person. Whatever transformation or arising and disintegration happened to the aggregates would also have to happen to the I. For example, since the body dies, is cremated, and does not go on to the future life, the I would also die, be cremated, and discontinue at the time of death. However, this is not the case: The I that exists by being merely labeled continues on to the future life. Conventionally, some things that happen to the aggregates also happen to the person. For example, if the mind thinks, we say that we are thinking. However, not everything that happens to the aggregates happens to the person.

Another way of explaining this point is to say if the I and the aggregates were one, just as the aggregates arise and cease, the self would as well. While a conventional I does arise and cease, an inherently existent I could not. It would be permanent.

Furthermore, the arising and ceasing of the I does not inherently exist. If it did, various faults would occur, such as (1) the persons of the previous life, this life, the future life, and so forth would not be part of the same continuum, (2) the karma a person created would go to waste, and (3) a person could experience the results of karma she did not create.

Regarding the first fault: All of us accept that the person is affected by a process of arising and perishing, such that earlier moments of the person arise and perish, thus giving rise to later moments of the person. There is an I of the present, an I of the past, and an I of the future. If they were inherently one, they would be inseparably one. If that were so, the past I could remember what the future I will experience, just as the future I remembers events experienced by the past I.

Alternatively, if the I's of the past, present, and future lives were inherently different, they would have to be totally unrelated. In that case, the future person could not remember what happened to him in the past because they would be two totally different people. It would be like John trying to remember Mary's experience. If the I's of the different lifetimes were totally separate and unrelated people, the Buddha could not say, as he did in the sutras, "I remember being a king in my previous life as a bodhisattva."

Regarding the second fault: The person in a future life could not experience the results of the actions done by the person in the past life. This would contradict one of the fundamental attributes of karma, which is that the result is never lost. If the I's of the different lifetimes were unrelated, the karma would go to waste. Even in this lifetime, if the I of one day were totally unrelated to the I of the next day, our actions today would not affect us tomorrow.

The reason for this is an I that arises and ceases inherently would utterly cease at the time of death, without any continuity to the next life, and in the next life a completely different person would arise who has no connection with the former life.

Regarding the third fault: If we insist that the future person experiences the results of karma that was done in the past life, then he would experience the results of actions he did not do. That is because the person of one life and the person of the next life would be completely unrelated. In that case, that person's past lives and the lives of other, distinct people would be equally unrelated. If that were so, Tashi could experience the results of actions done by a totally different person named Lobsang who was not part of his previous continuity. That would contradict another of the four general aspects of karma: that we don't experience the results of actions that we haven't done.

Thus if the person of the past and the future were two distinct, unrelated persons, two faults would occur: (1) The results of karma would be lost because the person who does the actions in one lifetime would utterly cease at the time of death and therefore would not experience the results of those actions in the future life and (2) the person in the future life, who is completely different and unrelated, would undergo experiences resulting from actions she did not do.

In fact, when a person experiences the results of her previous lives' actions in this life, she is not experiencing the results of karmas that were done by somebody who is totally unrelated to her. The persons of the past, present, and future are related in that the previous person is the cause of the present person, who is the cause of the future person. They exist in the same continuity. Due to this relationship, the person in the future life experiences the results of actions that have been done in previous lives of the same continuum. However, self-existent entities cannot have such relationships.

Because a connection exists between the I of today and the child that we were, we are able to remember events from our childhood. Likewise, due to this relationship of the past person to the future person in the same continuity, the Buddha was able to recollect who he was and what he did in his past lives when he was a bodhisattva.

All three of the above faults would follow if the I existed inherently and were one with the aggregates. The source of these three absurdities comes back to the way in which the innate I-grasping mind grasps its object. If the person that goes from life to life—the focal object of the I-grasping— were inherently existent, it would have to be either inherently one with or inherently different from the aggregates. If it were one, it would have to be inseparably one with the aggregates, and those faults would follow. Therefore, it cannot possibly be one with the aggregates.

When thinking about this, reflect on the absurd consequences that would come about, such as there being five selves since there are five aggregates.

It seems fairly straightforward to say that if the I were inseparable from the aggregates, there would be this fault and that fault. But what is more difficult is to see the source of these errors in our own mind, to know that all these absurd conclusions would follow if the I existed inherently in the way that our own innate I-grasping mind holds the I to exist.

These are very special and unique lines of reasoning that Chandrakirti used to refute the Svatantrika position. We should remember that the Prasangikas do posit the person in dependence on the aggregates—more precisely in dependence on the continuity of the mental consciousness—but do not posit the person on the aggregates in the context of that person being findable when searched for within the aggregates that are its basis of designation.

To recap, with the first essential point we get the image in our mind of what an inherently existent I would be like if it existed. We need to keep the image of the inherently existent I in the mind, without losing it, while we are analyzing to see whether it exists or not. If the image of the inherently existent I slips from our mind while we are doing this analysis, there is risk that instead of searching for the inherently existent I, we start to search for the conventionally existent I, which is the I that *does* exist. This I cannot be found when searched for within the aggregates because it is merely designated in dependence on the aggregates. However, not finding the conventional I under ultimate analysis does not mean it does not exist. Ultimate analysis negates *only* the I's ultimate or inherent existence.

THE FOURTH ESSENTIAL POINT: ARE THE I AND THE AGGREGATES TOTALLY UNRELATED?

If the person were inherently separate from the aggregates, various faults would follow. For example, if the aggregates were eliminated one by one, a person could still be identified. That is, if we imagine taking away the form aggregate, the feeling aggregate, the discrimination aggregate, the volitional factors aggregate, and the consciousness aggregate, the person would remain. But that's impossible, isn't it? Without the aggregates, there is no way to identify or establish the existence of a person.

The I and the aggregates are not totally separate and unrelated. When our stomach hurts we say, "I'm sick." When we feel pain in our hand, we say, "I'm in pain." Likewise when we take medicine and the illness is cured or the pain stops, we say, "I'm well." Saying this is possible because the person and the aggregates are related. Saying "I'm hot" when our body is hot would be completely impossible if the person were inherently separate from the aggregates and therefore totally unrelated to them. Similarly, if the person and the aggregates were unrelated we could not say "I'm thinking" when the mind is thinking or "I'm happy" when a happy feeling arises.

In general, two things can be different without being completely unrelated. The person and the body are different. But if two things were inherently different, or if an inherently existent thing were different from another thing, they would have to be not just different, but totally unrelated and distinct from each other. If you understand this, it will be not difficult to understand that there is no such thing as an inherently existing person separate from the aggregates.

Expanding the Analysis

The refutation of one and different can also be done with respect to cause and effect, and to agent and object. For example, smoke is what is produced (the result), and fire is what produces it (the cause). If smoke and fire existed inherently, they would have to be either inherently one or inherently different. If smoke were inherently one with fire, it would be inseparably one with the fire, and we would not be able to differentiate them. In addition, both of them could be that which is producing and that which is produced, and smoke would be able to produce fire. On the other hand, if the smoke and the fire were inherently different, they would be totally unrelated, in which case the fire could not cause the smoke.

Generally, two things that are different are not necessarily totally unrelated. Smoke and fire are different, but if they existed inherently, they would be totally unrelated because each one would exist independent of other factors. That is not the case since smoke and fire are causally related.

Another way to expand the analysis is to reflect on five or seven points. As mentioned above, Nagarjuna said there were five false views of the I in relation to each aggregate. To refute these, he presented a five-point analysis, as outlined in his *Precious Garland* (1:82):

> The aggregates are not the self, nor are they in it.
> It is not in them, without them it is not.
> It is not mixed with the aggregates like fire and fuel.
> Therefore how could the self exist?

To refute the designated object (in this case, the I) being inherently existent in relation to its basis of designation (the aggregates), seven points are usually taught:

1. The I is not one with the aggregates.
2. The I is not other than the aggregates.
3. The I is not dependent upon the aggregates.
4. The I is not what the aggregates depend upon.
5. The I does not possess the aggregates.
6. The I is not the collection of the aggregates.
7. The I is not the shape or arrangement of the aggregates.

Four of these points come from the sutras (1, 3, 4, and 5), one from Nagarjuna (2), and two from Chandrakirti's *Supplement to the Middle Way* (6 and 7). Together these form the sevenfold analysis.

Although I will not explain these seven points here, you can study them elsewhere. Je Rinpoche explains this analysis in both his *Ocean of Reasoning* and in his *Elucidation of the Thought*. These seven points can be distilled to form the last two points in the four essential points: The I is not inherently one with the aggregates or inherently different from them. Whether we meditate on two, five, or seven points, the conclusion is the same: The I is not inherently existent.

The Correct Conclusion

Gradually wearing away at our idea that the I exists inherently through this in-depth examination, you notice how the innate I-grasping functions and wonder if what it believes is true actually exists. You start to wonder, "Maybe there isn't an inherently existing person as I believed."

As you go about your day, while you are eating, drinking, walking, and talking, you think, "I am doing this and that." Based on that, the innate I-grasping arises. It focuses on the conventionally existing "I" and conceives it to be inherently existent. In meditation, when you search for that inherently existing I and don't find it, its existence disappears from your mind. At that moment, as an inevitable side effect, you also lose the appearance of the conventionally existing I. Having negated the inherently existing I through analysis, meditate on space-like emptiness. Only emptiness appears to this mind; there is no appearance of any conventionality, including the I. At this point in your meditation, you cannot and should not think about the existence of the I. Stay with the experience of emptiness.

There is no danger at this point of your meditation becoming nihilistic. Pabongkha Rinpoche and Dagpo Lama Rinpoche are clear about this in their writings. At that point, do not try to establish the existence of the conventionally existing I; just continue meditating on emptiness. This correct cognizer perceives only emptiness. It is only upon emergence from the meditative equipoise on emptiness that the conventional I reappears. Thus, during meditation don't worry that you've fallen to nihilism because the appearance of the conventionally existing I has ceased along with the appearance of the inherently existent I.

WHEN TO REFLECT ON DEPENDENT ARISING

The fact of a thing being dependent is the ultimate reason for saying it is empty. This is stated formally as "empty because of being a dependent arising," and "dependent because of being empty." Initially, insight into an object's dependent nature is crucial to understanding the impossibility of its being self-existent. At the beginning, we become familiar with thinking, "It is dependent, therefore it is not self-existent," and in this way we are able to correctly and confidently conclude that it is empty of self-existence.

However, in a meditation session, once we have successfully refuted the object of negation, we do not continue to reflect on the object's dependent nature. Rather, during meditative equipoise on emptiness, we focus only on the mere absence of inherent existence. At this time there is no sense of the dependent object. If this meditation produced a thought about the dependent nature of the I, that would mean emptiness was an affirming negation. However, emptiness is a nonaffirming negation; that is, it only negates inherent existence and does not establish anything else in its stead.

In short, when we first think about what it means for phenomena to be empty, we approach the topic in terms of dependent arising. But afterward, when we have identified the object of negation and are searching to determine if the object exists in this way, we do not think of the object's dependence. Instead we search to see if we can find the inherently existent thing that seems so real to us.

As we progress, the topic will become more and more clear for you. Because you are learning about emptiness, I am confident that even if it doesn't bring about a great change in your mind immediately in this life, the seeds it plants will certainly bring great results in future lives. Familiarity with reflecting and meditating on the teachings in this life will yield the result of having wisdom that is quick and incisive in future lives. What we gain from devoting our time and energy to understanding emptiness now is, in a sense, entrusted to our future lives. This is a wonderful legacy that benefits both ourselves and all sentient beings.

CHAPTER FOURTEEN

How Things Arise: Refuting the Four Extremes

Refuting the four extremes of arising—also called "diamond slivers" because each reason powerfully contradicts inherent existence—is one of the major reasonings used to establish the emptiness of inherent existence, especially the emptiness of phenomena. Nagarjuna presents this in the first verse of his *Treatise on the Middle Way* (1:1):

> Nothing ever in any way
> arises from itself, from another,
> from both (itself and another),
> or without a cause.

This refutes the inherently existent arising, or production, asserted by others. The Samkhya, a non-Buddhist school in India, asserts production from self. The lower Buddhist schools assert production from inherently existent others. The Jain, a school that was present at the Buddha's time and still exists today, says things arise from both self and others, while the material-ist Charvaka school says that things arise without causes. Nagarjuna refutes all four of these wrong views, thus demonstrating that there is no inherent production. In none of these four ways does anything whatsoever—be it an external or an internal phenomena, be it form or consciousness or anything else—inherently arise.

Not Arising from Self

The Samkhyas assert that from a cause that has the same essence as itself, an effect is produced that also has the same essence as itself. By this they mean that cause and effect have the same identity or entity, the same essence, and the same nature. To be the same essence or nature, however, two things must exist simultaneously. Thus Buddhists reply, "That means the effect must exist at the time of the cause," and the Samkhyas accept that. They say the effect is present at the time of the cause in an indistinct manner. That is, while present at the time of the cause, the effect is unmanifest; it does not appear clearly to the sense consciousnesses. For example, the sprout is present at the time of the seed, but in an indistinct or unmanifest way. Later, when the seed is watered, the ground is fertilized, and the temperature is warm, the seed grows into the spout, and at that time the indistinct sprout appears and we can see it.

Our system responds, "What do you mean when you say the effect is there at the time of the cause in a way that is not clear to the sense consciousnesses? All you can point out at the time of the cause is the potential or ability to produce the effect." When the Samkhyas say that the sprout is present in the seed in a way that is not clear to the sense consciousnesses, they seem to be saying that the effect exists at the time of the cause because the potential for the effect exists at that time.

We now say, "If you say that the effect exists at the time of the cause because the potential for the effect exists at that time, what do you think about the following? In the mental continuum of a tiny insect there is the potential—a karmic seed—to be born as an elephant thousands of times. In that case, are there thousands of elephants in the continuum of that insect?"

Do you feel comfortable saying that thousands of elephants are present in the tiny insect because the causal karma that will ripen into those resulting rebirths is there? When an ant stands on the tip of a fine blade of grass, are there thousands of invisible elephants there? Not even a very ignorant person would say that!

The Prasangika system asserts emphatically that cause and effect are different; they are different entities, natures, and substances, and the effect does not exist at the time of the cause. Cause and effect are never simultaneous, and therefore the sprout definitely does not exist at the time of the seed. This is quite different from the Samkhyas.

If the effect existed at the time of the cause, it would be pointless for the sprout to grow from the seed because it would already be there. Thus we say to the Samkhyas, "According to you, a sprout growing from a seed is merely a matter of making the identity of the sprout clear. Yet since the identity and entity of the sprout have already been attained at the time of the cause—because the sprout is there—why would it still have to arise? On the one hand you say that the effect exists there at the time of the cause, which means it has already arisen at that time. On the other hand, you say that the sprout has to arise from the seed, which would be a case of producing something that has already been produced! And if you say it still needs to be produced even though its entity is already present, that would lead to nonstop production."

The Samkhya position is hard to uphold. Again, in brief, if the effect exists at the time of the cause, it means cause and effect are simultaneous, in which case the effect would not arise from the cause. Since the effect is already present, it would be pointless for it to arise again. But if that which has already arisen must arise again, then it would arise again and again, endlessly. These are the absurd consequences that follow from asserting arising from self.

Some proponents of arising from self say that the cause is a prior movement in the mind of the creator deity, Ishvara (God). They believe that everything exists in Ishvara's mind in an unmanifest way. When there is movement in Ishvara's mind, things arise and become manifest. However, the same faults pertain to this position as to the position that the sprout is present in the seed in an unmanifest form—if something exists already, there is no need for it to arise again. If it must still arise again, then it would arise endlessly.

Not Arising from Other

Production from other means production of an inherently existent other effect from an inherently existent cause. All the Buddhist schools from Svatantrika-Madhyamaka down assert this type of production. These schools all accept inherent existence. They say cause and effect are inherently existent because according to them, the imputed object can be found when searched for. "Being able to find the imputed object when searched for in its basis of designation" is the meaning of a thing being inherently existent or existing from its own side. In addition, cause and effect are other because they are different, and thus they are inherently other, inherently different. The meaning of *arising from other* is an inherently existing effect that is other (than the seed) arises from an inherently existing cause that is other (than the sprout).

Refuting inherently different cause and effect requires the same thought process as the reasoning of freedom from one and many. This reasoning is based on the unique Prasangika position that if two things are inherently the same they must be indistinguishable, and if they are different they must be entirely unrelated. In the Prasangika system, inherently one and inherently different have those implications, and negating inherently one and inherently different only works when we stick to those implications. Insisting that such implications exist is not a case of being stubborn. They have a source in the Buddha's own scriptures, and many logical proofs establish them as well. They are not mere sophistry used to win an argument; they tell us something about how things really are.

The lower schools do not say that if two things are inherently different, they must be totally unrelated. Nor do they say that if two things are one, they must be inseparably one, having no difference at all. Nevertheless, because passages in the Buddha's scriptures as well as reasoning support it, the Prasangika system insists that those consequences follow from saying that two things are inherently one or inherently different. This type of reasoning is called *reasoning of unsuitability*, which means, "If you say this, that must be the case. If you say that, xyz must follow." In other words, a Prasangika follows a position to its logical conclusion.

The lower schools do not immediately accept what Prasangikas claim to be the logical conclusion of their position. As far as they are concerned, just because two things are inherently different doesn't mean they have to be totally unrelated. They will say, "A seed and sprout are inherently different, but they are not unrelated because they have a causal relationship. Likewise, a jug and 'functioning thing' are different, but they are not unrelated because they have a relationship of the same nature." For them, these things are inherently different and are still related.

However, according to the Prasangika system, this is not possible. Things that are inherently different must necessarily be totally unrelated, and things that are inherently the same must be inseparably one. On this basis, we direct our reasonings to them.

When the lower schools say that an inherently existing effect, which is other, arises from an inherently existing cause, which is other, we ask, "Does darkness arise from light?" Of course, they say, "No," and when we ask, "Why not?" they say, "Because darkness and light are unrelated." Then we ask, "Is an inherently existent child born from an inherently existing mother?" to which they say, "Yes." We reply, "But that can't be so because they are unrelated!" Shocked, they protest, "But they are related!" But we insist, "They can't be related because they are inherently different. If they are related, they can't be inherently existent. If they are related, they must be dependent and reliant, because when two things are related as cause and effect, it means that one arises depending on the other. Since one arises from the other and they are dependent, neither can exist inherently or from its own side."

In this way, our system brings the argument back to the fact of dependence. Explained in many sutras and treatises, dependence is certainly the intention of the Buddha. If you take your time and think carefully about this, it will become clear.

The principal fault in asserting that an effect that is other arises from a cause that is other lies not from saying that the cause and its effect are other. It's due to claiming that cause and effect operate in the context of existence from their own side. If production existed from its own side, it would not depend on anything else because something that exists from its own side does not depend on other factors. The birth of a child that existed from its own side would not depend on the mother. Since the child's birth depends on the mother, the child does not exist from his own side; he exists dependently. Seen in this way, it is clear that there is no such thing as an inherently existing effect that is other arising from an inherently existing cause that is other.

The lower schools' assertion that an inherently existent effect that is other arises depending on an inherently existing cause that is other has two parts: (1) the cause and effect being other and (2) their being inherently existent. Prasangikas do not refute the arising of an effect from a cause that is other. When a cause produces an effect, this is in fact a case of something that is other (the sprout) arising from something that is other (the seed). What the Prasangikas take issue with is the claim that arising exists inherently and exists from its own side. The reason for this is that inherently existent arising cannot involve reliance or dependence. The effect would not rely on the cause, and the two would have no relationship. But it is absurd to say that a sprout does not depend on a seed.

If a cause and its effect did not have to be related, then light could produce darkness and darkness could produce light. Anything would be able to produce anything. There would be no difference between something that produces a thing and something that does not, because everything would be equal in being other. For example, a sprout and a mountain would be equal in terms of being inherently other than a seed. In that case, the seed could be the cause of the mountain.

A question arises: "Of the four extremes, the most difficult to realize is 'no arising from other.' To realize this, we have to realize that no inherently existent effect that is other can arise from an inherently existent cause that is other. To realize that, do we have to realize that nothing is inherently existent? Do we have to realize emptiness? Isn't 'no arising from other' stated as a reason proving that there is no inherent existence? So aren't we involved in circular reasoning?"

Let's examine what *reason* means. We say, "In that place, there is fire because there is smoke." The presence of smoke is stated as a reason establishing the presence of fire in that place. Without fire, there will not be smoke. Smoke is the proof (reason) in that syllogism.

It is possible to know the proof without knowing that which is to be proved. A person who knows that there is smoke could be in doubt whether there is fire. If we point out to him, "In that place, there is fire because there is smoke," he would think, "Yes, of course; there couldn't be smoke there if there were no fire." In this case, the presence of smoke is easier to know so he understands that first, and with that as a reason, he then knows there is fire.

We state "no arising from other" as a reason to prove there is no existence from its own side. If understanding no arising from other means you simultaneously understand no existence from its own side, that would indicate that one is not known prior to the other and there would be no difference in how difficult these two were to ascertain. If that were the case, they would not be "proof" and "that which is to be proved." "Not arising from other" would not be able to act as a proof to bring about the realization of not existing from its own side.

In fact, "not arising from other" is easier to realize than "not existing from its own side." It is realized first, and it proves that existence from its own side does not exist. Thus to realize no arising from other, we do not have to realize that nothing exists inherently; we do not have to realize emptiness.

Furthermore, the reason to prove there is no existence from its own side is "because it is not produced from the four extremes," not simply "because it does not arise from other." Therefore, while realizing no arising from others is the most challenging of the four extremes, realizing it alone is not sufficient to realize no existence from its own side. We have to understand that production in all four extreme ways is impossible in order to realize emptiness.

NOT ARISING FROM BOTH

Arising from both means arising both from self and from other. When we negate arising from self, we also negate arising from both. Similarly, when we refute arising from other, we also have to say there is no arising from both. In other words, since both means both self and others, once we refute either arising from self or arising from others, we clearly cannot have arising from both of them. By analogy, if we want an orange and an apple, as soon as we find out there is no orange, we know we cannot have both. Similarly, if we know someone is missing a hand, we know that person does not have a pair of hands. We will not have realized that he has no hands at all, but we will not think he has a pair of hands. Thus as soon as we understand either that there is no arising from self or no arising from other, we have already put a stop to the idea of arising from both.

The reasoning of no arising from self refutes the position of arising from self. The reasoning of no arising from other refutes the position of arising from other. However, the reasoning refuting either one refutes arising from both. When someone asserts arising from both, all the faults of asserting arising from self accrue as do all the faults of asserting arising from other.

NOT ARISING CAUSELESSLY

Charvakas are non-Buddhist atheists who deny past and future lives and endorse the pursuit of sense pleasures. They assert arising without cause, saying, for example, that there is no cause for the roundness of a pea because no one makes peas round. Likewise, they say there is no cause for the various colors of a peacock's feathers, because no one made them that color. There is no cause for the blackness of a crow's feathers or for the sharpness of a thorn for the same reason. These things are the way they are without anyone making them that way, so they are without cause. While Charvakas certainly know that a sprout arises from a seed, they do not accept any cause and effect relationship that they cannot see with their eyes. For this reason, they also deny rebirth and the law of karma and its effects.

To their assertion that there is no cause for the various beautiful colors of a peacock's feathers, we reply, "In that case, why does a crow have black feathers and not beautiful feathers like the peacock? If there is no cause for the beautiful feathers, crows should have them too." They cannot answer because the colored feathers occur only when there are specific causes, and crows do not possess those causes.

We ask, "If a pea and a thorn do not need a cause for their roundness and sharpness respectively, why isn't the pea sharp and the thorn round?" They have no answer. They can't say that the cause of the pea being round is this, and the cause of the thorn being sharp is that, and that this cause is missing. Can you think of an answer they could give to our question? If there were a rule that something had to be either sharp or round and the pea was not sharp so therefore it must be round, that might work. However, there is no rule that everything must be either sharp or round.

If things happened causelessly, we could not explain why certain plants grow in the heat and not in cool weather, and why others grow when it is cool but not when it is very hot. We could not explain such events in terms of certain factors being present or absent. We would have to say that everything grows no matter the climate because its growth does not rely on anything else. As soon as we say, "It doesn't grow under these conditions," we have introduced some degree of dependence. But according to the Charvaka logic, dependence was already excluded by saying growth occurs without causes. So then we are left with saying anything we like and none of it makes sense!

If we say things arise randomly and without cause, we would have to say that the hardships people go through to sow seeds, work in the fields, and harvest the crops would be pointless because the crops could grow without causes. In the same way, creating virtue in order to have a good future life would be unnecessary because what we are born as in the future would not depend on causes. In that case our present fortunate rebirth would also have arisen randomly, without causes, and there would be no way to explain why one person is born in one set of circumstances and another person born in another.

Summary of the Four Extremes

Having examined the four alternatives for how effects could arise if arising were inherently existent, we find that none of them can be established either by reasoning or experience. The arising of something new cannot occur from itself, from a cause that is inherently other, from both, or causelessly. Yet we know that things arise. How do they arise? They arise in dependence on other factors. If we reflect well on dependent arising, we will understand this ever more clearly, and eventually the net of wrong views will vanish.

It is helpful to repeatedly reflect that because things arise by depending on other factors and exist by relying on other things, nothing is self-existent. Reflecting on dependence and reliance makes this point very clear. Dependent arising, the king of reasonings, proves that nothing exists inherently or by its own characteristics. Just as all the ministers turn to the king for final decisions and the king makes the matter clear, so too all other reasonings refuting the object of negation defer to dependent arising for the final say. When we turn to the reasoning of dependent arising, we see very clearly why there is no self-existence.

While seeds and sprouts are used as examples to help us become familiar with the reasoning, in our meditation we should contemplate these points with respect to our bodies, feelings, minds, the twelve links of dependent arising, bodhisattva deeds, and so on. Understanding the emptiness of these conditioned things will have a strong effect on our minds.

His Holiness the Dalai Lama often tells us that the ultimate view of the original founding masters of all four Tibetan Buddhist traditions is the Prasangika view. Of course, we cannot guarantee that the ultimate view of everybody who claims to represent any of the four traditions is Prasangika or that what they teach is the Prasangika view. A person may sincerely be trying to follow Nagarjuna and His Holiness, but they may make a mistake. While we cannot know for sure what another person's view is, we should study, reflect, and meditate well ourselves so that we will be able to navigate all the intricacies involved in gaining the right view free from the two extremes.

CHAPTER FIFTEEN

Ever-Deepening Understandings of Selflessness

THE THREE TURNINGS OF THE DHARMA WHEEL

The Buddha turned the Dharma wheel three times during his lifetime—that is, he gave three principal cycles of teachings. Each of these three sets of teachings was given according to the capacity and disposition of the audience at that time, and thus the view of selflessness was explained differently in each case. Viewed as a whole, these three cycles indicate the Buddha's marvelous skill as a teacher.

In the first turning of the Dharma wheel the Buddha introduced the idea of the person lacking identity. This was refined in the second turning of the wheel, when he explained the emptiness of inherent existence. However, some people make the mistake of thinking that emptiness means that phenomena do not exist at all. Thinking that names and labels are all that exist, not phenomena themselves, they fall to the extreme of nihilism. Therefore, in the third turning of the Dharma wheel, there is a special teaching differentiating which phenomena lack which kind of identity.

The Vaibhashikas and Sautrantikas follow the teachings of the first turning, saying that the Buddha taught a coarse selflessness (the lack of a permanent, unitary, and independent self) and a subtle selflessness (the lack of a self-sufficient, substantially existing person). According to the higher systems, this is not the final mode of existence of all phenomena. For the Prasangikas specifically, the subtle selflessness is the absence of inherent existence.

The first turning of the wheel didn't challenge the assumption that all phenomena—from form up to omniscient mind—are self-existent and inherently existent as they appear to be. Based on this belief, Vaibhashikas and Sautrantikas assert that causes produce effects. They say that the afflictions of attachment, hatred, and so on arise from grasping a self-sufficient, substantially existent person that does not rely on the aggregates. These afflictions produce karma, and sentient beings experience happiness and suffering as a result. These schools leave the grasping at the person as inherently existent intact. For them, the nonexistence of a self-sufficient, substantially existent person is the meaning of the teaching in the first turning that the person is identityless.

The Chittamatra Perspective

In the second turning of the wheel, the Buddha expanded on the selflessness he taught in the first turning, saying that all phenomena—persons and all other existents—are empty of inherent existence. According to the Prasangikas, the middle turning of the wheel is *definitive*; the way it describes phenomena as existing is the way they actually exist. For that reason they say the teachings of the second turning are definitive, not provisional. They do not need to be interpreted as meaning something else.

According to the Chittamatrins, however, if the teachings in the second turning are understood literally, they would mean that everything is empty of nature and therefore nothing exists. This would be nihilistic and a big mistake. Therefore, it cannot be taken literally and needs interpretation. From the Chittamatra perspective, when the Buddha taught that everything is empty, what he meant was that there are three natures, and each one is empty of identity in its own way. To clarify this, the Buddha taught the third turning to resolve inconsistencies that arise by taking the second turning of the wheel literally. For that reason, the Chittamatrins say the third turning is definitive—it contains the Buddha's final view—and the second turning is provisional and needs interpretation.

According to the Chittamatra, in teaching that all phenomena are devoid of identity in the second turning, the Buddha did not have in mind just one way in which phenomena were without identity. Rather, he had in mind three types of phenomena that lack three different types of identity. Vasubandhu explains this in *Thirty Stanzas* (*Trimshika*, verse 23):

> On the basis of the three natures of existence
> are established the three natures of identitylessness.

The Chittamatrins divide phenomena into three natures, or to put it another way, they say that each phenomenon has three natures:

1. The *imaginary* (or *imputed*) *natures* are mere superimpositions or exaggerations by the conceptual minds that apprehend them. They are mere imputations by conception.
2. The *dependent* (or "*other-powered*") *nature* includes everything that exists depending on causes and conditions. These are impermanent phenomena.
3. The *consummate* (or *thoroughly established*) *nature* is the actual nature. The absence of the imaginary nature in dependent phenomena is the consummate nature.

Each of these lacks its own type of identity:

1. Imaginary natures lack "character identity," an identity that exists by its own characteristics. This is because they exist by imputation and therefore cannot exist by their own characteristics. They are character identityless.
2. Dependent natures lack "production identity" because they are not produced from themselves. They also lack "ultimate identity" because they are not the ultimate nature of phenomena. They are production identityless and ultimate identityless.
3. The consummate nature is the absence of the imaginary ways of existing. It is ultimate identityless in that it is the actual, ultimate nature of phenomena.[45]

To understand the three natures more clearly, take the analogy of a reflection of a face in the mirror. The reflection of a face is dependent. That reflection being an actual face is imaginary. The reflection's lack of being an actual face in the way that it appears to be is analogous to the consummate nature.

Dependent phenomena are produced through depending on causes and conditions, not independently. This is the way in which they lack production identity. The production identity they lack is independent production.

Imaginaries lack a nature that exists by its own characteristics. For example, the reflection being an actual face is merely imputed by the mind; it is a mere projection by the mind. There is no actual face there existing by its own characteristics. Its being an actual face is a mere creation by the mind and does not exist by its own characteristics. It is in that sense we say that imputed phenomena are character identityless.

On the other hand, the dependent lacking a false nature imputed on it by conception—that is the way the dependent actually exists. This is its consummate nature.

With respect to dependent phenomena, there is an object to be negated. This object of negation is the imaginary nature, something that does not really exist, a mere exaggeration by conception. This imaginary or false nature is of two types: (1) dependent phenomena existing as having a different substance than the mind that cognizes them, and (2) dependent phenomena existing as referents of their terms by their own characteristics. Both of these ways of existing are mere imputation by the mind. Dependent phenomena do not in fact exist this way.

One of the imaginary natures that form and other dependent phenomena lack is their being a different substance from the mind that perceives them. According to the Chittamatrins, the cognizing mind and the object cognized in a perception come from the same substantial cause: a karmic seed on the foundation consciousness. The fact that we see the subject and object as separate phenomena is erroneous, according to the Chittamatrins. This is an imaginary nature we project on dependent phenomena.

The second imaginary nature that form and other dependent phenomena lack is existing as the referents of their names by their own characteristics. In actual fact, form is the basis of the name "form." However, it does not exist as the basis of the name "form" by its own characteristics. This means there are no characteristics from the side of form that necessitates the word "form" being applied to it. That form existing from its own side as the basis for the name "form" is completely imaginary; it is a superimposition that is merely imputed by the mind and does not exist by its own characteristics.

If it did exist by its own characteristics, form would be the basis for the name by its own characteristics. But this can be refuted. Asanga's *Compendium of the Great Vehicle (Mahayanasamgraha)* says, "Because an awareness does not exist prior to name..." If there were a substantial basis for names, then the name of an object would already be determined. In this case, it would be difficult to account for one person having several names or one name being applied to several objects. If an object existed from its own side as the referent for that name, then there would have to be several objects because there are several names. The names "apple," "fruit," "impermanent thing," and so forth could not all apply to that round, crunchy, tasty object.

There would have to be a different object for each name. Furthermore, in the case where different objects have the same name—every object in the basket is called "apple"—then there should be only one object because there is only one name.

To summarize, the Chittamatrins say that in the second turning of the wheel when the Buddha said all phenomena are empty, he really meant that each of the three natures are identityless in its own specific way. The dependent lack production independent of causes and conditions. Imaginaries lack existing by their own characteristics. The consummate is the actual ultimate identitylessness.

SUBTLER MEANINGS REVEALED IN THE THREE TURNINGS

Each subsequent turning of the Dharma wheel is in agreement with the teachings of the previous turning but refines its meaning. In the first turning of the wheel, for example, the Buddha taught that the true origins of duhkha are ignorance, afflictions, and karma. The teachings of the second turning are in accord with this; however, ignorance and afflictions are described differently and are identified on a more profound level. The truth of the origin explained in the second turning is more subtle, and because of this, the explanation of the duhkha produced from it is more subtle. The truth of the path, which is the antidote to those afflictions, is likewise more subtle, and the cessation achieved through meditating on that path is also more subtle.

One major difference between the first and second turnings of the wheel is the description of the four aspects of the first noble truth, the truth of duhkha. To review, its four aspects are: impermanent, duhkha, empty, and selfless. The meanings of *empty* and *selfless* were refined in the second turning, when the Buddha said they both referred to the lack of inherent existence of all phenomena.

Differences in subtle points such as this in the three turnings may lead us to wonder if contradictions exist among Buddhist scriptures. Once we understand the topic of definitive and provisional scriptures and definitive and provisional meanings, we discover there is no contradiction among the three turnings of the Dharma wheel.

Definitive meanings are those that cannot be harmed by reasoning or scripture, while *provisional* meanings are those that can be harmed by reasoning or scripture. Provisional or interpretable teachings need to be interpreted according to the context and level of reality to which they pertain. To understand this better, it is helpful to look at the four reliances.

THE FOUR RELIANCES

The great masters advise us to depend upon the four reliances in our Dharma practice. These four help us discern what is important and how to access the deepest level of reality. They are as follows.

1. Don't rely on the person of the teacher, but on what he or she teaches, the doctrine.
2. Don't rely on the words, but on the meaning.
3. Don't rely on provisional teachings that require interpretation, but on the definitive teachings.
4. Don't rely on the definite meaning as found by a dualistic consciousness, but on nonconceptual wisdom.

The first reliance means don't accept what the teacher says as true simply because he is famous, has many titles, or behaves in an elegant manner. Do not get infatuated with the teacher, accepting everything he says on blind faith. Instead listen to what he teaches and examine whether it is suitable.

The second reliance, "Don't rely on the words, but on the meaning," urges us not to accept what is taught just because the words are poetic, elegant, and exotic but to look at the meaning behind them. Accept teachings after analyzing them and discovering for yourself that they are true and that they will lead to the liberation and enlightenment you desire.

The third reliance reminds us that we can't simply say that a certain teaching must be literally true because the Buddha taught it. The Buddha taught in conformity with the values, dispositions, and capacities of his audience. He knew that certain people could easily misunderstand a particular teaching, and instead of benefiting them, it would harm them. For that reason he taught what was suitable and appropriate for specific people according to their level of spiritual development at that time. Sometimes he would say something, although his ultimate intention was another. But when that audience took his words literally, they would benefit.

Therefore, some teachings are provisional in that they require interpretation for their deeper meaning to become apparent, while other teachings are definitive because they present suchness, the way phenomena actually exist. This is the case with the explanation of identitylessness in the third turning of the wheel, a teaching that the Chittamatrins consider definitive and the Madhyamikas consider provisional.

The fourth reliance instructs us not to rely on the definitive meaning as found by a dualistic consciousness, but on nonconceptual wisdom. Rather than being content with a conceptual understanding, we should strive to realize the meaning with a direct valid cognizer.

To conclude, not all of the Buddha's teachings should be understood literally, and not all discuss the ultimate nature of phenomena according to the way the Buddha perceives it. A teaching could be provisional and require interpretation. This is similar to a skilled physician, who instructs one patient to eat a certain food and another patient not to eat it. The food and the physician are the same, but the situation and the patient are different. It would be extremely limiting and even damaging if the physician's advice to one patient were applied to all patients. While superficially the advice he gives to different patients may sound contradictory, it is not; the ultimate intention of the physician is to benefit both individuals.

In order to rely on definitive sutras, we have to first learn the criteria for differentiating definitive and provisional sutras and apply them correctly. From the viewpoint of how phenomena actually exist, the Prasangikas' teachings express the ultimate intention of the Buddha, whereas the lower schools' interpretations reflect the scriptural intention, but not the final understanding, of the Buddha.

Ever-Deepening Levels of Selflessness

We have heard about the three turnings of the Dharma wheel and about the various Buddhist tenet systems. I would like now to summarize these in order to illustrate the Buddha's skillful means in giving various teachings according to the dispositions and interests of the audience and in this way leading all sentient beings to full enlightenment. The summary will also give a broad and encompassing view of the main points of all these teachings and tenets.

The selflessness that is the nonexistence of a permanent, unitary, and independent person and the selflessness that is empty of a self-sufficient, substantially existent person were taught in the first turning of wheel and are accepted as the subtlest teaching by the Vaibhashika and Sautrantika systems. The emptiness of inherent existence—of phenomena existing in and of themselves—was taught in the middle turning of wheel. This is the Prasangika understanding of selflessness, and here emptiness is understood in terms of phenomena existing by reliance, dependence, and relation. This is what is meant by the "stages of emptiness explicitly revealed in the second turning of the wheel."

Those who think that because things do not inherently exist they do not exist at all risk falling to nihilism after listening to the teachings of the middle turning. To avoid this, the Buddha taught the third turning of the wheel. Here he explained what he said in the second turning about all phenomena being identityless as referring to three types of phenomena, each having its own type of identitylessness. Thus in each turning of the wheel, the Buddha explained selflessness in a different way, according to the dispositions and capabilities of the various audiences.

According to the lower schools, realizing the nonexistence of a permanent, unitary, and independent person is the coarse realization of the selflessness of persons, and realizing the nonexistence of a self-sufficient, substantially existent person is the subtle realization of the selflessness of person. However, according to the Prasangika school, realizing these two selflessnesses is not the realization of emptiness and will not free us from samsara because they are not the most subtle level of selflessness.

While all Buddhist schools refute an independent self, their meaning of *independent* varies. When speaking about a self that is permanent, unitary, and independent, *independent* means independent of causes and conditions. When speaking about a self-sufficient, substantially existent person, *independent* means independent of the aggregates. According to the Prasangikas, an even subtler meaning of *independent* exists: being independent of designation by term and concept.

Chittamatrins and Svatantrikas accept selflessness of persons as asserted by the Vaibhashikas and Sautrantikas, but they also assert a selflessness of phenomena. According to the Chittamatra system, the selflessness of phenomena has two aspects: (1) the emptiness of form and so forth existing by its own characteristics as the basis for their names, and (2) the emptiness of form and so forth and the valid cognizer realizing form and so forth being different substances. The Madhyamaka school does not accept the

Chittamatrins' assertion that form and its valid cognizer are empty of being different substances because they accept external objects.

Furthermore, Chittamatrins accept true existence as well as nontrue existence. In speaking about the three categories of phenomena, they say dependent things—all impermanent things—are truly existent. By negating external objects, Chittamatrins staunchly assert that the mind itself is truly existent. The emptiness of imaginaries in dependent phenomena is the consummate nature, which they say is also truly existent. Only imaginaries are said to be empty of true existence.

Madhyamikas, on the other hand, negate true existence across the board, saying everything that exists is posited by mind. Nothing can exist without being posited by mind.

Within the Madhyamaka school, the Svatantrikas say that phenomena must exist from their own side. If not, they would be totally nonexistent. Thus they assert the emptiness of true existence but accept inherent existence and existence from its own side on the conventional level. Prasangikas say that true existence and inherent existence are the same and negate both of them. Here again is a situation of different schools using the same word but defining them differently.

For Svatantrikas things are empty of true existence, but they exist by being posited through the force of appearing to a nondefective awareness. To prove this, they give the example of sexual attraction. The desirable person possesses an element of beauty from his or her own side. Inappropriate attention exaggerates this, making the other person seem 100 percent beautiful, and in this way attachment arises. If there were absolutely no beauty from the side of the other person, they say, this wouldn't happen. There would be nothing to exaggerate.

We can see that when attachment and anger arise, a change has occurred. With attachment the person now appears beautiful, with anger the person seems bad or wrong. The Prasangikas say that this change in appearance has nothing to do with the person having that quality from his or her own side. Those changes take place in our mind in dependence on various other factors.

The Prasangika approach is very different from the other systems. While they say it is important to realize the selflessness of persons propounded by the lower schools, meditating on that alone is not sufficient. Even if someone also accumulates vast merit on the bodhisattva path by engaging in the six perfections, the subtlest self-grasping of persons will not be harmed. The grasping at inherent existence and all the afflictions that arise depending on it will still remain in the person's mindstream. Even though some people realize that the person is not independent of causes and not independent of the aggregates, their minds still grasp both persons and phenomena as inherently existent. Following this, inappropriate attention arises, which produces afflictions. These create karma, and samsara is perpetuated.

In contrast, people meditating on the Prasangika view will realize there are no inherently existent persons or phenomena—they will know the apprehended object of the grasping at inherent existence does not exist— and in this way they will be able to cut the root of self-grasping ignorance. By doing this, the inappropriate attention that arises based on it, the afflictions, and the karma they create to be reborn in cyclic existence all cease. All duhkha in cyclic existence thus ceases and can never arise again.

By realizing the emptiness of each object of negation, they are able to reduce the force of more and more afflictions. Realizing the selflessness of a permanent, unitary, independent self and the selflessness of a self-sufficient, substantially existent person temporarily ceases the afflictions arising in dependence on them. This enables them to create more virtue and less negativity in their lives. By then going on to meditate on the two selflessnesses of phenomena asserted by the Chittamatrins, they lessen their attachment to external objects by seeing that a perceived object and the consciousness perceiving it arise from the same substantial cause, a latency on the mind.

If they then adopt the Svatantrika view of the emptiness of true existence, they will see that the mind, too, lacks true existence, which will further subdue, though not totally eradicate, their afflictions. Meditating on the views of the lower schools prepares these practitioners to then understand and realize the Prasangika assertions of the emptiness of inherent existence. At this point, they realize the actual ultimate nature of persons and phenomena, and by meditating on this over time they are able to eliminate all afflictions, their seeds, and the karma that causes samsaric rebirth. In this way they attain nirvana. If, in the process of deepening their understanding of selflessness by progressing through the views of the lower schools until they reach the Prasangika view, they also generate bodhichitta and practice the six perfections, this will enable them to create all the causes and conditions to become a fully enlightened buddha.

Deepening Understanding of Dependent Arising

In the same way that studying the various tenets systems in order of the sophistication of their view enables us to arrive at the correct view, contemplating the levels of dependent arising they assert enables us to understand the subtlest level of dependent arising.

All four philosophical schools accept existence through dependence and reliance. But when it comes to explaining *how* things are dependent and reliant, they differ. Proponents of the lower schools realize the two types of coarse selflessness of persons and understand that the person is dependent on causes and conditions and on the aggregates. However, they do not understand that because the person depends on causes and conditions and on the aggregates, the person cannot exist inherently. They do not understand the fact that all phenomena existing in dependence on other factors means they are empty of inherent existence. Therefore they do not understand the subtle level of dependent arising that the Prasangikas talk about.

The Vaibhashikas and Sautrantikas assert all products are dependent because results exist dependent on their causes. In this way, these two schools limit dependent arising as applying only to conditioned phenomena. Even in the realm of cause and effect, they only establish effects as being dependent upon causes. They are not able to understand that causes also depend upon their effects, as Prasangikas assert, and thus do not understand mutual or relational dependence.

Expanding the field of objects covered by dependent arising, the Chittamatra and Svatantrika systems say that all phenomena depend on parts. For example, a year depends on the twelve months that are its parts. Permanent space depends on the space in the east, the space in the west, and so on. Therefore, they say that both impermanent and permanent phenomena are dependent arisings.

In addition to this, Prasangikas accept that everything depends on being imputed by name and conception. In this way, all phenomena, permanent and impermanent, are mere name, which indicates they are also empty of inherent existence. When it is said that phenomena exist in mere name, *mere* negates self-existence, existence from its own side. The meaning of *dependent* is much more profound in the Prasangika system.

We may believe that because things appear to be the same from one moment to the next that their name inheres in them. Or we may think that their name is a solid factor that connects one moment of the object to the next moment of that object. Alternatively, we may think that because something changes in each moment, there is no basis that can be labeled.

All of these views are incorrect. The name follows the continuity of moments of a similar type. For example, this object that is used to tell time is called "clock," even though the basis of designation has changed from one day to the next in that the parts are arising and disintegrating in every nanosecond. While there is no point in which impermanent things remain unchanging, a basis of designation is still present over time as is the object that exists by being merely designated in dependence on that basis.

For example, there is the basis of designation—the collection of parts— that the word *clock* refers to. That collection of parts has to be something that can be used to tell the time. But if we look within that basis and try to find something that is the clock or something that by itself tells the time, there is nothing findable within it that could be identified as being the clock that is used to tell time. For that reason, the clock is said to exist by being merely imputed by name and concept in dependence on its basis of designation. When we understand this with respect to one object, it will be easy to transfer that understanding to other phenomena and to see that they also are mere name and therefore are unfindable on their bases of designation and do not exist from their own side.

Names and labels are sounds, specifically, expressive sounds. In accordance with that name, a conceptual mind arises that thinks, "That is a clock." It is in this sense that we say all phenomena are mere name, mere label, and mere imputation by conception. It is not the case that the clock is a sound or that only sounds exist.

Although the clock is unfindable in its basis of designation, it is findable in general. When someone asks us, "Where is the clock?" we point over there. While the clock exists on the table, it does not exist on its basis of designation. Conventionally, a clock is on the table, but when we search in its basis of designation for what the clock ultimately is, we cannot find anything. This is the subtle mode of existence of that object, and understanding dependent arising is indispensable for understanding this.

When we look at the relationship between the person and her aggregates and see the way in which the person depends upon these aggregates, this brings us to investigate the subtle levels of dependence. That, in turn, leads us to the subtlest way of being of the I, and through this investigation, we come to understand that there is no person that is self-existent or independent of all other factors.

In the monasteries we spend a lot of time and energy discussing the meaning of *mere name, mere label*, and *mere imputation by conception*. Gradually through this process of debate and discussion, we gain clarity about this topic. Likewise, if you think about these topics and discuss them, they will become clearer to you.

Phenomena Are Self-Liberated

Sometimes we hear it said that phenomena are "self-liberated" or that "the appearing and the possible are self-liberated, like illusions and dreams." What does this mean? The person and the elements that are its basis of designation are self-liberated in that they are primordially free or liberated from self-existence. In fact all permanent and impermanent phenomena—everything that exists—are self-liberated; they are primordially free from or liberated from existing in and of themselves because they are dependent.

Person, being, self, and I are synonyms. The being is imputed depending on the assembly of the six elements—earth, water, fire, air, space, and consciousness—which are its basis of designation. In his *Precious Garland* (1:80) Nagarjuna refutes the person being any of these elements that constitute the basis of designation of the person:

> A person is not earth, not water,
> not fire, not wind, not space,
> not consciousness, and not all of them.
> What person is there other than these?

The four or five aggregates are also the basis of designation of the person, and the person is what is imputed depending on the assembly of four or five aggregates.

You may say, "Wait a minute! First you said the four or five aggregates are the basis of designation of the person, and now you are saying the six elements are." The six elements fit into the five aggregates. Five elements—earth, water, fire, air, and impermanent space—are included in the form aggregate. The hardness in the body is due to the earth element, the cohesion in the body is due to the water element; it makes the earth particles form a mass. The heat in the body comes from the fire element. The air element in the body flows through various channels, and in this way, the person can move around. The air is able to move in the body due to the presence of the empty spaces inside it. Lastly, the consciousness element consists of the four mental aggregates.

Nagarjuna continues in the following verse:

> Just as a person is not real
> due to being a composite of six elements,
> so each of the elements also
> is not real due to being a composite.

The person arises in dependence on the assembly of the six elements. Because of this, the person is not established in and of itself; the person is not self-existent. This shows the selflessness of persons. Likewise, each of the elements is also merely labeled in dependence on the assembly of parts that are its basis of designation. Therefore the elements, which are the basis of designation of the person, also are not self-existent. This is the selflessness of phenomena. Because neither the person nor other phenomena are self-existent, all phenomena are self-liberated.

SELF-EMPTINESS AND OTHER-EMPTINESS

Phenomena are not only self-liberated, they are also self-empty. That which is empty of self-existence we call *self-empty* (*rangtong*). This is the emptiness taught in the middle turning of the wheel, the emptiness asserted by the Prasangikas, and it means all phenomena do not exist in and of themselves; they exist dependent on other factors. Impermanent things rely on causes and conditions, they are composed of parts, and they depend on the mind conceiving and labeling them. Permanent phenomena also rely on parts and exist by being merely labeled by term and concept.

Self-emptiness does not mean that something is empty of itself. If it did, then a table would be empty of table. If the table were empty of table, the table would not be a table. The table is not anything else either. Saying that a table is empty of being a table would mean that in dependence on the basis of designation where "table" is labeled, the table would be nonexistent. If table is nonexistent there, where would it exist? One would end up saying that the table is totally nonexistent and that nothing at all exists. There are great scholars who assert self-emptiness as meaning that a conventional truth is empty of being itself, but we disagree.

Regarding *other-empty* (*shentong*), His Holiness the Dalai Lama says that there is one explanation of other-emptiness that is correct and another that is incorrect. In the remainder of this section, I will discuss the incorrect explanation.

In the late thirteenth and early fourteenth centuries in Tibet, Dolpopa Sherab Gyaltsen, a lineage guru in the Kalachakra practice and the founder of the Jonang tradition, taught a view of other-emptiness. His teachings on tantra are wonderful, but his explanation of emptiness—self-emptiness and other-emptiness—is very different from the Prasangika explanation.

According to his view, all conventionally existent phenomena are self-empty in the sense of being empty of themselves. This is a very different meaning of *self-empty* than that held by the Prasangika system. Prasangikas negate these assertions by saying that if the jug were empty of being the jug, then in the place where there is the flat-based, round-bellied water pourer—which is the definition of a jug—there would be no jug. The only place a jug can exist is where there is a flat-based, round-bellied water pourer. A jug cannot exist in any other place. If it does not exist there, where else could it exist? It would not exist at all. The jug would be totally nonexistent. Prasangikas see those who assert this view as having fallen to nihilism by saying that conventional phenomena do not exist because they are empty of being themselves.

According to Dolpopa, *other-emptiness* means that something is empty of being something else. This would be like saying the temple is empty of being a human. Here the basis of the negation (temple) is empty of being something other than itself (humans, statues). When the object that is the basis of the negation (temple) is other than what is being negated on it (humans, statues)—that is, the basis of the negation and the thing negated are mutually other—that is other-emptiness. For example, a pillar is not a jug, and so the pillar is empty of being a jug. Other-emptiness is similar to this.

Of course, the proponents of other-emptiness do not say the temple being empty of being humans is the realization of the ultimate nature. I am merely using the temple as an example. Once we have understood the principle in the context of an example, we can then understand it in connection with what the example is intended to illustrate.

As soon as we know what the temple is, we will know that the temple is not humans. By knowing that, will we be able to negate the object of negation, true existence, on the temple? When we realize the temple is empty of being humans, we realize it is not humans. Is this the realization of the emptiness of the temple? No, because to realize the emptiness of the temple involves realizing it is empty of self-existence. Thus, the realization of the other-emptiness of the temple is not the realization of its emptiness of inherent existence. The way of realizing emptiness is not complete because the actual object of negation has not been negated.

Realizing the temple's self-liberation and self-emptiness are realizations of its emptiness, because in both cases the temple's emptiness of self-existence has been realized. Realizing the self-emptiness of a phenomenon is the realization of its emptiness. Realizing its other-emptiness is not the realization of its emptiness.

Most scholars accept that investigating a thing's emptiness is investigating its self-emptiness, because they agree that its self-emptiness is its emptiness of self-existence, its emptiness of existence from its own side. Self-emptiness and self-liberation are the same. Self-emptiness means emptiness of inherent existence, liberation from inherent existence, liberation from existence through its own identity. Realizing this is realizing emptiness. While there are texts that advocate other-emptiness, saying that it is Nagarjuna's intention, that is incorrect.

In particular, proponents of other-emptiness assert that ultimate phenomena are other-empty, meaning they are empty of being conventional phenomena. While it is true that ultimate truths are empty of being conventional truths, the Prasangikas say this is irrelevant to the subtle meaning of emptiness. One object being empty of another object other than itself does not capture the full meaning of emptiness. They also disagree with the proponents of other-emptiness who say that the ultimate truth is empty of conventional phenomena, because this implies that ultimate truth is independent and absolute, whereas according to the Prasangikas, emptiness also is dependent. Therefore, when Prasangikas analyze and establish emptiness, they do not use the term *other-empty*.

It is not that there is no such thing as other-emptiness. It is not that things are not other-empty, because of course they are empty of being what they are not. It is true that cold is empty of being hot. Ultimate truths are empty of being conventional truths. However, realizing other-emptiness does not help us progress on the path. It is missing the mark of refuting the object of negation. The emptiness we need to meditate on is an object's emptiness of existing from its own side.

While some scholars claim the meaning of emptiness is other-emptiness, most scholars agree that other-emptiness does not meet the criteria necessary for realizing emptiness. They agree that by just realizing other-emptiness, a person has not fully realized emptiness. The reason certain scholars seem to consider other-emptiness so important is because they have not gone into it in fine enough detail. They do not see that understanding other-emptiness does not negate the subtle object of negation, inherent existence.

It is similar to someone who believes that meditating on the absence of a permanent, unitary, and independent self is meditation on the subtlest level of reality. That is not the subtlest selflessness because to realize it, one only needs to realize that the person is impermanent and relies on causes and conditions. Meditating on other-emptiness is like this. By realizing it, one has not yet negated the subtlest object of negation and thus has not yet realized emptiness.

In short, we have two main differences with those who assert other-emptiness:

1. They say that *self-emptiness* means "empty of itself," or that conventional phenomena are empty of being conventional phenomena. For example, the jug is empty of a jug. We disagree, saying that if the jug were empty of being a jug, it would be nonexistent. We assert that self-emptiness is the emptiness of self-existence, the emptiness of inherent existence.

2. They say that other-emptiness is the real meaning of emptiness, and assert that other-emptiness is something being empty of being something else, specifically the ultimate truth being empty of being conventional truths. This is similar to saying a temple being empty of being humans. We respond that this does not negate the subtlest object of negation, inherent existence, so it cannot be a complete realization of emptiness.

CHAPTER SIXTEEN

Appearances

THINGS DO NOT EXIST AS THEY APPEAR

In our studies about emptiness, we often hear that "things don't exist in the way they appear." This statement can have more than one meaning depending upon the situation. First, there are true and false phenomena, in which their truth or falsity is discerned according to the principal consciousness that cognizes them. Here "existing or not existing the way they appear" involves whether or not they appear truly existent to their principal cognizer.[46] *True* phenomena exist the way they appear in that they do not appear truly existent to their principal cognizer. Ultimate truths such as emptinesses are true phenomena; they appear empty of true existence to their principal cognizer—a valid cognizer[47] analyzing the ultimate—and they are empty of true existence. *False* phenomena appear truly existent to their principal cognizer. Conventional truths—all phenomena except emptiness—are falsities because while they appear truly existent to their principal cognizers—conventional valid cognizers—they are not truly existent. In unpacking this, we move into an interesting discussion of what consciousnesses, to which people, and at what time things exist the way they appear.

In another way of speaking about "existing in the way they appear," the consciousness that cognizes the object in question is a conventional valid cognizer in the continuum of someone who has not realized emptiness. This mind can discern things that are *real from a worldly perspective*—things that a worldly cognizer knows exist the way they appear, for example a table. It can also discern things that are *unreal*, such as a reflection in a mirror, the appearances on a television screen, a mirage, and so on. These things do not they exist the way they appear because there is no face in the mirror, no people in the television, and no water on the asphalt.

These two ways of speaking about things existing or not existing in the way they appear points to a distinction that is made between true and false, on the one hand, and real and unreal from the perspective of the worldly mind, on the other hand.

TRUE AND FALSE

Something is true if the way it appears and the way it exists are concordant. Something is false if the way it appears and the way it exists are discordant. Emptiness is true because the way in which it appears and the way in which it exists are concordant. The way emptiness appears is just as it is. Conventional phenomena, on the other hand, are false because the way they appear is not in accord with the way they exist.

Someone might object, "According to these criteria, emptiness is false because to the mind grasping true existence that takes emptiness as its object, emptiness appears truly existent whereas it is not. So it does not exist in the way it appears." This is something that is worth thinking about.

It is true that when emptiness appears to the mind grasping true existence, it appears to be truly existent whereas in fact it is empty of true existence, and therefore it does not actually exist in the way that it appears to that mind. Any phenomenon that appears to the mind grasping true existence appears truly existent, and this mind grasps whatever appears to it as truly existent. Emptiness is no exception: To the true-grasping mind it appears to be completely independent of all other factors, and this mind believes that appearance to be exactly how emptiness exists. Thus emptiness does not exist in the way it appears to the true-grasping mind.

But if true-grasping were the yardstick for measuring whether something is true or false, we would have to say that everything that exists is false, because everything that appears to true-grasping appears to be truly existent, whereas in fact it is empty of true existence. Everything is false in relation to true-grasping. However, determining whether a phenomenon is true or false is not done in relation to the true-grasping mind. It is done in relation to the wisdom of meditative equipoise of an arya. That mind directly and nonconceptually realizes emptiness.

An arya's wisdom of meditative equipoise and an arya's subsequent attainment—the period when she arises from meditation and engages in daily activities—are arya paths. If you haven't had the opportunity to study the grounds and paths—the progressive stages one actualizes in order to become an arhat or a buddha—I will give you a brief overview so that you will understand them.

There are three vehicles: the vehicles of the hearers, solitary realizers, and bodhisattvas, each of which has five paths. One enters the first path when one has firm renunciation in the case of the first two vehicles or spontaneous bodhichitta in the case of the bodhisattva vehicle. The names of these five paths are the same in each vehicle, although what exactly is realized and attained on each path differs in some respects according to the vehicle and according to the tenet system describing it. The five paths are:

1. Path of accumulation
2. Path of preparation
3. Path of seeing
4. Path of meditation
5. Path of no-more learning

The first two of the five paths are called *ordinary paths*, or paths of ordinary beings, whereas the last three paths of each vehicle are called *arya's paths*, or paths of the superior or noble ones, because on these paths one realizes emptiness directly. "The wisdom of meditative equipoise of the arya" refers to the direct nonconceptual realization of emptiness. During this equipoise, an arya directly and nonconceptually realizes emptiness, and to that mind there is no appearance of true existence. There is no dualistic appearance at all to that mind. Here *dualistic appearances* includes all of the below:

- The appearance of true existence
- A conceptual appearance through which a conceptual mind knows its object
- The appearance of subject and object being different, i.e., of the perceiving mind and its object being different
- The appearance of conventional phenomena

An arya's wisdom of meditative equipoise is free of all of these types of dualistic appearance. Emptiness is the object of that mind, and when that wisdom of meditative equipoise takes emptiness as its object, emptiness does not appear truly existent to it. There are no dualistic appearances at all to that mind. It is with respect to this mind that emptiness is true because the way it appears to that mind and its actual way of existing are the same.

In fact, that arya's meditative equipoise goes into the object, emptiness, just like water being mixed with water.

Thus the arya's meditative equipoise on emptiness is the mind that determines whether emptiness, an ultimate truth, is true or false. We can see this from the definition of ultimate truth: It is the object found by a valid mind experiencing the ultimate, and that valid mind experiencing the ultimate is a valid mind experiencing the ultimate with reference to it.[48]

Apart from emptiness, every other phenomenon is a conventional truth. Conventional truths are false because there is disparity between the way they exist and the way they appear. They are not said to be false in relation to the mind grasping true existence or in relation to the arya's wisdom of meditative equipoise because that is not the principal mind that realizes conventional truths. This determination of their being true or false has to be made in relation to the principal mind that realizes conventional objects. What are these minds?

MINDS AND THEIR OBJECTS

Among conventional truths, some are conditioned phenomena and others are unconditioned or permanent phenomena. Conditioned phenomena include visual forms, sounds, smells, tastes, tangibles, and *dharmas*, or "objects of mental consciousness." Each type of phenomenon has a principal mind that realizes it: the visual consciousness for visual forms up to the mental consciousness for objects of mental consciousness.

When a visual form appears to the visual consciousness, it appears as if it existed from its own side. Likewise, when a sound appears to the auditory consciousness, it appears to be truly existent. It is the same with the other objects appearing to the other sense consciousnesses and to the mental consciousness apprehending objects of mental consciousness. Although those objects appear to be truly existent—as if they were completely independent of all causes and conditions and any other factor whatsoever—to the consciousnesses that apprehend them, not all of the consciousnesses believe or grasp that appearance as true. In other words, while true existence *appears* to them, not all of these consciousnesses *grasp* or believe in true existence.

For example, none of the sense consciousnesses conceive, think, or grasp that form is truly existent as it appears to be. They are not minds grasping true existence. Even though visual form appears truly existent to the visual consciousness apprehending it, that visual consciousness does not grasp it as truly existent. This mind is a valid mind because it realizes that visual form. It is valid with respect to the visual form and is not erroneous in the way it apprehends visual form. It is the same with the other sense consciousnesses; they are valid with respect to their apprehended objects—visual forms, sounds, and so forth. However, while this visual consciousness is not erroneous with respect to its apprehended object, it is a mistaken mind. Its mistake is in terms of its appearing object, because the visual form appears truly existent.

However, the true-grasping mind that has a visual form as its object grasps truly existent form. It grasps that visual form as being truly existent; it believes the appearance of true existence and conceives that form exists that way. Thus it cannot be posited as a valid mind and is a wrong consciousness with respect to its apprehended object, which, in this case, is truly existing form. Only mental consciousnesses can be true-grasping minds, although not all mental consciousnesses are minds grasping true existence.

To review, the *focal object* of a mind is the main object that the consciousness is concerned with, the *appearing object* is the object appearing to that mind, and the *apprehended object* is the object the mind apprehends or grasps. For both the visual consciousness realizing form and the mental consciousness grasping form as truly existent, the focal object is visual form and the appearing object is truly existent form.[49] However, these two minds differ in terms of their apprehended object. For the visual consciousness seeing form, the apprehended object is visual form; but for the mind grasping form as truly existent, the apprehended object is truly existent form. It is from the viewpoint of the apprehended object that we distinguish minds as either valid or erroneous. Thus the visual consciousness apprehending visual form is a valid cognizer while the mind grasping it as truly existent is erroneous.

Mistaken and *erroneous* have different meanings. Minds are deemed *mistaken* in relation to their appearing object—that is, whether true existence appears to it. Minds that are erroneous are distinguished in relation to their apprehended objects. A visual consciousness is erroneous if it perceives white snow as blue or the landscape moving when we're in a train. A mental consciousness is erroneous when it grasps true existence or when it thinks incorrectly. Both the visual consciousness apprehending a visual form and a mental consciousness grasping it as truly existent are mistaken because their appearing object is truly existent form. However, the mind grasping true existence is erroneous while this particular visual consciousness is not. Here we see that although a mind is mistaken, it can be valid. In other words, a valid cognizer can be mistaken.

Similarly to the valid I-apprehending mind, the I appears inherently existent, so this mind is mistaken with respect to its appearing object. In fact, every conventional valid mind of sentient beings is mistaken in terms of how things appear to it because its object always appears to it as if it were existing from its own side. However, as we have discussed, the valid I-apprehending mind is not mistaken in the way it apprehends the I because it does not *grasp* the I as existing inherently as it appears. Thus it is a valid mind. The I-grasping, on the other hand, not only has the appearance of an inherently existent I, but it also grasps that appearance as true; it thinks the I exists inherently as it appears. While this mind is mistaken with respect to its appearing object, it is also erroneous because it grasps the conventional I to exist inherently.

Thus things vividly appear as self-existent even to valid minds, but such minds do not grasp the object as being self-existent as it appears. If all minds grasped their objects as existing in the way that they appear, no mind would be valid. But that is not the case.

The only mind of a sentient being that has no appearance of true existence at all is the arya's wisdom of meditative equipoise. When the arya comes out of meditative equipoise, things still appear truly existent, but they do not believe or grasp at things as existing in that way. For example, when we watch television, all sorts of things appear to us to be there, on the screen. However, we do not think there are real trees and people inside the television although there appears to be. In the same way, when an arya comes out of meditative equipoise on emptiness and engages in daily activities, things appear to exist from their own side, but she does not believe in those appearances for a moment.

Not only aryas in post-meditation time but also anyone who has realized emptiness—even inferentially, conceptually—realizes that there is a disparity between the way things appear and the way they actually exist. This is because they realize that things are not truly existent and do not exist from their own side because they are dependent arisings, relying on many

CHART: THE OBJECTS OF VARIOUS TYPES OF MINDS

	Focal object	Appearing object	Apprehended object	Mistaken	Erroneous
Visual consciousness apprehending blue	Blue	Blue	Blue	Yes	No
True-grasping mind apprehending blue	Blue	Truly existent conceptual appearance of blue	Truly existent blue	Yes	Yes
I-apprehending mind	Conventional I	Truly existent I	Conventional I	Yes	No
I-grasping mind	Conventional I	Truly existent I	Truly existent I	Yes	Yes
Inferential realization of emptiness	Emptiness	Truly existent conceptual appearance of emptiness	Emptiness	Yes	No
Arya's meditative equipoise on emptiness	Emptiness	Emptiness	Emptiness	No	No

factors. Although things appear truly existent to these people, they do not believe in that appearance. Instead, they practice seeing such appearance as illusory.

Phenomena whose way of appearing and way of being are concordant in relation to the mind that directly realizes them are called *ultimate phenomena*. These phenomena—emptinesses—are true. Phenomena whose way of appearing and way of existing are discordant to the mind that directly realizes them are conventional phenomena. Conventional phenomena are false. They appear to be self-existent but they are empty of self-existence.

By definition, conventional phenomena are objects found by a valid mind distinguishing conventionalities. The mind that determines whether they are true or false is the principal mind that realizes those objects. For sense objects, it is their respective sense consciousnesses. For the aspects of impermanent and unsatisfactory—two of the four aspects of true duhkha—the main mind realizing them is the mental consciousness or inference. In either case, their way of appearing to those minds and their way of existing are discordant.

There are three types of conditioned phenomena: (1) form or matter, (2) consciousness, and (3) abstract composites. Visual forms, sounds, smells, tastes, and tangibles are included in matter. All other conditioned phenomena are realized by the mental consciousness; that is the principal mind realizing them, and in many cases this is an inference. Phenomena that are realized by the mental consciousness include impermanence, unsatisfactory nature, time, and so forth.

To recapitulate, the determination whether a phenomenon is true or false—whether it exists the way it appears or does not—is done in relation to the principal mind cognizing that object. There are two types of phenomena, ultimate truths and conventional truths. Ultimate truths are emptinesses, and the principal mind cognizing them are an arya's meditative equipoise on emptiness. Emptiness is true because there is no disparity between the way that it appears to the arya's wisdom of meditative equipoise focused nonconceptually on emptiness and the way that it exists. Emptiness appears empty to this mind and it is, in fact, empty of true existence.

The principal mind cognizing conventionalities are conventional valid cognizers, which are of different types because their objects are of different types. There are two types of conventional phenomena: conditioned and unconditioned. For an unconditioned phenomenon, such as space, the principal mind realizing it is an inferential consciousness. There are three categories of conditioned things: matter, consciousness, and abstract composites. The five sense objects—visual form, sounds, smells, tastes, and tangibles—are included in matter. The principal mind realizing these things is their respective sense consciousness. The principal mind realizing consciousness is an inference. The principal mind realizing abstract composites such as impermanence, unsatisfactory nature, and so forth is also an inference. All these consciousnesses to which conventional truths appear have the appearance of true existence and thus are mistaken consciousnesses. Some but not all of these consciousnesses at certain times may also be associated with grasping true existence, in which case they become erroneous as well as mistaken.

ANALOGIES

Reacting to the people we see in movies as if they were real people is a modern example of grasping false appearances as true. The classical texts often use the example of a magical illusion. In ancient times magicians could cast a spell so that sticks and pebbles would appear as horses and elephants to the audience.[50] All the people present, including the magician, would see horses and elephants where in fact there were only sticks and pebbles. The audience did not know a spell had been cast, so they thought the appearances of these large and magnificent animals was real. The magician, on the other hand, knew that even though horses and elephants appeared to him, they were simply the result of the spell and were not real. Someone who came along later, after the magical show was over, would see only sticks and pebbles. Horses and elephants would not appear to her, and she definitely would not believe they were there.

There are three possible ways to experience this situation.

1. To people in the audience, horses and elephants appeared, and they believed this appearance to be true. The audience is analogous to ordinary beings, to whom things appear truly existent and who believe those appearances are true, grasping things as truly existent as they appear.

2. To the magician, horses and elephants also appeared, but he did not believe this appearance to be true. Though he saw horses and elephants, he knew they were not really there. The magician resembles a person who has realized emptiness, even someone who has not yet entered a path. To this person, things may appear to be truly existent, but she does not believe them to be true. Instead, she knows the appearances are produced by causes and conditions and sees them as illusory.

3. To the person who came later, horses and elephants did not appear, and the belief that they were there did not arise. This person is analogous to an arya in meditative equipoise who has neither the appearance of nor the grasping at true existence.

REALIZING IT DOES NOT EXIST AS IT APPEARS

What does, "It does not exist as it appears to the mind" mean? We could say, "There is no appearance of true existence to the arya's wisdom of meditative equipoise." We could also say, "At the time of meditative equipoise on emptiness, there is no appearance of true existence to the arya himself." In the first case, we are referring to the mind realizing emptiness and in the second case to the person realizing emptiness at that time.

To realize emptiness, we have to realize that the mind grasping true existence is a wrong consciousness and that there is a disparity between the way things appear to it and the way they actually are. To realize emptiness we have to realize that things do not exist as they appear to the mind grasping true existence. Yet, in order to realize emptiness, we do not have to realize that things do not exist as they appear to us or to our mind at that moment. That is, the mind directly realizing emptiness does not have to realize that things are empty of existing truly as they appear *to it*, because that mind realizing emptiness does not have the appearance of true existence. It does not realize that things do not exist truly as they appear to it because things do not appear truly to the arya's wisdom of meditative equipoise. In short, when we say, "Things do not exist as they appear to that mind," it implies that truly existent things are appearing to that mind. However, there is no appearance of true existence to an arya's meditative equipoise on emptiness. This is in terms of the mind realizing emptiness.

Similarly, in terms of the person realizing emptiness, she realizes there is a disparity between the way of appearing and the way of existing. Although she realizes that the object does not exist as it appears, the object does not have to appear *to her*. In the case of an ordinary person, "realizing that the object does not exist as it appears" implies realizing it does not exist as it appears *to that person*, because true existence still appears to that person. But in the case of a buddha or an arya in meditative equipoise, it does not imply that. Both the buddha and the arya realize that the object does not exist as it appears, even though the object does not appear truly existent to them at that time. In other words, an arya does not need to realize that phenomena do not exist truly as they appear *to him or her*. This is because there is no appearance of true existence to the arya in meditative equipoise.

An analogy might make things clearer. Due to the light, someone looks at a snow mountain and the white snow appears blue to him. But to people standing elsewhere, the white snow mountain does not appear blue, and they realize that it isn't blue in the way that it appears to someone seeing a blue snow mountain. These people do not realize that the snow mountain does not exist as blue in the way that it appears *to them*, because it does not appear blue to them. What they have realized is that the snow mountain does not exist as blue in the way it appears to that other person.

The question I'm raising here is: When aryas are in meditative equipoise directly realizing emptiness, are they or are they not realizing that there is a disparity between the way of appearing and the way of existing? In other words, things do not exist truly as they appear. To realize that, do they have to realize that things do not exist truly as they appear to them? That's the question.

Real and Unreal

Let's leave ultimate phenomena aside for a moment and focus on conventional phenomena. Here a further distinction can be made between things that are real from a worldly perspective and things that are unreal from the worldly perspective.

Worldly perspective or *worldly consciousness* here refers to a conventional valid cognizer not directed toward emptiness in the continuum of a worldly being. Worldly beings are those who have not realized emptiness either inferentially or directly. Included among worldly beings are people who have not yet entered the path as well as people who have.

What is the range of people who have not realized emptiness? Most people who have not entered the path have not realized emptiness, even inferentially. Beings on the first path, the path of accumulation, have not necessarily realized emptiness, even inferentially, although some may have. The demarcation line for entering the path of preparation is the union of serenity and insight on emptiness, which in this case is an inferential realization of emptiness. So those who have entered the path of preparation have realized emptiness inferentially.

What is the range of people who have realized emptiness? It is possible to realize emptiness inferentially before entering a path, and beings with sharp faculties often do this. They realize emptiness before generating unfabricated bodhichitta, which is the demarcation line for entering the Mahayana path of accumulation. In addition, the realization of emptiness may exist on all five paths. But only those on the path of seeing and above have the direct, nonconceptual realization of emptiness.

A visual form is an example of something that is true from a worldly perspective—that is, from the perspective of the mind of a worldly being. Even though that visual form appears to that person to be truly existent, he is not able to realize at that point that this visual form does not exist in the way that it appears. For him, that visual form exists truly as it appears because he hasn't yet realized that it is empty of true existence.

The appearance of two moons when we stretch our eye is an example of something unreal from the perspective of a worldly being. Another example is a white conch that appears yellow. In these cases, we know there is disparity between the way of appearing and existing. We can realize that the appearance of some things is wrong, that they do not exist the way they appear, even before we realize emptiness. These things are unreal from a worldly perspective. Both ordinary people and aryas have conventional valid cognizers that can distinguish reflections, mirages, and so forth as unreal.

Real and unreal things are distinguished according to whether or not a worldly being is able to see that it does not exist as it appears. Here "does not exist as it appears" does not mean that it appears truly existent although it is not. Rather, things are real or unreal from a worldly perspective depending on whether someone who has not realized emptiness can see that they do not exist as they appear. Here "does not exist as it appears" refers to mistaken ways of appearing that even a conventional valid cognizer can know are mistaken.

In the previous discussion of true and false phenomena, the table is an example of a false phenomenon. It is a conventional truth that appears truly existent to its principal cognizer although it does not exist that way. However, from the perspective of a person who has not realized emptiness, the table is considered real because it exists the way it appears to a worldly being who has not realized emptiness. That is, it appears as a table to this person and it exists as a table.

But what about the people and events that appear on a television screen? What about reflections in a mirror and mirages? Apart from perhaps a very young child, people who haven't realized emptiness can discern that they are unreal, that they do not exist as they appear. They know that people appear to be in the television but that there are no people there. They know that the face in the mirror and water on the asphalt are only appearances and that nothing real is there.

Although worldly beings know that people in the television, holograms, reflections, and mirages do not exist as they appear, does that mean that they have realized emptiness? Is realizing that things do not exist as they appear the same as realizing their emptiness of true existence? No, it isn't. Realizing that the face in the mirror is not a real face is a coarse, superficial way of knowing that things do not exist as they appear. To know this, realization of emptiness is not necessary. Realizing that phenomena do not exist truly although they appear to is a much deeper understanding, and to know this, one must have already realized emptiness either inferentially or directly.

INFERENTIAL AND DIRECT REALIZATION OF EMPTINESS

As we've seen, there are many ways to meditate on emptiness, including refuting inherently existent arising, using the logic of the four essential points, and meditating on dependent arising. It is helpful to approach emptiness from different angles, repeatedly reflecting on how things appear to exist inherently but do not exist as they appear. The more we think about this and meditate on it, the more we understand that it is impossible for them to exist the way they appear.

Someone first realizes emptiness by means of an inferential realization. While an inferential realization of emptiness is still conceptual, it is very different from a correct assumption regarding emptiness, which is also conceptual. A correct assumption is not very strong. While it is going in the right direction, it is not stable and it does not comprehend emptiness incontrovertibly in the way an inference does. In fact someone who is a good debater could even convince someone with a correct assumption that phenomena are truly existent! However, this cannot happen with someone who has realized emptiness by means of an inference.

An inferential realization of emptiness is an understanding that arises due to reasoning. It understands emptiness by way of a conceptual appearance, which also acts like a veil separating the mind and emptiness. The conceptual appearance is an obscuration that prevents the meditator from realizing emptiness clearly. It is like fog—when we look in the distance, we cannot see clearly.

While this inferential realization lacks the directness of a nonconceptual realization of emptiness, it is nevertheless valuable as a step on the path. Once we have an inferential realization of the emptiness of one object, just by turning our minds to another object we will easily realize its emptiness using the same reasoning without having to go through a long process.

Over time, as we continue to meditate on emptiness with the union of serenity and insight, to purify, and to accumulate merit, the obscuration of the conceptual appearance will become thinner and thinner, until eventually it will disappear. At that time we will have the direct realization and enter the path of seeing. When we directly perceive the emptiness of one object, simultaneously we will realize the emptiness of all phenomena.

For us ordinary beings who have not realized emptiness directly, changing from meditation on the emptiness of one thing to the emptiness of another requires us to think, "Now I'm going to change meditation object," and this causes a break in our meditation during which a conventional mind is operating. But for aryas, who have realized emptiness directly and nonconceptually, that is not necessary. Their mind remains merged with emptiness, like water mixed with water. To this mind there is no appearance of subject (the meditating mind) and object (emptiness) being different. They are inseparable to this mind.

The points we are studying are those that are studied and debated by monastics at the great monasteries. Emptiness is not a topic that new people are taught during the first few years of their studies. At the beginning, the young monastics do not know very much, and if their teachers explained emptiness to them, they wouldn't understand. However, you Westerners have already received a good education and know how to think critically, so it is not so difficult for you to understand these things even though you have not spent many years learning them. Nevertheless, to turn your understanding into a realization that has the capacity to uproot ignorance, you must persevere in your studies and go over the material repeatedly, thinking about it from various angles.

Two Levels of Mistaken Appearance

There can be two mistaken appearances in relation to one object. In the simile of the mirage, its appearance as water is its coarse mistaken appearance, while its appearance as truly existent is its subtle mistaken appearance. Similarly, its nonexistence as it appears could be on two levels. The mirage not existing as water as it appears is the coarse level. The mirage not existing from its own side is the subtle level. When we clearly realize the coarse level of its mistaken appearance, we come closer to understanding the subtle one, which is the actual meaning of the mirage simile.

To realize that the reflection in the mirror does not exist as an actual face, we have to realize that the reflection does not exist as it appears. That reflection has two appearances: (1) its appearance as a face, which is the coarse appearance, and (2) its appearance as self-existent, which is its subtle appearance. When we realize the reflection is empty of existing as a face as it appears, we realize it is empty of its coarse appearance. At that time, we have not even come close to negating its subtle mistaken appearance, its appearance as truly existent. When we realize the reflection is empty of true existence as it appears, we realize its subtle emptiness.

The reflection is given as a simile to help us understand the emptiness of other objects, such as a table. Someone could make the syllogism, "The table does not exist as it appears; for example, like a reflection." The example—the reflection of a face is empty of being a real face—is coarse. The point it is illustrating—the emptiness of inherent existence of the table—is subtle. The example itself cannot be the subtle emptiness, because if it were, we would have had to already realize emptiness just to understand the example.

"The table is empty of existing as it appears, like the reflection of a face in a mirror does not exist as it appears." It only says, "It doesn't exist as it appears," which is a fact. Only that is said because there are multiple levels on which the reflection of a face in a mirror does not exist as it appears. Thus, even if a person has not yet realized the subtle one, he can get at it by contemplating the coarser level indicated by the simile.

If a mirage were actually water, as we came closer to it, we would see the water ever more clearly. Wild creatures believe it is water and go running toward it. But as they approach, the appearance of water vanishes because in fact there is no water. Dependent on the combination of sunlight and the asphalt, an appearance arose of what from a distance seems to be water. Similarly, if we do not analyze closely, inherent existence appears, but the more we investigate, the more we discover it is not actually there. Like a mirage, the appearance of inherent existence is an illusion that does not persist if we look closely.

Similarly, when the sky is clear on a full moon night, the form of the moon will appear reflected in a still body of water, though there is no moon in the water as there appears to be. Likewise, things are not existent from their own side as they appear, because if they were, when we searched for them in their basis of designation, we would find them.

CHAPTER SEVENTEEN

Refining Our Understanding of Emptiness

SIMILES SHOWING THE FIVE AGGREGATES ARE EMPTY

Like the similes of things not existing as they appear, the Buddha explained some similes showing that the five aggregates are empty of inherent existence. These poetic analogies inspire us to think deeper and to see that form and even perception lack inherent existence. When we realize emptiness, nothing new is added to phenomena and nothing that was already there is removed. Rather, from the beginning phenomena have been empty of existing from their own side.

Each of the five aggregates, which are the bases of designation of the person, is empty because each is a dependent arising. In talking about the emptiness of each aggregate, the Buddha used a simile unique to each one:

> Form is like a ball of foam,
> feeling is like a water bubble,
> discrimination is like a mirage,
> volitional factors are like a plantain trunk,
> and consciousness is like an illusion.[51]

The Vaibhashika system uses these five similes for the five aggregates to illustrate impermanence. They say, for example, that the body is not permanent just like a ball of foam. The Prasangika system takes these as similes for selflessness. In this case the body is not inherently existent as it appears to be.

Form is deceptive, like a ball of foam.
The form aggregate does not exist in the way it appears, like a ball of foam. A ball of foam is fragile and cannot withstand contact. Our body is like that. It is contaminated in that it is a product of afflictions and karma. It is fragile,

feeble, and easily harmed by small things. A pin can easily scratch it, a thorn can easily pierce it, and a microscopic virus or bacteria can make it violently ill. If the body were tough, the situation would be different, but it is not. As the contemplation on death in the stages of the path tells us, our body is easily harmed, and a great deal of effort is required to keep it alive.

How does this illustrate the selflessness of the form aggregate? When we look at a ball of foam, it looks sturdy; it looks like there is something that we can take hold of. But when we touch it, ever so gently, it bursts. It is not hard and strong as it appears to be. Like a ball of foam, the appearance of the body is false. Although it appears inherently existent, it is not.

Feeling is dependent, like a water bubble.

The feeling aggregate is dependent and therefore empty, like a water bubble. The feeling aggregate consists of the three different types of feeling: pleasant (happy), unpleasant (painful), and neutral (neither pleasant nor unpleasant). When rain falls on water, bubbles form momentarily on its surface, only to vanish immediately. Feelings are like that; they are not stable at all. Fleeting, they arise and, just as soon as they do, they vanish.

Let's look at the example of the pleasant feeling that arises when we are hungry and begin to eat. The Buddha said this pleasant feeling is the duhkha of change. This means that a pleasant feeling from eating arises and the very next moment a change takes place, and the suffering of being full begins. Of course, at first the suffering of being full is imperceptible; it comes on gradually. We experience this ourselves when we overeat. At first eating is enjoyable, but at a certain point a noticeable feeling of discomfort begins. That unpleasant feeling did not arise suddenly out of nowhere. It was built up little by little, bite after bite. When it first began we did not notice it, but later on it became quite evident.

Like a water bubble, a pleasant or painful feeling appears so real and we think it will last a long time. Yet in reality it is dependent and fleeting. It's here and then it's gone. The feeling of pleasure seems to exist from its own side; that experience appears to be inherently pleasurable. But this appearance is false. The pleasant feeling is not independent; it is so designated in relation to a painful feeling. Anything that is relationally dependent does not exist from its own side. Furthermore, just like a water bubble, a pleasant feeling is dependent on causes and conditions. Its causal dependence is another reason it is empty of independent existence.

Discrimination is false, like a mirage.

As we've seen, discrimination is the mental factor that apprehends the distinguishing characteristics of a phenomenon. For example, it can identify white and yellow, long and short, what to practice and what to abandon.

Some animals—not to mention weary and thirsty desert travelers— are susceptible to the visual illusion of a mirage and run toward it, eager to drink the water they believe to be there. However, although the water appears, no water is actually there. In the same way, the myriad features that discrimination distinguishes appear to be self-existent but do not exist as they appear. In addition, discriminations themselves appear to be truly existent and "solid," whereas they are dependent like a mirage. Just as there is an appearance of water that animals run toward, our discriminations appear to be objectively real, and we chase after them. However, this appearance is false, just like the appearance of water in a mirage. Just as a mirage is dependent on the interaction of sunlight and asphalt, so too are discriminations dependent on other factors.

Volitional factors are empty, like a plantain tree.

This aggregate consists of conditioned things that do not fit into any of the other aggregates. Volitional factors include a wide variety of mental factors—emotions, afflictions, intentions, views, attitudes, and so forth—as well as abstract composites such an impermanence, duhkha nature, arising due to causes and conditions, and so forth. The simile for this aggregate is a plantain tree, the trunk of which is said to be essenceless. When the outer bark of other trees is peeled away, the wood—the essence of the tree—inside is revealed. But the outer layer of a plantain tree is peeled away to reveal one layer after another, and when no layers remain, its core is hollow. While a superficial look at a plantain tree leads us to believe it has a wooden core, no wooden essence is ever found. The aggregate of volitional factors is like this. Our emotions appear truly existent and very real, but actually they lack any intrinsic essence whatsoever.

Consciousness is unreal, like an illusion.

The consciousness aggregate consists of the six primary consciousnesses: visual, auditory, olfactory, gustatory, tactile, and mental. These consciousnesses know the general aspect of the object, while the mental factors perform more specific functions and fill in the details of each mental state.

Just as a magician can conjure appearances of horses and elephants when no animals are actually there, so too the objects of the six consciousnesses appear to the consciousnesses as if they were objectively real, although they are not. Similarly, consciousness itself appears to exist as totally independent from its objects when, in fact, it is not. All these appearances are false, like an illusion.

Contemplating these analogies can help us gain a better understanding of phenomena's false appearance, what that entails, and its implications. The five aggregates are empty of true existence because they do not exist as they appear, and they are not truly existent because they are dependent arisings.

THE REFUTATION OF ONE AND MANY

When we examined the four essential points, I mentioned that "one and many" could be viewed in different ways: as same and different or as singular and multiple. Whereas previously I explained them as same and different, now I would like to explain them as singular and multiple. In this case, the four points are: (1) ascertaining the object to be negated, (2) ascertaining the pervasion, (3) ascertaining there is no truly existing singular one, and (4) ascertaining there is no truly existent "many," which means more than one. Since the first two points were explained previously, here we will focus on the last two.

We can establish there is no truly existent one by the reason that everything, even the smallest particles, possesses parts. Once we have established that, establishing freedom from truly existent many is easy because many is a collection of parts, each of which is "one." If there is no truly existent one, there cannot be a collection of truly existent ones to make truly existent many.

If the form aggregate—specifically our body—were truly existent, it would have to be either truly existent one or truly existent many. The Prasangikas say that the body is not a truly existent one single thing because it is composed of parts. In addition, "one" exists by being merely labeled. The idea of one cannot exist unless there is the idea of more than one, because they are relationally dependent. Therefore, the body is not truly existent one.

It also does not exist as truly existent many, because in order to have truly existent many, there has to be truly existent one. In general, "many" depends on "one"—there cannot be many of something if there is not first one of that thing. Many is a collection of ones. Therefore the body is neither truly existent one nor truly existent many, in which case it can't be truly existent at all.

Similarly, even the tiniest subatomic particles we can imagine are not truly existent, because they are not truly existent one or truly existent many. They, too, have parts. If they were partless, there would be no location for them to exist. Since they must have parts that compose them, they are dependent on these parts. Thus they are not independent of everything else and cannot be truly existent.

We can apply this same reasoning to the other four aggregates. When we have understood the reasoning establishing the aggregates as being empty of true existence, we can apply that very same reasoning to the eighteen elements and the twelve sources. In that way we will easily be able to understand that all these phenomena also lack true existence.

PERCEPTION IS NOT TRULY EXISTENT

Those who say that phenomena are self-existent—that they exist from their own side—say, for example, that the color blue can only produce the visual perception of blue if it exists from its own side. To refute this view, we must first understand that any consciousness depends on three conditions: objective, dominant, and intermediate.

In the case of a visual perception of blue, the *objective* condition is the color blue itself. The *dominant* condition is the eye sense power—the subtle material in the eye that allows perception to occur—and the *immediate* condition is an immediately preceding moment of consciousness. The same applies to a perception of the ringing of the bell: The objective condition is the sound of the bell ringing, the dominant condition is the ear sense power, and the immediate condition is an immediately preceding moment of consciousness. In this way, the different consciousnesses are produced depending upon their own specific sets of three conditions.

The lower schools say that all these conditions are inherently existent and that together they give rise to an inherently existent perception. That is, inherently existent blue produces an inherently existent perception of blue by means of an inherently existent eye sense power. They say this because they conflate existence and inherent existence, thinking that if something exists, it must inherently exist, and if it is not inherently existent, then it doesn't exist at all. Prasangikas accept that blue can produce a perception of blue and that no other color can, but for blue to produce a perception of blue, it does not need to be self-existent. In fact, it cannot be self-existent because something that is self-existent cannot interact with other factors to produce something new. Furthermore, blue itself is not self-existent because it is a dependent arising, coming into existence through depending upon causes and conditions. It is precisely because blue is a dependent arising and exists through depending upon other factors that it can interact with other factors and produce the perception of blue.

Nothing to Remove, Nothing to Add

In the *Ornament for Clear Realization* (5:21), Maitreya says:

> Nothing whatsoever is to be removed,
> not the slightest thing is to be added.
> Flawlessly view the flawless.
> Seeing the flawless will liberate completely.

When meditating on emptiness, we do not realize the nonexistence of something that previously existed. Rather, meditating on emptiness involves realizing the nonexistence of something that has never existed. True existence has never existed, has it? Therefore, meditation on emptiness does not destroy true existence because things never have been truly existent. There is nothing whatsoever being removed from objects because they never were truly existent. Meditation on emptiness also does not add something new, such as emptiness, onto an object that previously was not empty. It is not the case that previously the object was not empty and now we are making it empty.

Thus when we realize emptiness, we realize that something which has never existed (true existence) does not exist. That's all. Our problem was that previously, due to the true-grasping, we thought that true existence existed. Now we see that we were wrong.

We have various erroneous minds, such as thinking a scarecrow is a person. Such wrong conceptions can be overcome by a valid mind. When we see the scarecrow is not a person, it is not the case that a person was once in the field and we are now removing the person and putting a scarecrow there in his place. Rather, there was never a person to remove in the first place. The scarecrow was there all the time, so there was nothing new to add.

To give another example, our body is impermanent. It has always been impermanent, and yet our minds mistakenly think that it is permanent. When we eliminate that mistake by understanding that the body is impermanent, it is not the case that the body was initially permanent and that permanence has been eliminated. In addition, realizing that the body is impermanent does not add the quality of impermanence onto the body.

Similarly, when meditating on emptiness we are not removing true existence from objects and replacing it with emptiness. The objects never were truly existent and they have always been empty of true existence. What is being removed and added is in relation to our minds. Meditation on emptiness eliminates the ignorance that grasps inherent existence from our minds and enhances the wisdom factor in our minds, transforming it into the wisdom realizing reality.

Avoiding the Views of Nihilism and Absolutism

We discussed the danger of misunderstanding emptiness and falling to the extremes of nihilism and absolutism earlier in the book, but now that we have learned about emptiness and dependent arising, let us return to this topic, for we will understand it better now.

The nihilistic view holds that phenomena do not exist, or if they do exist, then causality does not. Instead of meditating on things being empty of true existence, a person with this view meditates on things being nonexistent. This erroneous view comes about through searching for the imputed object in its basis of designation, not finding it, and then drawing the erroneous conclusion that the object does not exist at all. That person incorrectly believes that meditating on emptiness means meditating on phenomena not existing at all. This is a very heavy wrong view.

Liberation is attained through the meditation on emptiness that eliminates true-grasping ignorance, its seeds, and all mental afflictions derived from true-grasping. But if our meditation on emptiness is mistaken and we fall to a nihilistic extreme thinking that nothing whatsoever exists, that will in no way harm the true-grasping ignorance that is the root of cyclic existence. That means we will have no way at all to eliminate the root of cyclic existence.

Instead, when we meditate on the emptiness of cause and effect or karma and its result, we contemplate that none of these things can be found when searched for in the designated object. We understand that meditation on their emptiness does not mean meditating on their total nonexistence, because we know everything is a dependent arising. Because things depend on other factors, and have various functions that they perform, we know they exist.

We need to be very careful in our way of thinking, because it is a fact that when we look for the imputed object, we cannot find it. But remember that is a sign of it not existing from its own side. The danger is thinking that since phenomena cannot be found when searched for in their basis of designation, they obviously don't exist at all. That is a huge mistake.

When those of limited intelligence grasp emptiness wrongly, it brings about their downfall. Not falling to this view is so important that a root bodhisattva downfall warns against it. This precept is to abandon revealing emptiness to somebody who is untrained in the Dharma, which means someone who lacks an understanding of causality, specifically karma and its effects. This is a person who would think that nothing exists if we explained to them that things are empty and that the imputed object cannot be found when sought in its basis of designation. If we explain emptiness to such a person there is a risk that he will think enlightenment and the path to it do not exist and therefore turn away from enlightenment. If he gives up his quest for enlightenment, we receive a root bodhisattva downfall.

For this reason, we should prepare people by first teaching them the dependent nature of things. Explaining cause and effect and how things function in the world, we teach them there is benefit and harm. We explain the interrelationship among the topics in the stages of the path, how they depend on each other, and that one realization on the path leads to another. Having given them this firm basis, we then explain that because all these things exist dependently, they are not self-existent. In this way, they are protected from the danger of nihilism.

The other extreme is the view of absolutism, permanence, or eternalism. Here a person also errs in thinking that if things are empty, they don't exist at all. Unlike the nihilists, adherents to this view say there has to be something that exists from the side of the object and phenomena are self-existent. This is also a big mistake, but it is not as bad as falling to the extreme of nihilism. All the lower schools hold this absolutist view. The Svatantrikas say that although things do not truly exist, they do inherently exist. The imputed object can be found when sought. The Chittamatrins also hold an absolutist view, saying that although imaginaries do not exist by their own characteristics, it is going too far to say that nothing is truly existent. They assert that dependent things—especially the mind—and the consummate nature both are truly existent.

If there is a choice between falling to the extreme of nihilism, thinking that nothing exists, and falling to the extreme of absolutism, thinking phenomena exist from their own side, it would be better to fall to the extreme of absolutism. On the basis of thinking there is something findable from the side of the object, someone will still do purification practices, accumulate merit, listen to teachings, and meditate. Eventually, through doing these activities, his mind will develop, and he will start to wonder if things really exist in the way he assumes them to. At that time, he will be better prepared to meditate on emptiness and realize that things are completely nonexistent from their own side.

ABANDON MEDITATING ON THE NONEXISTENCE OF ANYTHING AT ALL

There is a type of meditation called "the view of focusing on nothing at all" or "meditating on the nonexistence of anything at all." There are two ways of explaining this; one is a correct view, the other is not. The expression "focusing on nothing at all" is found in certain Dzogchen texts, which explain that when meditating on emptiness, we should not focus our attention on things being truly existent or conventionally existent. We are simply to focus on the nontrue existence of the object. If the view of meditating on the nonexistence of anything at all or the view focusing on nothing at all is explained in that way, it is acceptable to all four traditions of Tibetan Buddhism. At the time of nonconceptual meditation on emptiness, there is no appearance of true existence. At that time also we do not establish the conventional existence of phenomena; we simply focus on the nonexistence of true existence.

The view of meditating on nothing at all that is to be rejected was brought into Tibet by a few Chinese masters many centuries ago, and it was the topic of a great debate held at Samye Monastery in Central Tibet at the end of the eighth century. According to this view, all thoughts, be they good thoughts or bad thoughts, are to be completely rejected. "Good thoughts" are conceptual consciousnesses such as bodhichitta, love, and compassion. Bad thoughts are attachment, anger, confusion, jealousy, conceit, and other such afflictions. The proponents of this view say that all thoughts are like clouds. Be they white or black, all clouds function to obscure the sky and block the sunlight. Therefore, according to this view, all thoughts are to be rejected because taking any of them to mind will harm one's meditation on emptiness.

They also assert that banishing all of these thoughts from one's mind will bring sudden enlightenment. They compare their view to ours saying that ours is like the view of a monkey climbing from the bottom of a tree to the top. The monkey is lower down and looks upward through the branches. He can neither see the top nor get there quickly. Their view, on the other hand, is like the view of a garuda suddenly landing on the top of the tree from above. This great bird does not have to go to the effort of climbing up the tree step by step. Likewise, they say, theirs is a view that arises simultaneously in that defilements are eradicated suddenly, at once. This view was present in Tibet at the time of the great abbot Shantarakshita (725–88) and seems to have taken hold in one of the centers of meditation in Tibet.

The sutras prophesize that the degeneration of the Buddhadharma will not come from outside but from inside. In other words, people who claim to be Buddhist will propound wrong views and engage in wrong actions and in this way damage the existence of the Dharma in the world. Wary of this possibility, the Dharma King Trisong Detsen invited Shantarakshita's disciple, Kamalashila, to Tibet to debate with the proponents of this view. Like Shantarakshita, Kamalashila had studied at Nalanda University in India.

Having invited both Kamalashila and Hashang, the Chinese proponent of the view of not focusing on anything at all, to debate, the king attended as did many ministers. Hashang and his many followers were asked to sit on the right, while Kamalashila sat on the left with his followers. The king offered a flower garland to each of them and said, "Debate this view to determine if it is correct or not. The one who loses will offer the victor his flower garland without any sense of pride or anger. Furthermore, the loser must return to the place from which he came—if Kamalashila loses, he will return to India, and if Hashang loses, he will return to China."

Many people came from the surrounding areas to watch the debate. When asked who would ask the first question, Hashang said, "Since I am a more senior monk and am older in the trainings, and since I came to Tibet first, you should ask me a question." At Hashang's request, Kamalashila began the debate, asking, "You said the garuda is in the sky and settles on the peak of the tree. Was the egg of this garuda first laid in a nest perched up on the mountain? After hatching, did the garuda gradually grow until it was eventually able to fly in the sky and land on the tree? Or did the egg appear in the sky, and the garuda suddenly hatched and immediately flew on the top of the tree?"

Kamalashila answered his first question himself, "In fact, the garuda hatched from the egg on the mountain and grew gradually. When its wings were strong enough, it flew and landed on the tree. Thus your idea that our view is like the progress of a monkey that gradually makes its way up the tree, while your view is like a garuda with simultaneous abandonment of everything, is completely wrong, isn't it?"

Let me pose some questions to you. Imagine you are a proponent of this view of focusing on nothing at all. This view discourages any kind of conceptualizing mind. You are supposed to think of nothing at all. Does all conceptualization cease or only some? If you say only some, then there is no difference between your view and what happens when a person faints or falls asleep. In both cases, some conceptualization stops. Would you say that someone in a faint who has lost consciousness and that someone who is asleep are meditating on focusing their minds on nothing at all, since in each case, some conceptualizing minds have stopped?

If you say that all conceptualizing minds must cease, then must even your motivation—thinking to yourself, "Now I am going to meditate on this view"—be abandoned? If you say yes, it would mean that no sentient being would have to cultivate the intention to do this meditation. Everyone would have it spontaneously and effortlessly, even though sentient beings currently lack the thought, "Now I am going to meditate on this view."

If you say the motivation is needed, then you must begin your meditation session by thinking, "I am going meditate on this view." In that case, it would be contradictory to say that it is a view where all conceptualizing minds are stopped.

Let's think about a person who is practicing the fasting retreat, Nyung Nay, where the participants keep silence for a day. Would it conflict with her not speaking if she said, "I am not speaking"? What do you think? This seems similar to the issue of the meditator needing a motivation. Does it harm the meditation or help?

When examined closely, it becomes difficult to uphold the view of focusing on nothing at all. The proponents of this view say just as the garuda does not need to climb the tree gradually, a practitioner does not need to cultivate the view gradually. But when we study at school, don't we have to start in first grade and gradually work our way up to the higher levels of study? How would it be possible to gain the results of this meditation suddenly without having created any causes over a period of time?

Through this kind of discussion and examination, the view of meditating on nothing at all was rejected at the Samye debate and did not spread in Tibet. Hashang offered his garland of flowers to Kamalashila and then returned to China.

In summary, sometimes we find a scriptural passage that says, "Meditate on total nonexistence." What this refers to is the total nonexistence of the object of negation, true existence. That is, we should meditate on the total emptiness of true existence. Do not understand such passages to mean meditate that nothing at all exists. Emptiness never means the total non-existence of conventional things, because for emptiness to exist, there must always be an existent object that is empty. For the emptiness of the I to exist, there must be a conventionally existent I that is empty of true existence.

We may also come across scriptural passages saying, "Not seeing is the perfect seeing." This means that when we search for the object of negation, we will not find it. That "not seeing" of inherent existence is the perfect seeing. In not seeing the object of negation—in not seeing inherent existence—we will see the perfect phenomenon, emptiness.

Emptiness is said to be like space. However, this does not mean that meditating on nothingness or on nothing existing at all is meditation on emptiness. Rather, emptiness is like space because it is a nonaffirming negative, a mere lack of self-existence. So meditating on emptiness is like meditating on space in that only a nonaffirming negative is realized, not a positive phenomenon.

CHAPTER EIGHTEEN

The Two Truths

BASIS, PATH, AND RESULT

All the Buddha taught can be encompassed under the headings of basis, path, and result, so understanding them well indicates that we have a good understanding of the Buddha's teachings. The *basis* is what we have to work with, the *path* is the correct minds we develop as we practice, and the *result* is what we aim to actualize. In the explanation below, the two truths are the basis, method and wisdom are the path, and the two bodies of a buddha are the result.

Whenever we begin a new project, establishing a firm basis is necessary. When building a house, the foundation needs to be stable, otherwise the house will tilt and crumble before too long. Similarly, if we have a mistaken understanding of the two truths, our practice of the path—which is done in reference to the two truths—will also be faulty, and the two bodies of a buddha will elude us.

Each of the aspects of the result corresponds with an aspect of the path and with one of the two truths. Attaining the form body depends mainly on the practice of method, and the method aspect of the path correlates mainly with the practice of conventional truth. Once we have understood conventional truths, we will be able to practice the method aspect of the path, and it is mainly through this practice that we will attain a buddha's form body. Likewise the truth body is attained mainly by the practice of wisdom, and this practice is done mainly in reference to ultimate truths. A correct understanding of the ultimate truth is the basis for practicing wisdom, and it is mainly through the practice of wisdom that we will attain the truth body. For this reason understanding both conventional and ultimate truths is so important.

CHART: BASIS, PATH, AND RESULT, AND THE TWO TRUTHS

Basis	Path	Result
Conventional truth	Method— collection of merit	Form body of a buddha
Ultimate truth	Wisdom— collection of wisdom	Truth body of a buddha

THE TWO TRUTHS

The two truths are objects of mind, not facts or beliefs accepted as correct as the usual meaning of *truth* implies. The two truths are the conventional truths and the ultimate truths, and all phenomena are either one or the other. There is nothing that is both and nothing that is neither. Conventional truths include causes and effects; karma and its results; birth, aging, sickness, and death; coming and going; persons and aggregates—in short all the evident phenomena we see around us. Conventional truths include all impermanent phenomena—I, our body and mind, and the environment around us. Any permanent phenomenon that is not emptiness is also included in conventional truths.

Emptinesses are ultimate truths. Everything that exists is empty, so everything has its own emptiness. Each one of those emptinesses is an ultimate truth. An ultimate truth is the way of being, the actual mode of existence. In short, conventional truths are objects known by consciousnesses that perceive falsities—objects that appear to exist from their own side to minds influenced by ignorance.[52] Ultimate truths are objects known by wisdom consciousnesses that perceive reality—their actual mode of existence.

All four systems of tenets speak of the basis, path, and result but differ in how they define them. Due to these differences, what is considered a conventional truth and an ultimate truth also differ in each system.

When we understand the two truths according to the Prasangika system, we will have understood phenomena's way of existence as it really is because this is the most subtle presentation of the two truths. Studying the explanations of the two truths in the Vaibhashika, Sautrantika, Chittamatra, and Svatantrika systems gradually leads us to an understanding of the most subtle presentation of the two truths found in the Prasangika system. Nevertheless, the proponents of each of the lower schools characterize their explanation as the most profound and the most subtle view describing the real way that things exist.

Both Madhyamaka systems—the Svatantrika and the Prasangika—assert that the two truths are one nature[53] but different isolates. The concept of an *isolate* is important in Buddhist philosophy, but it is complicated to explain. For our purposes here, it suffices to know that "one nature but different isolates" means they are the same nature but are nominally different; in other words, we approach them through distinct conceptual pathways. "One nature" means that one cannot exist without the other. The fact that the two truths are one nature does not mean that they are the same thing. Two things that are the same have to be not just the same thing but also nominally the same, which means that even their names are identical.

Are the phenomena referred to by the names *table* and *chogtsé*, the Tibetan word for table, the same? Yes. It is like one person who has two different names. There is just the one person to which those two names refer. You may get confused, thinking, "Earlier it was said that for two things to be the same, they could not have different names. Now you're saying *table* and *chogtsé* are the same even though they have different names." In general, two things that are referred to in different ways are different. But the things *referred to* by the names *chogtsé* and *table* are the same. If not, it would be difficult to say that there is anything that is the same, because we have so many different languages with so many different words and ways of referring to things. So while the words *table* and *chogtsé* are different, they refer to the same object. In fact, they are synonyms.

Table and *chogtsé* are different isolates because they have different names. But these two names refer to the same object. In the case of *table* and *emptiness of the table*, they are one nature but have different names. However, they are not synonyms because they each refer to different objects. If the emptiness of the table and the table were the same, then when we wanted to refer to the emptiness of the table we could just say, "table." Similarly, when we said, "emptiness of the table," it would refer to the table. But *table* and *emptiness of the table* are not synonyms.

Thus not all sets of objects that are one nature and nominally different are synonyms. Like *table* and *chogtsé*, *impermanent* and *product* are one nature and nominally different, and they are synonymous. However, while a table and its emptiness are one nature and nominally different, they are *not* synonymous. In fact, they are mutually exclusive. Something that is a table is not an emptiness of a table, and something that is the emptiness of a table is not a table.

Each conventional phenomenon—permanent or impermanent—is empty of inherent existence. The conventional phenomenon and its emptiness are one nature; one cannot exist without the other. Furthermore an ultimate nature cannot be posited or identified separate from a conventional nature and vice versa. In other words, a table and the table's emptiness are one nature.

However, they are not the same. They have different names and are different phenomena. The names *conventional truth* and *ultimate truth* are different, and a conceptual consciousness understands them to be different. In addition, a conventional truth is not an ultimate truth and vice versa. While a table is empty, it is not emptiness. This is because a table is a conventional truth and the emptiness of the table is an ultimate truth. What is one truth cannot be the other.

Any phenomenon—a conventional truth or an ultimate truth—has both an ultimate nature and a conventional nature. Its conventional nature is that it exists conventionally, by mere name. Its ultimate nature is that it is empty of self-existence.

CONVENTIONAL TRUTHS

The Tibetan term for conventional truths is *kundzob denpa. Kun* means "all" and has the connotation of a variety and of many. *Dzob* has the meaning of being false, of concealing. The reason that conventional truths are regarded as false is because their way of appearing and their way of existing are discordant. *Denpa* means "truth," and in the case of conventional truths, it means "true from the perspective of the true-grasping mind" or "true as far as the true-grasping mind is concerned."

In actual fact, nothing exists as it appears to the true-grasping mind, so there is nothing that is truly existent. Even though from the perspective of the true-grasping mind they are true, they are not actually true because they do not exist as they appear.

For example, a jug appears to exist from its own side to the true-grasping mind. That mind grasps the jug as existing from its own side, just as it appears. Thus, for that mind, the jug is true, because for it the jug exists as it appears. In fact the jug is not true; it is false. If it were true, it would have to exist just like it appears to the true-grasping mind. But it doesn't; it is a falsity. In fact, being true from the perspective of a true-grasping mind is the very meaning of being false.

Emptiness also appears truly existent to the true-grasping mind. But it is not false, because whether it is true or false is judged from the viewpoint of an arya's wisdom of meditative equipoise, which is the principal mind that knows emptiness. To that mind, emptiness appears empty and is empty. It exists as it appears to that mind.

You may wonder, "Can the table also be an ultimate truth, because even though it appears true to the true-grasping mind, it is not truly existent?" No, because the table does not appear true to an arya's wisdom of meditative equipoise on emptiness; in fact, it does not appear at all to this mind.

ULTIMATE TRUTHS

For ultimate truths, however, the situation differs. They are not judged as true from the perspective of the true-grasping mind. Rather it is the arya's meditative equipoise on emptiness that determines that. To that mind, emptiness is true because it exists as it appears.

The Tibetan term for ultimate truth is *dondam denpa. Don* means "fact" or "object." An ultimate truth is a fact or object found by the arya's wisdom of meditative equipoise on emptiness. *Dam* means "amazing" or "supreme," and *denpa* means "truth." Ultimate truths are true from the perspective of the arya's wisdom of meditative equipoise directly realizing emptiness, which is a supreme and amazing mind. To that mind there is no discrepancy between the way an object exists and the way it appears. The way that it appears is exactly the way it is. Emptiness is such an object and thus is the supreme and most amazing way of being.

Emptiness is an ultimate truth that has three features: (1) It is a fact or object realized by the arya's wisdom of meditative equipoise; (2) it is something supreme and amazing; and (3) it is true. The emptiness of any phenomenon is an illustration of an ultimate truth because everything that exists is empty. Everything that exists has its own emptiness, which is an ultimate truth.

The word *truth* in "conventional truth" and the word *truth* in "ultimate truth" refer to two very different things. Conventional truths are said to be true from the perspective of a mind that does not see reality. Here things are true from the perspective of a mind contaminated with ignorance. Ultimate truths are true for the wisdom that directly sees the way phenomena exist. From this perspective, conventional truths are falsities.

The great masters recognize these points as very important. To understand them well, we must think deeply and precisely about these topics. Keep investigating them, and they will become clearer.

SAME NATURE, NOMINALLY DIFFERENT

Now that we understand a little more about what conventional and ultimate truths are, let's look again at why they are said to be the same nature but nominally different.

Any object and its emptiness are one nature. For example, the table and the emptiness of the table are one nature. We may wonder, "What about emptiness? Is it empty? Is it one nature with its emptiness?" Although emptiness is an ultimate truth, not a conventional truth, it too is dependent on other factors, and it too is empty of inherent existence. Emptiness and its emptiness are the same nature.

Four Faults That Would Arise If an Object and Its Emptiness Were the Same

Let's use the table and the emptiness of the table as an example. They are the same nature, but they are not the same. If they were the same, four faults would arise:

1. The table is an object of a direct perceiver for us ordinary beings. If the table and its emptiness were the same, the emptiness of the table would also be an object of an ordinary being's direct perceivers. However, emptiness can be directly seen only by an arya's meditative equipoise on emptiness. It is not an object that can be known by the direct perceivers of us ordinary beings. Our visual consciousness, for example, cannot perceive emptiness; only an arya's direct, nonconceptual wisdom can.

2. When ordinary beings look at a table, attachment, hatred, and various other mental afflictions may arise. If the table and its emptiness were the same, when an ordinary being's mind focused on the emptiness of the table, those afflictions could

also arise. But that is not what happens. In fact the reverse occurs; the afflictions are subdued when the mind focuses on emptiness.

3. Great meditators put much effort into listening, reflecting, and meditating in order to realize the emptiness of the table. If the table and its emptiness were the same, they would have to strive just as hard to listen, reflect, and meditate in order to realize the table. But they don't; in order to realize the table they just open their eyes.

4. Just as the table has various attributes such as shape, color, texture, and so on, if the table and its emptiness were the same, the emptiness of the table would have shape, color, texture, and so on. But emptiness does not have these attributes of form.

As we have seen, to be the same, two things must fulfill two requirements: (1) They must have the same name and (2) their name must refer to the same object. As long as names are different, even if what they refer to is exactly the same thing, they are considered different and not the same. As noted above, the table and its emptiness are one nature but are not the same. If they were the same, the above four faults would ensue.

Four Faults That Would Arise If an Object and Its Emptiness Were Different Natures

Even though an object and its emptiness are one nature, they are nominally different. They have "different isolates," which means they have different names and are therefore conceptually distinct. If the table and its emptiness were not only nominally different but also were different natures, they would be unrelated like a horse and a cow. In that case, four faults would follow.[54]

1. The valid mind realizing the nontrue existence of the table would not harm the mind grasping the table as truly existent. The conceived object of the true-grasping mind is the truly existent table. The valid mind realizing the emptiness of true existence of the table negates a truly existent table; it refutes the existence of the conceived object of that true-grasping. The true-grasping mind and the wisdom realizing emptiness focus on the same object—the table—but apprehend it in contradictory ways. If the

two truths were not the same nature, the wisdom realizing the emptiness of the table would not counteract the mind grasping the table to be truly existent.

2. The emptiness of true existence of the table would not be the reality (*dharmata*) of the table. The absence of true existence of the table would have no relationship to the table. In that case, the emptiness of the table would not be the ultimate nature of the table. However, true existence is negated in relation to the table, and the emptiness of true existence is the ultimate truth of the table. The table and its emptiness being one nature means the two do not exist separately. That which conventionally exists is itself empty of ultimate existence, and that which is empty of ultimate existence is itself conventionally existent. If the table were not empty, it would be independent of causes and conditions. That clearly is not the case. If the two truths were different natures and unrelated, the conventional nature of the table (its being a dependent arising) would not have to be concordant with its ultimate nature (its being empty of inherent existence). However, because the table has a dependent nature on the conventional level, it lacks inherent existence on the ultimate level.

3. We would not need to rely on a conventional truth (table) in order to understand an ultimate truth (the emptiness of inherent existence of the table). The true-grasping mind focuses on the table and grasps it to be truly existent. To realize the lack of self-existence of the table, we have to focus on the table, which is the basis of that emptiness, and understand that the conceived object of that grasping—a truly existent table—does not exist. The way to do that is by focusing on the table and understanding that the table is a dependent arising. Only by focusing on the table can we understand the emptiness of the table. However, if the ultimate truth of the table and the conventional truth of the table were different natures, they would be totally unrelated like a horse and a cow, and we wouldn't need to rely on the table (the conventional truth) in order to understand the emptiness of true existence of the table (the ultimate truth).

4. The Buddha would see the two truths as different natures. As a fully enlightened and omniscient being, he would know the two truths are different natures; but that is not the case. The mind seeing the two truths as different natures is actually a cognitive obscuration that prevents the attainment of the omniscient mind. If the Buddha had the mind believing the two truths are different natures, it would mean he would not have abandoned all obscurations and would not be fully enlightened. However, just understanding that the Buddha does not have the obscuration believing the two truths to be different natures does not mean we have abandoned that obscuration.

Before abandoning either the acquired or innate true-grasping and afflictions, we can understand through a correct assumption that the two truths are the same nature. In fact, it is even possible to have developed a valid cognizer realizing the two truths are the same nature and a valid cognizer realizing emptiness before abandoning any of the afflictions. But doing so does not mean we have necessarily abandoned true-grasping or the mind grasping the two truths as different in nature.

Being able to make the distinction between saying the two truths are the same and saying they are the same nature is important. They are the same nature but they are not the same. If they were the same, they would be the same in name and meaning. However, as we have seen, the two truths have different names and refer to different objects. They are mutually exclusive. Nevertheless, they are the same nature, which means that the conventional nature of the thing—its nature of being nominally existent, its nature of depending upon causes and conditions—is the nature of being empty of true existence.

As the great master Nagarjuna says, there is nothing that is not dependent, and for that reason there is nothing that is not empty. All existents depend upon various factors; therefore they are dependent. If something is dependent, it cannot be independent. Therefore, it cannot be self-existent; it must be empty of self-existence. This is, in brief, what is to be understood from the statement that the two truths are the same nature. This is extremely important to understand. Nagarjuna says that if we do not understand the distinction between the two truths—that all existents are empty of self-existence and that all phenomenon are conventionally and nominally existent—there is no way that we can understand the Buddha's definitive explanation of emptiness.

TRUTH AND TRULY EXISTENT

Truth exists, but there is nothing that exists truly. That sounds odd to say at first, but when we understand the meaning it makes sense. Truth does exist because emptiness is true and because ultimate truth is true. Emptiness is true because it is the meaning discovered by the wisdom of meditative equipoise of an arya directly realizing emptiness. It is also true because it is undeceiving in that its way of appearing and its way of existing are in harmony.

Although emptiness is true, it is not truly existent, because to be truly existent means to exist independent of everything else. Nothing exists in that way. All phenomena have their own entity, nature, and characteristics, which mean they have unique functions. Different objects perform different functions according to their different characteristics. Yet being able to perform that function is not something that exists in and of itself, independent of anything else. That is the reason for saying that even though everything has an entity or nature, nothing exists by its own entity or by its own nature. Similarly, each phenomenon *has* its own characteristics, but it does not *exist* by its own characteristics because it exists dependently.

Each phenomenon has its own nature. That it has that nature is established by a valid cognizer, because that phenomenon is realized by that valid cognizer. Does it exist by its own nature? Its nature exists, a valid cognizer establishes it, but it does not exist by its own nature. While things have their own conventional nature, they do not exist by their own nature. In fact, *own-nature* (*svabhava*) is the object of negation. Existence by its own nature is not realized by a valid cognizer. In addition, a valid cognizer analyzing the ultimate realizes the nonexistence of things existing by their own nature. Thus the nature of a phenomenon exists, and at the same time it does not exist by its own nature. Similarly, each phenomenon has its own characteristics, but it does not exist by its own characteristics.

As we have discussed, there are two meanings of *true*. One is established relative to the arya's wisdom of meditative equipoise on emptiness. The other is established relative to conventional valid cognizers. In the case of the former, emptiness is true. Conventional objects such as the table are false because they appear truly existent whereas they are not. Thus they are false. Everything other than emptiness is false.

The other meaning of *true* and *false* applies to conventional valid cognizers knowing conventionalities. Here, the meaning of "not existing as it appears" differs. In this case, a table is true (real) because it is known by a conventional valid cognizer, and a reflection of a table is false (unreal) because there is not a table there although there is the appearance of a table in the mirror.

A table is a conventional truth, but that does not make it a truth. The use of the word *truth* in the term *conventional truth* reflects the fact that an object is true for the true-grasping ignorance. However, that does not make it true for the wisdom of meditative equipoise of an arya. The word *truth* in the term *ultimate truth* means it is true for an arya's wisdom of meditative equipoise on emptiness. This is why emptiness is an ultimate truth; it exists the way it appears to that wisdom. Thus the reason for calling something "truth" in the terms *conventional truth* and *ultimate truth* is different; it is judged according to different criteria.

Some dependent arisings are conventional truths, others are ultimate truths. For example, emptiness itself is a dependent arising, and it is an ultimate truth. The table, the people in this room, love, compassion, and wisdom are dependent arisings, and they are conventional truths.

Conventional and Ultimate

Each phenomenon has a conventional nature and an ultimate nature. So both ultimate truths and conventional truths have both an ultimate nature and a conventional nature. Their ultimate nature is their actual mode of existence, their emptiness. Their conventional nature is that they exist by being merely labeled and exist dependently. With respect to both table and the emptiness of table, each one's conventional nature is that it exists by being merely labeled, and each one's ultimate nature is that it is empty of inherent existence. Don't think that emptiness is some faraway absolute, independent existence unrelated to ourselves and everything around us.

In addition, while nothing exists ultimately, all phenomena, including emptiness, exist conventionally. If something exists, it exists conventionally. That is the only type of existence there is. Ultimate existence is the same as inherent existence, and that does not exist at all. Initially it may sound strange to say, "Emptiness exists conventionally," but when we think about the meaning of these terms, it becomes clear.

CHAPTER NINETEEN

Similes from the *Diamond Cutter Sutra*—Part I

In the sutras, the Buddha often gave similes to help his disciples understand an underlying principle. A concise but powerful verse from the *Diamond Cutter Sutra* contains nine similes that help us understand dependent arising, emptiness, impermanence, and the nature of duhkha. This verse is often recited before teachings to help guide our minds and make them receptive.

> A star, a visual aberration, a flame of a lamp,
> an illusion, a dewdrop, a water bubble,
> a dream, a flash of lightning, a cloud,
> see conditioned things as such.

The first three similes—a star, a visual aberration, and the flame of a lamp—illustrate conditioned things' emptiness of inherent existence as well as their nature of dependent arising. The simile of an illusion, while also illustrating emptiness and dependent arising, specifically indicates the way in which we are drawn into duhkha by believing these false appearance to be true. The simile of the dewdrop illustrates the impermanence and instability of the conditioned things of cyclic existence, while the simile of the water bubble indicates that feelings—be they pleasurable, painful, or neutral—all have the fault of being unsatisfactory in nature. The similes of a dream, a flash of lightning, and a cloud illustrate the emptiness of inherent existence.

The meaning of the similes is potent. In addition to using reasoning to reflect on emptiness or impermanence, you can include any of these nine similes in your meditation. The fact that we often observe stars, dewdrops, water bubbles, dreams, lightning, clouds, and so forth in our daily lives will spark the memory of the meaning of these similes to arise in our minds when we are not in formal meditation too.

THE SIMILE OF A STAR

The simile of a star illustrates that conditioned things both appear and are empty. That is their nature. Stars do not appear in the daytime; so too conventional truths do not appear to an arya's meditative equipoise on emptiness. However, stars appear at night; similarly conventionalities appear to conventional consciousnesses.

In terms of its ultimate way of existence, everything is empty of existing from its own side. In terms of its conventional way of existence, it exists nominally and performs its own functions. For example, the nature of fire is to burn, and the nature of water is cohesion.

Here we are talking about the two truths—ultimate truth and conventional truth—or the ultimate and conventional natures in terms of one object. With respect to a book, the lack of its inherent existence is its ultimate nature and the dependently arising book itself is its conventional nature.

A thing's ultimate way of existing is the object realized by the arya's nonconceptual wisdom focused on emptiness. In other words, its ultimate way of existing is the object found by an arya's nonconceptual meditative equipoise mind directly realizing the ultimate. This is a valid mind realizing the ultimate. Phenomena's conventional or nominal nature is the object found by a valid mind realizing conventionalities.

The simile of a star gives us insight into these two aspects of phenomena. In the daytime, we cannot see the stars. All we can see is the open and empty sky. Just as no stars appear in the empty sky during the daytime, no conventional phenomenon appears to the arya's wisdom of meditative equipoise. For that wisdom, there are no dualistic appearances—no appearances of a difference between subject and object, no appearance of true existence, and no appearance of conventionalities. There is no conceptual appearance that acts like a veil that obscures the mind from directly perceiving emptiness. All such appearances have been pacified; there are no such appearances to that mind. The arya's wisdom of meditative equipoise sees only the empty nature of phenomena, without seeing the phenomena themselves.

The wisdom of meditative equipoise itself is a conventional truth, so it does not appear to the arya's wisdom of meditative equipoise. In other words, the mind that is meditating on emptiness does not appear to the mind that is meditating on emptiness. Only emptiness appears to that mind.

Prior to being able to see a thing's ultimate nature, we must go through the process of investigating and understanding that the object cannot be self-existent as it appears because of being a dependent arising. However, the arya's wisdom of meditative equipoise that arises due to this investigation does not see the object as dependent. All it sees is the emptiness of the object.

If the wisdom of meditative equipoise could see conventional phenomena and the dependent nature of the phenomena, it would mean that instead of being a nonconceptual realization, that wisdom would be a conceptual mind. In this context, *conceptual* and *nonconceptual* have different meanings than usual. Here, *nonconceptual* specifically refers to there being no superstitions, no preconceptions, and no conceptualization of inherent existence in the mind at that time. This mind is nonconceptual in the sense that it is free from dualistic appearances—the appearance of true existence, of subject and object being different, and of conventional phenomena. The mind that realizes the conventional existence of the object—its dependent nature—is a conceptual mind in the sense that it has these three dualistic appearances.

In the daytime only the sky appears and not the stars, even though the stars exist during the day. Similarly, only emptiness and no conventional phenomena appear to an arya's wisdom of meditative equipoise, even though conventional phenomena still exist. However, just as the stars not appearing during the day does not mean they are totally nonexistent, conventional truths not appearing to an aryas's meditative equipoise does not mean they are totally nonexistent.

The sky or space in the simile also recalls the advice of the great masters to meditate on space-like emptiness, which means meditating on the nonexistence of any inherently existent object. We know that we are not meditating on the total nonexistence of anything whatsoever but on the nonexistence of the thing existing from its own side. The object of our meditation is only the emptiness of true existence; it is not the emptiness of all existence. At this time, we are not thinking about the object; we are not considering that although it is empty of self-existence, it does exist as a dependent arising.

Outside of meditative equipoise, all sorts of conventionalities appear to the various conventional consciousnesses. Due to the influence of true-grasping ignorance, things appear to be truly existent and to exist from their own side. These appearances are false—they do not exist in the way they appear. Due to having realized emptiness, we will know these appearances as false and will not believe that they exist truly as they appear.

A visual consciousness realizing blue is a valid mind realizing blue; it is a valid cognizer realizing a conventional phenomenon. Nevertheless, it is a consciousness that is contaminated by one or both of two factors: ignorance or the latencies of ignorance. The reason we say it is contaminated by one or both of these is that even an arhat—somebody who has completely abandoned ignorance—has some consciousnesses that are contaminated by the latencies of ignorance.

We have so many conventional consciousnesses that engage with such a wide spectrum of objects. To each of these consciousnesses, its object appears to be truly existent. All these consciousnesses are mistaken in this way. Nevertheless, among them, many will be valid minds, because from the point of view of realizing their objects, they are valid. The visual consciousness apprehending blue sees blue; it does not see yellow. But it is mistaken because the blue appears to exist inherently.

In the simile, stars appearing at night are like those same conventional phenomena appearing to those consciousnesses that are contaminated by ignorance or the latencies of ignorance. Bearing in mind the three types of dualistic appearance, we can also say that the stars not appearing during the daytime is like the absence of any appearance of true existence to the arya's wisdom of meditative equipoise. The stars appearing during the night is like the appearances of true existence to those consciousnesses that are contaminated by ignorance or the latencies of ignorance.

THE SIMILE OF A VISUAL ABERRATION

The term *rabrib*, translated here as "visual aberration," is sometimes translated as "cataract," although that is not its actual meaning. *Rabrib* refers to a condition found in the elderly, although it can affect others as well. A person with this ailment may have a clean bowl in front of him but see fine hairs falling into it. The appearance of falling hairs is true for the person who has that illness and to whom the hairs appear. However, it is not true from the perspective of somebody whose sight is unaffected by such an illness. If it were true in general, then even people who are not afflicted by that illness would have the appearance of failing hairs, which is clearly not the case.

Likewise, to a consciousness contaminated by ignorance or its latencies, the object appears truly existent, and for that contaminated consciousness, the object truly exists as it appears. Of course, that does not mean that the object actually is truly existent. The appearance of things as existing from their own side is not true from the perspective of the arya's wisdom of meditative equipoise. Just as healthy eyes do not see falling hairs, an arya's meditative equipoise on emptiness does not see existence from its own side.

Both of the examples so far—the star and the visual aberration—show that things are not self-existent. If things were truly existent as they appear to the mind affected by ignorance and its latencies, that true existence would be the ultimate mode of existence of that phenomenon, and it would be found by an arya's wisdom realizing the ultimate way of existence. But, in fact, that wisdom realizes the nonexistence of truly existent things.

Think about it: A person with an eye disease feels very strongly that falling hairs are there. For him the very fact that he can see them so clearly seems proof that they exist. We need to reason with this person, saying, "Look, if it were true that falling hairs are present the way they appear to you, then everyone else should be able to see them. Somebody whose eyes are healthy should be able to see those hairs falling even more clearly than you do. Yet this is not the case. Not only does she not see the hairs more clearly, she does not see them at all!"

Although there are no hairs falling as they appear to that visual perception affected by this illness, the appearance of falling hairs does exist. Likewise, although things appear truly existent to a mind contaminated by ignorance or its latencies despite the fact that things are not truly existent, that appearance does exist. This is important: In terms of the simile, the *appearance* of hair falling exists, even though the falling hairs do not. Likewise, the appearance of true existence to our everyday consciousnesses exists, even though there is no true existence.

We may think that things are truly existent simply because that's the way they appear to us. But we need to be able to reason to ourselves and understand that true existence appears only because the consciousness to which it appears is flawed in that it is contaminated by ignorance and its latencies.

An omniscient mind definitely realizes conventional truths. Conventional truths exist, and because a Buddha's mind is omniscient, it knows everything that exists. Conventional truths appear to an omniscient mind, but they do not appear to it as if they were truly existent. In other words, conventional truths do not appear truly existent to all minds to which they appear.

Since enlightened beings are forever free from all obscurations, things do not appear truly existent to them. Buddhas are omniscient and perceive everything that exists. Since the appearance of true existence is an existent phenomenon (although true existence itself is not), it must appear to a buddha's mind. Since the mistaken appearances that appear to each sentient being do exist, a buddha realizes those appearances and at the same time realizes that although things appear truly existent to those sentient beings, they are not truly existent. Just because the appearance of true existence appears to a buddha and a buddha realizes that appearance does not mean that things appear as if they were truly existent to a buddha. A buddha realizes the appearance of true existence because it appears to sentient beings and a buddha knows what appears to sentient beings. There is huge difference between having the appearance of true existence because one's mind is contaminated by ignorance or its latencies and realizing the appearance of true existence because it is an existent phenomenon appearing to the minds of others.

All aryas, including bodhisattvas on the seven impure grounds and the three pure grounds, still have the appearance of true existence after they arise from meditative equipoise on emptiness. Bodhisattvas who have initially entered the Mahayana—as opposed to those who became hearer and solitary-realizer arhats before entering the Mahayana—do not eliminate the grasping at true existence until the eighth ground, and they, too, have the appearance of true existence when not in meditative equipoise on emptiness. The bodhisattvas on the three pure grounds—the eighth, ninth, and tenth grounds—have eliminated the grasping at true existence and its seeds, but they still have cognitive obscurations and thus also have the appearance of true existence when they are not in meditative equipoise.

Only at buddhahood has the subtle obscuration of the appearance of true existence been totally eradicated from the mind. Enlightened beings realize the two truths simultaneously and directly, unmediated by conceptuality. They do not have to think about ultimate truths in order to realize them. Nor must they switch their focus and think about conventional truths in order to realize them. Thus only a buddha can realize the four noble truths directly at the same time and with one mind. That is because three of the four noble truths—the noble truths of duhkha, origin, and path—are conventional truths, while the noble truth of cessation is an ultimate truth. Only buddhas can directly perceive the two truths simultaneously.

THE SIMILE OF THE FLAME OF A LAMP

The third simile is the flame of a butter lamp or an oil lamp. It illustrates that phenomena need to be properly and correctly posited on a conventional level despite the fact that they are empty of self-existence. The flame of a lamp does not naturally exist in the lamp. It arises due to the assemblage of a variety of causes and conditions, such as the oil, the wick, matches, and so on. In the same way, all phenomena—dharmas—of cyclic existence and nirvana do not inherently exist but come into being due to the aggregation of many factors. Within knowing they are empty, we still need to be able to posit them unmistakenly.

Nirvana means "liberation." The dharmas of nirvana are the factors that nirvana depends upon. They include the practices that we do in order to attain liberation. The dharmas of cyclic existence are what cyclic existence depends on—the afflictions and karma that lead us to take rebirth in fortunate and unfortunate realms.

In many sutras, the Buddha says:

> When this exists, that comes to be;
> with the arising of this, that arises.
> When this does not exist, that does not come to be;
> with the cessation of this, that ceases.[55]

In the context of the twelve links of dependent arising, the first two lines indicate how cyclic existence evolves. With ignorance as the condition, karmic formations arise. Depending upon that, consciousness arises. With each successive link depending on the previous one arise name and form, the six sources, contact, feeling, craving, clinging, existence, birth, and aging and death.

In the last two lines the Buddha indicates how cyclic existence is ceased: When ignorance is overcome, karmic formations cease. When karmic formations stop, consciousness ceases, and so forth. In short, by stopping ignorance, all twelve links cease, cyclic existence ends, and nirvana is attained.

Due to ignorance and its latencies, phenomena appear to us to exist truly. Although we do not necessarily grasp things as truly existent in the very next moment after the appearance of true existence, in many cases that grasping often follows the appearance. This is the first of the twelve links, ignorance. Based upon this grasping, other afflictions such as attachment and anger arise. Motivated by these afflictions, we engage in all sorts of actions, which constitute the second link, karmic formations. These karmas cause us to be born again in cyclic existence and to experience its multitude of duhkha, as found in the links of consciousness, name and form, six sense sources, contact, feeling, birth, and aging and death. So all the miseries that sentient beings experience arise due to grasping things as existing in a way that is the complete opposite to how they really exist.

The above describes one series of events—one set of twelve links— beginning with the ignorance that is the root of cyclic existence, which leads to the arising of disturbing emotions, which create karma, which results in rebirth in cyclic existence with all its attendant duhkha. The second series begins in the opposite way; it begins with the wisdom understanding that phenomena are empty of inherent existence and it leads to liberation.

The flame of a lamp is the simile for the arising and ceasing of things due to the presence or absence of their causes and conditions. Even though the flame does not exist from its own side, it does exist through depending upon various factors. In the same way, all dharmas of cyclic existence and nirvana lack any true existence whatsoever, but they still arise and cease depending upon various causes and conditions. Just as the flame burns brightly when all of its causes are assembled, so too does our cyclic existence burn with the three types of duhkha when afflictions and karma are present. Just as the flame sputters and goes out when its fuel is consumed or when a strong wind blows, so too is the misery of cyclic existence extinguished when ignorance is destroyed or when wisdom eliminates craving and clinging.

The Simile of an Illusion

We have previously discussed the simile of a magician's illusion, but we will revisit it here. A magician has the idea to conjure up the illusion of horses and elephants, for example. The magician recites some words and casts a spell so that the sticks and pebbles—the bases of the illusion—appear as horses and elephants. Perhaps he must apply some ointment or special substance to the sticks and pebbles as well. By his completing the procedure correctly, the sticks and pebbles then appear as horses and elephants. When the audience sees the illusory horses and elephants, not knowing that the magician has cast a spell, they believe the illusion to be real. The horses and elephants appear to the magician as well, but he does not believe them to be real, and a person who arrives later sees only sticks and pebbles, no horses and elephants.

The experience of watching television is similar. We see all sorts of things in it. Although no one has cast a spell enabling us to see the people, animals, jungles, forests, science labs, cities, and so forth, the television has the ability to show all of these faraway things and places. When an adult looks at the television screen, she knows that even though people appear in it, there are not people there the way it appears. She knows that whatever she sees is simply an appearance on the television. However, someone who is very young or does not know what a television is might think there are real people there and want to go talk with them! A third person arrives later, after the television has been switched off. He does not see anything on the screen, and he also does not believe anyone or anything is there inside the television.

To understand this simile, we need to understand the three people. Two experience the appearance, and one does not. Of the two that have the appearance of people on the screen, one believes it to exist as it appears, while the other one does not. The third person has neither the appearance of the illusion nor does he believe it is true.

If the magician conjures up something very beautiful, attachment arises in the minds of the audience. If he conjures up something ugly, the audience becomes upset and angry. Similarly, someone watching the television who does not know or forgets that it is only an appearance on a screen will be filled with attachment when seeing something desirable and will react with fear or anger when seeing something repulsive. While nothing on the television will actually benefit or harm him, by believing the appearances to be true he is drawn into duhkha.

Just like in these examples, in real life things appear to us as if they exist from their own side. Then we grasp that appearance as real. We believe in, assent to, and do not question that appearance, and grasp things as existing from their own side. Then when some things appear attractive to us, we yearn for them with craving; when other things appear frightening, we recoil with fear or anger. All of our emotions and the actions they motivate stem from things appearing to us as existing from their own side and our grasping at them as existing in the way they appear.

Like the audience in the simile who has the appearance of horses and elephants and believes them to be true, ordinary sentient beings who have not realized emptiness not only have the appearance of inherent existence but also grasp things to exist inherently. Like the magician to whom horses and elephants appear although he does not grasp them as real, people who have realized emptiness but are not in meditative equipoise on emptiness at the moment have the appearance of inherent existence but do not grasp things to exist that way. They know that as vivid as the appearance of inherent existence is, it is false. Like the latecomers who neither see horses and elephants nor believe them to be there, aryas in meditative equipoise on emptiness neither have the appearance of inherent existence nor grasp at inherent existence. In addition, all consciousnesses of a buddha have no appearance of true existence and also no grasping at true existence.

Things appear truly existent, don't they? When a person says, "There is nothing that is truly existent," somebody might reply, "But they appear truly existent. So aren't they truly existent since they appear that way?" This person needs to understand that things can appear to exist in a certain way without actually existing in that way. These appearances are deceptive and false. Although we may know this on an intellectual level, we often forget it, especially when something appears to us that gives us pleasure or pain.

Although the illusions that a magician creates do not exist as they appear, the audience members will still feel desire toward an illusion that is beautiful and fear or aversion toward horrible scenes. The attachment and fear they feel are really there. Similarly, we may feel craving or disgust after watching a movie even though there were only appearances on the screen.

Similar to the audience at a magic show or a child in front of a television, who are frightened by the appearance of stampeding animals, sentient beings are tormented by the duhkha of cyclic existence. Not knowing that things do not truly exist as they appear, sentient beings grasp beautiful and disgusting appearances as true, and based on that grasping, their mental afflictions arise. Once the mental afflictions have arisen in their minds, even though they want happiness and they do not want suffering, they act in ways that cause unwished-for suffering. As a result, sentient beings are continually reborn in cyclic existence and are tormented by the various types of duhkha. This huge tragedy is all due to the mistaken appearances and our grasping them to be true as they appear. When we realize that these appearances are false and that things do not exist truly as they appear to, we will be released from the tumultuous emotional reactions we have toward them. The actions motivated by those disturbing emotions will cease, as will the karma and perplexities of life in cyclic existence.

In the simile, there is a cause for the appearance of the illusory horses and elephants. Likewise, in the case of things appearing truly existent, there is a cause. It is a deep cause, one that is not easily evident—the mind grasping true existence itself. This does not mean that this moment's grasping at true existence is itself creating the appearance of things being truly existent. Rather, we have been grasping at things as truly existent since beginningless time, so things appear truly existent due to ignorance and its latencies. Previous moments of the ignorance grasping true existence are responsible for later appearances of things as truly existent. Even if someone has eliminated the grasping at true existence, he or she can still have the appearance of true existence due to the latencies of ignorance. These latencies are responsible for the appearance of true existence, whether we have realized emptiness or not.

In the case of illusory horses and elephants and appearances of people in the television, a superficial condition brings about their appearance. In both cases, it is possible for someone who has not realized emptiness to know that the appearance is false. Even though the deep cause—true-grasping or its latencies—may still exist in that person's mind, it is not responsible for the illusory animals and the spectacular things appearing on the television. Rather the spell and substance that helps to cast the spell are the superficial cause for the appearance of illusory horses and elephants, and the television, electricity, and film studio are causes for the appearances on the television.

Let's take it a step further. The horses and elephants in the illusion also appear to be truly existent. The appearance of the horses and elephants being truly existent is due to the deep cause, the true-grasping ignorance and its latencies. In other words, the audience has two mistaken appearances. One is the appearance of horses and elephants where there are none;

the other is the appearance of true existence where there is none. The first appearance is caused by a superficial cause of error—the spells and substances used by the magician. The second is caused by a deep cause of error—the true-grasping ignorance and its latencies. The first appearance can be realized as false by someone who arrives at the magic show late. The second appearance—the appearance of true existence—is known to be false only by someone who has realized emptiness.

In summary, the simile of the illusion illustrates that things do not exist truly as they appear. Just as these false appearances appear to the audience due to causes (the spell and special substance of the magician) so too does the appearance of true existence appear to sentient beings due to causes (ignorance and its latencies). Once we realize emptiness nonconceptually, we will begin the process of eradicating the true-grasping ignorance and then its latencies that cause the false appearance of true existence. The peace of nonabiding nirvana—the nirvana of a buddha in which one abides in neither samsara nor personal liberation—will follow.

CHAPTER TWENTY

Similes from the *Diamond Cutter Sutra*—Part II

THE SIMILE OF A DEWDROP

If we look outside in the early morning, we see dewdrops on the tips of the blades of grass. Twinkling in the sunlight, they look so beautiful. But they are unstable; once the sun rises and its warm light shines on the grass, the dewdrops dry up. This simile illustrates that conditioned things do not endure for long. They come into existence and perish in the same moment.

When we make something—let's say we construct a building or cook a meal—from the very moment it is made, it is constantly changing until eventually it falls apart and totally vanishes—the building falls down, the food is eaten. This is coarse impermanence. Subtle impermanence is the arising and vanishing of things in each moment, never remaining for another instant. Due to their subtle impermanence, which we are usually oblivious to, one day they will totally disintegrate and fall apart, manifesting their coarse impermanence.

Impermanent things change moment by moment, without our having to do anything to cause that change. It is their nature not to remain in the next instant. The Buddha taught that all conditioned things have the aspect of *nonexistence* in that they do not exist as something that will endure. Because they do not endure, they are not reliable or secure. For this reason, we should not count on the things and people of cyclic existence to remain the same. They are constantly changing—arising and ceasing—disintegrating from one moment to the next. True cessations and nirvana, on the other hand, are permanent. Once attained, we need not fear that they will dissolve and leave us bereft.

The Simile of a Water Bubble

This same simile appeared above when we discussed the similes the Buddha gave to illustrate the emptiness of the five aggregates. Here, again, feelings are described by the simile of a bubble of water. While a water bubble remains, its nature is water. Even after it has burst and has absorbed into the rest of the water, its nature is still water. So it is with feelings too. As a sutra said, "All feelings whatsoever are unsatisfactory."[56]

Contaminated feelings are so called because they are associated with ignorance and afflictions. They arise under the influence of ignorance and exist in a mindstream that has not yet eliminated ignorance. Because they are under the influence of ignorance, afflictions, and karma, these feelings—be they pleasant, painful, or neutral—experienced by samsaric beings are unsatisfactory by nature.

It is not difficult to understand that painful feelings are unsatisfactory—all sentient beings recognize that. It is harder to understand that contaminated feelings of happiness and pleasure are also unsatisfactory, because when we experience samsaric happiness we think it's great. In order to get it, we try to get all sorts of possessions, travel to beautiful places, and have many friends, believing these will give us the experience of happiness. When we get what we seek, we are satisfied and satiated for a time. But if we keep doing what seemed so pleasurable, it eventually becomes painful. In addition, even if these pleasant feelings fade naturally, painful disappointment arises in their stead.

We ordinary beings think there is a difference between the feelings of happiness (pleasure), pain (suffering), and neutrality. We believe some feelings are better and more desirable than others. We consider painful feelings as bad and do not like them; we believe that contaminated happiness is really great. However, for an arya there is no difference between any of these feelings because they are all unsatisfactory and aren't desirable in the least. To these beings who have realized reality directly, there is not enough happiness in cyclic existence to fit on the tip of a needle. Having abandoned attachment to all of cyclic existence and therefore to all the enjoyments of cyclic existence, they do not seek these things and do not derive contaminated happiness from them. For example, when aryas eat what we consider to be delicious food, they do not think, "Wow, this is fantastic," and become attached to it. They simply regard it as temporary happiness and enjoy it as such. While we run around pursuing contaminated pleasure, they see it as useless and would much rather turn their attention to more worthwhile things, such as ethical conduct, concentration, bodhichitta, and wisdom.

However, this does not mean aryas are bereft of happiness. In fact, they experience immense happiness; much more than we beings in cyclic existence do! For example, they have the happiness of true cessation and the happiness of the true path. They are close to the everlasting happiness of liberation or full enlightenment. For us, happiness means the short-term pleasures of samsara, the good feelings from having possessions, talking to friends, receiving praise, having a good reputation, and so on. Aryas are not seduced into believing these things will bring them ultimate happiness and are therefore not upset when they are separated from them. Seeing them as helpful to sustain the body and therefore attain liberation, they make use of these items.

These three contaminated feelings are included in the first of the four noble truths, which is called "true duhkha for the aryas" or "what is in truth unsatisfactory for the aryas." For aryas, who have firm determination to be free from cyclic existence and have directly realized emptiness, all contaminated feelings of happiness, pain, and neutrality are the same. As said in the four seals, "All contaminated phenomena are unsatisfactory." While painful feelings are the duhkha of pain, pleasant feelings are the duhkha of change. Contaminated neutral feelings are also unsatisfactory because they are the basis for all duhkha. Being unstable, neutral feelings give way to pain or contaminated pleasure and are therefore considered the pervasive duhkha of conditioning. Aryas want nothing to do with contaminated feelings; they seek the lasting fulfillment, bliss, and joy of liberation and enlightenment.

As the simile expresses, feelings—happy, painful, and neutral—are as transient and unstable as water bubbles. No sooner do they appear than they are gone. They change easily, with the slightest alteration in conditions, and therefore cannot provide stable joy and security. It is far better to turn our minds to nirvana.

The Simile of a Dream

A dream is a simile for things being false and not existing as they appear. Sleep is the condition that brings about the mistaken appearance in dreams.

All sorts of things appear in a dream—some are attractive and pleasant, some aren't. But whether we have a good or a bad dream, once we wake up it is no longer there. We realize that what appeared, what we thought was real, was only a dream. The people and things that appeared so vividly to us in the dream are not real at all.

For example, a young woman may want to have a child. When she is asleep, she dreams she gives birth to a child and is elated. But later in the dream, the child dies and she is devastated. However, on waking, she sees that neither the exhilarating appearance of having a child that brought her joy nor the horrible appearance of the child's death that caused her anguish is real.

Likewise, just as the child appears in the dream due to causes and conditions yet is unreal, our experiences in life appear due to our past actions even though they are not truly existent. Just as the unreal dream child invokes happiness and grief in the woman, our actions—which are unreal and do not exist from their own side—bring results which likewise do not exist from their own side.

In *Treatise on the Middle Way* (7:34) Nagarjuna said:

> Like a dream, like an illusion,
> like a city of gandharvas,[57]
> so have arising, enduring,
> and ceasing been explained.

Bhavaviveka in his *Lamp of Wisdom* (*Prajnapradipa*) explains the simile in this way: Since when we wake up from a dream, all the things that we dreamed about have disappeared, the dream is a simile connected to the past. In other words, the simile of the dream illustrates that phenomena of the past do not inherently exist.

The Simile of a Flash of Lightning

The simile of the flash of lightning illustrates that the phenomena of the present are not inherently existent. First the sky is clear; storm clouds gradually gather. Due to this, lightning flashes across the sky, appearing ever so quickly before vanishing. Thinking of the flash of lightning, we cannot say, "It came from here," and "It went there." Likewise, while it remains, we cannot say, "It is in this spot," because it occurred so very briefly. Occurring occasionally, it vanishes straightaway.

Likewise, all phenomena of the present are merely appearances to our minds. They arise due to the coming together of their causes and conditions; they do not exist at all from their own side. Just as we cannot say, "This is where the lightning came from," "There it is," or "That's where it went," from whatever angle we analyze the phenomena of the present, we are not able to find them. We may examine them from the viewpoint of agent, action, and object; scrutinize the nature of the phenomena themselves; or investigate their causes and its effects; but we will still not be able to find them. There is nothing to point to as being findable under analysis. Like the lightning, phenomena of the present disappear as soon as we start to search for them.

THE SIMILE OF A CLOUD

The simile of the cloud is connected to phenomena of the future and illustrates their lack of existence from their own side. Rain cannot fall from a completely clear sky. For rain showers to happen, first clouds must gather in the sky. Then the rain falls, and that has the potential to make crops grow, trees become full, and fruit ripen. Nevertheless, the sky itself has been clear all along. The clouds are adventitious; they arise dependent on causes and conditions.

In the same way the nature of the mind is clear light in that it totally lacks self-existence. Yet within the clear light and empty nature of the mind, the clouds of afflictions and their latencies gather. They motivate us to engage in many actions, which produce the various ripening results that we experience in the future. Like the simile of a cloud, this is a dependently arising process: Ignorance, afflictions, karmas, happy and miserable results all occur through dependence. Being dependent, they do not exist in the way they appear. They gather and disperse just like clouds, yet they seem real while they are present.

All of these causes and results exist by being merely imputed by term and concept. If they were inherently existent, causes and their results would exist at the same time. It would be as the Samkhyas believe when they assert arising from self: The results would exist in a nonmanifest form in the cause. In that case, the crops, trees, and fruit would have to already exist inside the rainclouds that are their cause, and there would be no need for the rain to produce them.

The Tibetan word for future means "that which has not yet come." If any resultant phenomenon were inherently existent, it would not need to depend on a cause to arise. That is because something that exists inherently already has its own entity. Something that already has its own entity does not need to arise; it already exists and so doesn't need to be produced.

Conventionally existent causes and results do not need to meet, but inherently existent ones would have to meet. If they didn't meet, how could one produce the other? There would be a time gap between them. But if they met, they would occur at the same time, in which case a sprout would already exist, and it wouldn't be necessary for a seed to produce it.

In general, for a result to arise, its cause must cease. That means that the result comes about through the ceasing of its cause. There are two ways in which a cause gradually transforms into the result. In one way, the cause ceases to be seen. For example, when a huge tree grows from a seed, the seed has disappeared, and we no longer see it. In the second way, there is a continuity of a similar type. For example, when we cook rice, the rice undergoes a transformation by changing constantly, moment by moment. At the end, we still see something that we call "rice," although it is not the same as the rice before it was cooked.

We may think, "My mother is the cause of me. Are you saying that she has to cease for me to be born?" Of course not. However, our mother when we were born was not the same as our mother when we were a toddler. She had changed moment by moment, even though she still had the same label, "my mother."

The ceasing of the cause and the arising of the result are simultaneous, yet we know that when we were born our mother did not cease to exist. So when we say the cause ceases when the result arises, it does not mean the cause utterly ceases to exist or the person dies. Rather, it means that it undergoes momentary change in which case the earlier moments in the continuity cease while later moments of that continuity arise. The continuity of our mother exists after we were born.

Causal dependence—causes producing results and results arising from causes—is one type of dependent arising. This demonstrates that things do not exist from their own side, independent of anything else. It also proves that things do not exist as they appear. This resembles the simile of the cloud: First there is the clear sky, then clouds form in it, the rain falls, and the crops and plants in the earth below are nourished and grow. All along one thing happens depending on another. None of this could take place if things existed from their own side.

Conclusion: See Conditioned Phenomena as Such

The last line of this verse, which also marks the conclusion of the *Diamond Cutter Sutra*, says, "See conditioned things as such." That is, all conditioned phenomena are like these nine similes, from the star down to the cloud. We should look at all conditioned phenomena in this way.

In addition, unconditioned phenomena, such as emptiness and unconditioned space, are not self-existent, because they, too, are dependent. Emptiness depends on its basis. That is, the emptiness of the table depends on there being a table that is empty of true existence. The emptiness of John depends on John.

Seeing all phenomena as such means to see them as empty of inherent existence, not existing as they appear and not findable when searched for in their basis of designation. That is, although they are empty they appear, and while they appear they are also empty. These two are not contradictory.

All nine similes are applicable to all phenomena because all phenomena do not exist as they appear and all of them cannot be found when we search for them just as shown in these similes. This is true in the case of the self, others, cyclic existence, and nirvana. These are the same in that they are all mere imputation by name and do not exist inherently on their basis of designation. Nevertheless, because the six consciousnesses—from the visual consciousness up to the mental consciousness—are contaminated by ignorance and its latencies, the objects of those consciousnesses all appear truly existent to them. The way conventional phenomena appear and the way they exist are discordant because ignorance and its latencies, which have colored our minds since beginningless time, distort the way those things appear to us.

CHAPTER TWENTY-ONE

How Fortunate!

I have explained emptiness as best as I am able, sharing with you some of the aspects of this profound topic that I believe to be most meaningful. Some of you have been studying and meditating on emptiness for many years and know how to meditate on it and the benefits of familiarizing your mind with emptiness and dependent arising. But some of you are newer to this topic, and so it will be helpful to review why it is important to learn, think about, and meditate on emptiness. When you understand this, you will know the value of putting effort and time into doing this. Then gradually you will develop the ability to think for yourselves, using the Buddha's teaching as a reliable guide directing you to where you want to go—enlightenment.

During his lifetime, the Buddha gave 84,000 sets of teachings. Be they sutra or tantra, the most important points in these teachings are renunciation, bodhichitta, and the correct view of emptiness. Of these three, the Buddha emphasized the teachings on emptiness right from the time he began to teach. Throughout his life, up until the time he passed into parinirvana, he continued to stress the importance of understanding emptiness.

While the Buddha taught emptiness to some extent in all three turnings of the Dharma wheel, he primarily explained it in the middle turning of the wheel in the Perfection of Wisdom sutras. Before giving these teachings, Buddha put on a display of miraculous manifestations that I have never heard of him doing before any other teachings. He made his tongue spread out expansively to the size of the three worlds. Light radiated from his tongue, and through this he made it known in all the buddha fields[58] that this teaching was about to begin.

Aware that something special was going to occur, the bodhisattvas in the retinues of these buddhas asked them what these special signs signified, and the buddhas indicated that Buddha Shakyamuni was about to give teachings on the Perfection of Wisdom in the world system called Fearless (Abhaya). Our world system has this name because the beings in it lamentably do not fear the afflictions. Rather than see the afflictions as the source of duhkha, they are friendly with their afflictions and are not afraid when they inhabit their minds. The bodhisattvas then requested permission from the principal buddha in their pure land to go to the Fearless world system in order to meet the Tathagata Shakyamuni, make offerings and prostrations to him, and listen to him teach emptiness. They were given permission, and so the audience became enormous.

MEDITATING ON EMPTINESS IS CRUCIAL FOR LIBERATION

As we learned before, the Buddha said to his disciple, the highly learned Ananda, who had listened to so many of the Buddha's words, that it was imperative that the Perfection of Wisdom teachings be preserved properly, without any alteration in words or meaning. Although the Buddha had given many explanations on a wide variety of topics, he spoke this way especially in regard to the teachings on emptiness. Having said this, the Buddha then gave the discourses that make up the *100,000 Verses Perfection of Wisdom Sutra* (*Shatasahasrika Prajnaparamita*), the *25,000 Verses Perfection of Wisdom Sutra* (*Panchavimshatisahasrika Prajnaparamita*), and the *8,000 Verses Perfection of Wisdom Sutra.*

This indicates just how important the Buddha considered these teachings to be. It is not as if the other teachings of the Buddha are unimportant. But somehow the Buddha considered the teachings on emptiness to be especially precious and critical to learn, preserve, and realize. This is because the understanding of emptiness is the most essential realization that sentient beings need to cultivate in order to free themselves from all of the duhkha of cyclic existence. It is only the realization of emptiness that has the ability to cut the root of cyclic existence so that it never returns. The Buddha clearly explained that without the realization of emptiness, it is impossible to attain any of three levels of enlightenment—the enlightenments of the hearers, solitary realizers, or the complete enlightenment of a buddha.

In Je Tsongkhapa's writings, he quoted the *Questions of Rashtrapala Sutra*, which presents the three doors of liberation.[59] It says that the Buddha taught emptiness out of compassion for sentient beings, who wander endlessly in cyclic existence due to not understanding the three doors of liberation—that all phenomena are empty, peaceful, and unborn. To liberate sentient beings, the Buddha taught emptiness using many different methods and hundreds of reasonings to show that everything lacks inherent existence.

For lifetimes without beginning, we have wandered in cyclic existence, continually taking births in each of the different realms of cyclic existence, from the peak of samsara down to the lowest hell. Why does this happen and why has it gone on for so long? It is because we have not understood the three doors of liberation. Because we have not understood emptiness, our beginningless duhkha has continued for so long. And we will keep experiencing all the frustration, unhappiness, and disappointment that cyclic existence brings until we realize the lack of inherent existence.

Why does this happen? The root of all afflictions is the true-grasping ignorance. Based on this, all other mental afflictions of attachment, anger, jealousy, arrogance, anxiety, and so on arise. These motivate us to engage in various actions or karma. While some are constructive actions, others are harmful: physical actions such as killing, stealing, and sexual misconduct; verbal actions such as lying, divisive speech, harsh speech, and idle talk; and mental actions such as covetousness, maliciousness, and wrong view. Engaging in these actions, we accumulate karma and as a result are born again and again in cyclic existence, experiencing the myriad sufferings of each realm and each rebirth.

Think about it—absolutely every single experience of physical and mental suffering we have ever had and ever will have while in cyclic existence is the result of destructive karma. That karma was created in dependence on the afflictions, and the root of all afflictions is true-grasping ignorance. This ignorance not only does not know the true nature of reality, but it also grasps phenomena to exist in the exact opposite way from how they actually exist. Whereas phenomena are empty of true existence, true-grasping ignorance grasps them as being truly existent.

If the roots of a particular tree are poisonous, the trunk and all the branches, leaves, flowers, and fruit that grow from it will also be poisonous. True-grasping ignorance is like the root of that poisonous tree, the afflictions are the branches and leaves that grow depending on it, and our misery is the flowers and fruit that are the result. The only thing that can damage that root is a mind that refers to the same object as ignorance but engages it in the completely opposite way. Since true-grasping refers to objects and holds them to be truly existent, what opposes it is the wisdom mind that refers to the same object and realizes that it is empty of true existence.

Other practices such as meditating on bodhichitta, love, and compassion are virtuous, but they are not able to harm the true-grasping ignorance that is the root of cyclic existence. That is because they do not refer to the same object as that ignorance and grasp it in a completely opposite way.

Once we realize emptiness, we will be able to free ourselves from having to take birth again and again under the control of afflictions and karma, and the miseries of cyclic existence—birth, aging, illness, death, and so on—will forever cease. For that reason, the great masters who authored the profound treatises request all those who wish to be completely free of the duhkha of cyclic existence to aspire to gain the wisdom realizing emptiness and to do their utmost to cultivate that wisdom.

Just as a blind person who wants to go home will hold on to a cow from his household who will lead him home, those of us who want to attain liberation and enlightenment need to hold on to the wisdom realizing emptiness that will lead us to our spiritual goals. All the buddhas and bodhisattvas, the dakas and dakinis, the heroes and heroines agree and make this request with one voice, "Those who wish to be liberated from duhkha, try your utmost to develop the wisdom realizing emptiness."

If an archer shoots a poisonous arrow at a person and it strikes him in such a way that it cuts off his life force, all the other faculties and all his organs will cease to function. In the same way, the wisdom realizing emptiness will destroy the life force of the true-grasping ignorance and, along with that, all the mental afflictions that rely on it.

The very purpose of the Buddha coming into the world was to liberate sentient beings from the duhkha of cyclic existence and show us the way to nirvana—the peace in which all afflictions and duhkha have been pacified. It is said that the Buddha has more compassion for us than we have for ourselves, and thus his heartfelt desire was that all sentient beings be able to experience the joy and happiness of nirvana, the state beyond sorrow.

Since the method to attain this state is the wisdom realizing emptiness, he emphasized this. Of all the discourses he gave, the Buddha considered the Perfection of Wisdom sutras to be the most precious, the most amazing, and the most excellent. These sutras are praised so highly and are said to be peerless and auspicious because they reveal not only the profound but also the extensive aspects of the path. The profound aspect is emptiness and the extensive aspects are all the magnificent deeds of the bodhisattvas. The Perfection of Wisdom sutras are so important that a place where they abide is considered to be a place where the Buddha abides. Even writing out the Perfection of Wisdom sutras and making offerings to them creates a huge, inexpressible amount of merit.

Without the realization of emptiness, we may practice pure ethical conduct and remain in deep concentration for tens of millions of years, but we will not attain liberation. While the practices of generosity, ethical conduct, fortitude, joyous effort, and concentration are extraordinary, if they are not combined with insight into wisdom, they alone cannot take us forcefully and rapidly toward enlightenment. The *Condensed Perfection of Wisdom in Stanzas* (*Prajnaparamita Samchayagatha*) states:

> Those millions and billions of blind ones who are bereft of sight,
> ignorant of the roads, how can they go to the towns?
> If wisdom is lacking then these five perfections
> cannot reach enlightenment, since they have no sight.

In his *Supplement to the Middle Way* (6:2), Chandrakirti continues this theme, saying:

> Just as a blind multitude is easily led to the place
> where they desire to go by a single person with eyes,
> likewise wisdom sustains the blind virtues [the other five
>   perfections]
> and journeys to the state of the conquerors.

Someone who is blind cannot get where he wants to go without help. It is as if he were traveling in the dark, where everything is obscured. The first five perfections are like that. While they are essential to attain buddhahood, they alone cannot get us to our goal. However, just as a blind person can be led to his destination with the help of someone with sight, if we combine the practice of the first five perfections with the wisdom realizing emptiness, we will arrive at full enlightenment.

Even if we do not attain full enlightenment in this life, making an effort to understand and meditate on emptiness will inflict huge damage on our true-grasping. Even if we do not understand emptiness very well, just having doubts about it, thinking, "Probably everything is empty of true existence," begins to ruin the root of cyclic existence, making it unstable, soft, and weak.

POWERFUL PURIFICATION

If you find understanding the way in which things are dependent and empty of self-existence is difficult to understand, ask knowledgeable people, read authoritative explanations, and listen to teachings. As you spend time thinking about these points, gradually they will become clear to you, and you will derive many benefits from this. Your understanding will increase, and many good seeds will be planted on your mindstream. This is also powerful purification of negativities. By continuing your contemplation, you will eventually gain a full understanding.

Having some understanding of emptiness is extremely useful when practicing tantra. In most, if not all, tantric sadhanas, there is a point where we say, "*Om svabhava shuddha sarva dharma svabhava shuddho ham*. Everything becomes empty." At this point, we pause and contemplate emptiness. Then, within emptiness—within an awareness that all phenomena lack true existence—the generation of the mandala and central deity occurs. After meditating on emptiness, we combine it with dependent arising, thinking that from *yam* comes the wind mandala and so forth, generating the inner and outer offering, the mandala, and the deity.

Meditation on emptiness is also an incredibly powerful method to purify negativities—afflictions, destructive karma, transgressions of precepts, and so forth—when done as part of the four opponent powers:

1. Having regret for the destructive actions we have done in the past
2. Making a determination not to engage in the same actions in the future
3. Taking refuge and generating bodhichitta
4. Applying the antidote: meditating on emptiness, reciting mantras, and doing any other virtuous practice

The fourth opponent power includes meditating on such topics as bodhichitta and emptiness, which are powerful ways to purify.

People who think deeply on these matters start to wonder how meditation on emptiness is relevant when purifying. They understand that being empty does not affect the fact that a given object still exists conventionally. Conventionally a cause gives rise to its result, and meditation on emptiness does not change that fact. So meditating on the emptiness of nonvirtue is not going to affect the fact that conventionally the nonvirtue exists and that conventionally nonvirtue produces unpleasant ripening results. How, then, does meditation on emptiness lead to purification of destructive karma?

Destructive actions are motivated by afflictions, and the root of all these afflictions is true-grasping ignorance. Karma is a product of afflictions, which arise due to true-grasping ignorance. Meditating on emptiness harms true-grasping ignorance. When that is damaged, all the mental afflictions that are based on it are also harmed, and all of the karmas that were created as a result of those afflictions are also harmed; they are purified and cleansed. This is similar to a painting done on canvas. When the canvas is ruined, everything that was painted on it is also ruined. Similarly, by destroying ignorance, the afflictions and karma that are based on it and rely on it are also destroyed.

The *Engaging in the Power of Faith Sutra* (*Shraddhabaladhanavatara Sutra*) says that if one has understood emptiness clearly, there is more benefit to meditating on emptiness for one session than in providing all sentient beings of the three realms—the desire, form, and formless realms—with everything they need for an entire lifetime. Why is meditation on emptiness so much more worthwhile? While it is certainly wonderful and very virtuous to provide sentient beings with food, clothing, shelter, and medicine, this does not prevent them from experiencing birth, aging, sickness, and death under the control of afflictions and karma. However, if we think in the long term, meditating on emptiness can do that.

Furthermore, when meditation on emptiness is combined with bodhichitta and the practices of the method aspect of the path, the benefits are inconceivable. Thus, do not neglect to meditate on bodhichitta by thinking that meditation on emptiness is more important. In fact, realization of both bodhichitta and the wisdom realizing emptiness are essential to the attainment of enlightenment. Just as a bird needs two wings to fly, we need bodhichitta and the wisdom realizing emptiness to reach full enlightenment.

Please rejoice at your great fortune to have encountered the Buddha's doctrine, especially his precious teachings on emptiness. Since you now have so many conducive conditions to study and learn, make good use of them to benefit yourselves and others and to progress on the path to full enlightenment.

Notes

1 Tsongkhapa [rJe Tsong khapa], *Ocean of Reasoning: A Great Commentary on Nāgārjuna's Mūlamadhyamakakārikā*, trans. by Geshe Ngawang Samten and Jay L. Garfield (New York: Oxford University Press, 2006), p. 16.

2 The I is the person, and the aggregates—the body and mind—are what the person depends on and clings to. These will be explained in future chapters.

3 The First Dalai Lama, Gyalwa Gendun Drub, says that the expression "particles in the River Ganges" can be understood in two ways: It can refer to the molecules of water in the River Ganges or to the particles of sand that make up the riverbed.

4 In *Ocean of Reasoning*, Je Tsongkhapa paraphrases this quotation.

5 Tib. *ka dag*: literally, "pure from the letter *ka*," which is the first letter in the Tibetan alphabet.

6 Translation from Tsongkhapa, *Ocean of Reasoning*, p. 17.

7 Adapted from Tsongkhapa, *Ocean of Reasoning*, p. 17.

8 In the seven-point instruction of cause and effect, practitioners contemplate: (1) that all sentient beings have been their mothers, (2) the kindness of those beings as their mothers, (3) the wish to repay that kindness, (4) love, (5) compassion, (6) the great resolve, and (7) the result, bodhichitta. When following the method of equalizing and exchanging self and others, practitioners meditate on equalizing themselves and others, the disadvantages of the self-centered thought, the benefit of cherishing others, exchanging self and other, and love and compassion through the meditation on taking and giving (*tonglen*).

9 The eight freedoms are not being born (1) as a hell being, (2) as a hungry ghost, (3) as an animal, (4) as a long-lived god, (5) as a barbarian in an uncivilized society, (6) where the Buddha's teachings are not available, (7) with physical or mental impediments that restrict one's ability to learn and practice the Dharma, (8) with stubborn wrong views. The ten fortunes are being born (1) as a human being, (2) in a central region where the Buddhadharma is present, (3) with complete and healthy physical and mental faculties, (4) not having done the five heinous actions, (5) having faith in what is worthy of respect, (6) where and when a Buddha has come, (7) where and when a Buddha has taught the Dharma, (8) where and when the Dharma still exists, (9) where and when there is a monastic sangha that is following the Buddha's doctrine, and (10) where and when there are others with loving concern who help us on the path: teacher, sponsors, and so forth.

10 The six root afflictions are attachment, anger, ignorance, conceit, doubt, and wrong views.

11 The twenty auxiliary afflictions are wrath, resentment, spite, jealousy, harmfulness, miserliness, haughtiness, agitation, concealment, dullness, laziness, lack of faith, forgetfulness, nonintrospective awareness, pretension, dissimulation, lack of integrity, inconsideration for others, negligence, distraction.

12 Śāntideva, *A Guide to the Bodhisattva Way of Life*, trans. by Vesna and Alan Wallace (Ithaca: Snow Lion, 1997), p. 18.

13 Tsongkhapa, *Ocean of Reasoning*, p. 498.

14 Geshe Sonam Rinchen, *Yogic Deeds of Bodhisattvas: Gyel-tsab on Āryadeva's Four Hundred*, trans. by Ruth Sonam (Ithaca: Snow Lion, 1994), p. 188.

15 These four are (1) being generous and giving material aid, (2) speaking pleasantly, (3) giving encouragement and leading followers on the virtuous path by teaching the Dharma, and (4) acting congruently and living the teachings through example.

16 Rinchen, *Yogic Deeds of Bodhisattvas*, p. 193.

17 The twelve links of dependent origination describe the process through which sentient beings are born in cyclic existence. They are: ignorance, formative action, consciousness, name and form, six sense sources, contact, feeling, craving, clinging, renewed existence, birth, and aging and death. By ceasing these, we attain liberation.

18 Note that here *designate*, *label*, and *impute* are used synonymously.

19 Many of us who grew up in theistic religions or in a culture where that is the norm may have remnants of the acquired self-grasping of the person as permanent, unitary, and independent in our mindstream. We may not initially recognize it, but it will come up from time to time and interfere with our taking refuge in the Three Jewels or our understanding emptiness. For that reason, it's good if we spend some time contemplating whether there actually is an everlasting soul that neither is born nor dies, that is partless or unitary, and that is independent and not influenced at all by causes and conditions.

20 Sometimes the analogy of the carrier and burden is used to illustrate the belief that the person and aggregates are different entities. Here the analogy is not being used to indicate that, but to show that the person depends on the aggregates because it is imputed in relation to them.

21 Both the Sautrantika and Chittamatra have branches, those following scripture and those following reasoning. Similarly, the Svatantrika-Madhyamaka school has two branches, Yogacharya-Svatantrika and Sautrantika-Svatantrika. While describing the various assertions of each branch is too detailed for the scope of this book, their positions are noted in the chart above, "Illustration of the Person." In general, in this book, *Sautrantikas* refers to those following reasoning, and *Chittamatrins* refers to those following scripture.

22 The Tibetan phrase "merely imputed in dependence on the continuity of the aggregate(s)" does not specify whether *aggregate* is singular or plural. So literally translated it could mean either "merely imputed in dependence on the continuity of the aggregate" or "merely imputed in dependence on the continuity of the aggregates." When speaking of the mere I that goes from one life to the next, *aggregate(s)* refers to the mental consciousness because its continuity spans one life to the next, even though it is not an inherently existent person. The illustration of the I that goes from one life to the next cannot be imputed in dependence on the continuity of the aggregates, because the body from this life does not go on to the next life.

23 When the person is alive and all the aggregates are functioning, we say the mere I is imputed in dependence on the collection of the aggregates, and when we speak in the context of what connects one life to the next, we say the mere I is imputed in dependence on the mental consciousness. There is no contradiction.

24 Since realizing emptiness by a valid inference does not eliminate I-grasping and its seeds from the mindstream, it may still arise.

25 It is not contradictory to say a wrong consciousness is erroneous with respect to its apprehended object. This implies that its apprehended object does not exist.

26 These three types of independence correspond with the three objects of negation in the meditation on the selflessness of person. For the Svatantrikas, the meaning of *independent* in the meditation on the selflessness of phenomena would be "not being posited by the force of appearing to a nondefective mind" and refers to true existence. When they refute true existence, they use the reason "because of being dependent and related," which negates true existence as they conceive it.

27 See José Ignacio Cabezón, *A Dose of Emptiness* (Albany: State University of New York Press, 1992), p. 334, for more about this example.

28 The Tibetan term *cha* literally means "part," but it is a misleading term here in that we tend to mistakenly think that the top third of the fluid is nectar, the middle third is water, and the bottom third is pus and blood. Then we think that if one of the three sentient beings drinks his or her share, the other two parts should remain in the glass. But that is not the case. To avoid this misunderstanding it is better to translate *cha* as "facet." When a god drinks that facet of the fluid that appears to him or her as nectar, there will be nothing left in the glass—no water, no pus and blood.

29 It is important to remember that this example has to do with sentient beings with very powerful karma, so powerful that it made them take the physical and mental aggregates of a particular realm of existence. The facet that appears as water to a human being does not do so because of some inherent quality from the side of the fluid. Rather, that person's karma affects how the object appears to him and how his mind perceives and labels it. The same is true for the facets that appear to the hungry ghosts and gods.

30 Samyutta Nikaya I.5:10.

31 See chapter 13 for more on the sevenfold reasoning.

32 As distinct from impermanent things, which arise and cease due to causes and conditions, permanent phenomena do not depend on causes and conditions. Examples of permanent phenomena are unobstructed space, emptiness, selflessness. See Jeffrey Hopkins, *Meditation on Emptiness* (Boston: Wisdom Publications, 1996), p. 217, for more on permanent phenomena.

33 This reasoning investigates whether an effect arises from itself, a cause which is other, both, or causelessly.

34 This reasoning investigates whether a cause produces an effect that is (inherently) existent, nonexistent, both, or neither.

35 These are: (1) *Refutation of Objections*, (2) *Seventy Stanzas on Emptiness*, (3) *Six Stanzas of Reasoning*, (4) *Treatise Called "The Finely Woven,"* and (5) *Treatise on the Middle Way.* Sometimes a sixth text—the *Precious Garland*—is added.

36 Translation adapted from Tsongkhapa, *Ocean of Reasoning*, pp. 503–4.

37 Translation with minor style changes from Tsongkhapa, *Ocean of Reasoning*, pp. 24–25.

38 Translated by Thupten Jinpa.

39 The ten directions are the four cardinal directions, the four intermediate directions, above, and below.

40 This latter meaning of *one and many* will be explored in chapter 17.

41 Majjhima Nikaya 44, the *Sutta of Shorter Series of Questions and Answers* (*Culavedalla Sutta*). This sutta was spoken by Bhikkhuni Dhammadinna.

42 In relation to form these four are: (1) viewing forms (e.g., the body) as a self, (2) viewing the self as inherently possessing forms, (3) viewing the self as inherently existing in form (form is inherently a support for the self), and (4) viewing form as inherently existing in the self (the self is inherently a support for form). The same four are outlined in relation to feelings, discriminations, volitional factors, and consciousnesses.

43 See Hopkins, *Meditation on Emptiness*, pp. 176–77. The innate view of the perishing

aggregates does not grasp the I and the aggregates to be either one or different, so all twenty-five views are acquired views. However, if the I existed in the way the innate view of the perishing aggregates grasps it to exist, it would have to exist in one of the twenty-five ways. Thus when searching for the inherently existent I, we examine all these points.

44 Although "action" is the literal translation, the meaning is the object of the action or that acted upon.

45 The meaning of *ultimate identityless* in the context of the dependent and the consummate is different. The dependent are ultimate identityless because they are not the ultimate nature of phenomena while the consummate is ultimate identityless because it is the ultimate nature of phenomena.

46 A principal cognizer of an object is the main mind that cognizes that object; for example, the visual consciousness is the principal cognizer of colors.

47 A valid cognizer is a mind that is incontrovertible with respect to its apprehended object. See "Valid and Mistaken, but Not Erroneous" in chapter 7.

48 The last clause is given in order to include a buddha's perception of ultimate truth when definitions are used on the debate ground.

49 Technically, we can't say truly existent form is an appearing object or an apprehended object because truly existent form doesn't exist, and to be an object, something must exist. However, for ease we often speak like this.

50 It is unclear whether the spell is cast on the sticks and pebbles or on the people in the audience. However, the result is the same.

51 This quote is found in the Pali Canon, Samyutta Nikaya III 22.95.

52 Buddhas perceive conventional truths although their minds are not influenced by ignorance. Buddhas perceive falsities because sentient beings perceive them and buddhas perceive everything that exists. However, from the buddhas' side, they do not perceive phenomena as false—i.e., as not existing in the way they appear—because buddhas have no appearance of true existence.

53 This refers to the two truths with respect to one object, for example, a table and its emptiness. It does not mean that any conventional truth is one nature with any ultimate truth.

54 The four faults of asserting that the two truths are different natures apply to those who incorrectly speak of other-emptiness (*shentong*), saying that the ultimate truth is empty of being a conventional truth.

55 This version is from the *Sutta on the Many Kinds of Elements* (*Bahudhatuka Sutta*) in the Pali Canon, Majjhima Nikaya 115:11, translated by Bhikkhu Ñāṇamoli and Bhikkhu Bodhi.

56 Adapted from Jeffrey Hopkins's translation in *Maps of the Profound* (Ithaca: Snow Lion, 2003), p. 726.

57 Spirits with great musical abilities. They live in illusory cities.

58 There are innumerable buddha fields, or pure lands, each with its own buddha teaching a retinue of bodhisattvas. The Land of Great Bliss (*Sukhavati*) is the pure land of Buddha Amitabha, and the Array of Turquoise Leaves Pure Land is the pure land of Buddha Tara.

59 See chapter 1 for the quotation.

More Reading

Bodhi, Bhikkhu, trans. *The Connected Discourses of the Buddha: A Translation of the Saṃyutta Nikāya*. Boston: Wisdom Publications, 2000.

Cabezón, José Ignacio. *A Dose of Emptiness: An Annotated Translation of the sTong thun chen mo of mKhas grub dGe legs dpal bzang*. Albany: State University of New York Press, 1992.

Dalai Lama. *Essence of the Heart Sutra*. Trans. and Ed. by Thupten Jinpa. Boston: Wisdom Publications, 2005.

———. *How to See Yourself as You Really Are*. Trans. by Jeffrey Hopkins. New York: Atria Books, 2006.

———. *The Middle Way: Faith Grounded in Reason*. Trans. by Thupten Jinpa. Boston: Wisdom Publications, 2009.

———. *Practicing Wisdom*. Trans. by Thupten Jinpa. Boston: Wisdom Publications, 2005.

Gyatso, Lobsang, and Graham Woodhouse. *Tsongkhapa's Praise for Dependent Relativity*. Boston: Wisdom Publications, 2011.

Hopkins, Jeffrey. *Maps of the Profound*. Ithaca: Snow Lion, 2003.

———. *Meditation on Emptiness*. Boston: Wisdom Publications, 1996.

———. *Nāgārjuna's Precious Garland: Buddhist Advice for Living and Liberation*. Ithaca: Snow Lion, 2007.

———. *Tsong-kha-pa's Final Exposition of Wisdom*. Ithaca: Snow Lion, 2008.

Jinpa, Thupten. *Self, Reality and Reason in Tibetan Philosophy*. New York: Routledge Curzon, 2002.

Ñāṇamoli and Bodhi, Bhikkhus, trans. *The Middle Length Discourses of the Buddha: A Translation of the Majjhima Nikāya*. Boston: Wisdom Publications, 1995.

Newland, Guy. *Appearance and Reality*. Ithaca: Snow Lion, 1999.

———. *Introduction to Emptiness*. Ithaca: Snow Lion, 2008.

———. *The Two Truths*. Ithaca: Snow Lion, 1992.

Rinchen, Geshe Sonam. *Yogic Deeds of Bodhisattvas: Gyel-tsab on Āryadeva's Four Hundred.* Trans. by Ruth Sonam. Ithaca: Snow Lion, 1994.

Śāntideva. *A Guide to the Bodhisattva Way of Life.* Trans. by Vesna and Alan Wallace. Ithaca: Snow Lion, 1997.

Sopa, Geshe Lhundup, and Jeffrey Hopkins. *Cutting through Appearances.* Ithaca: Snow Lion, 1989.

Tegchok, Geshe Jampa. *Transforming Adversity into Joy and Courage.* Ithaca: Snow Lion, 2005.

Thakchoe, Sonam. *The Two Truths Debate: Tsongkhapa and Gorampa on the Middle Way.* Boston: Wisdom Publications, 2007.

Tsering, Geshe Tashi. *Emptiness.* Boston: Wisdom Publications, 2009.

———. *The Four Noble Truths.* Boston: Wisdom Publications, 2005.

———. *Relative Truth, Ultimate Truth.* Boston: Wisdom Publications, 2008.

Tsong-kha-pa. *The Great Treatise on the Stages of the Path.* 3 vols. Ithaca: Snow Lion, 2000–2004.

Tsong khapa, rJe. *Ocean of Reasoning: A Great Commentary on Nāgārjuna's Mūlamadhyamakakārikā.* Trans. by Geshe Ngawang Samten and Jay L. Garfield. New York: Oxford University Press, 2006.

Index

Terms in **bold** are followed only by those pages where that term is defined, rather than simply used, since their pervasiveness in the book would otherwise render their entries unhelpful.

Biographies

KHENSUR JAMPA TEGCHOK RINPOCHE became a monk at the age of eight. He studied all the major Buddhist treatises at Sera Monastery in Tibet for fourteen years before fleeing his homeland in 1959. After staying in the refugee camp at Buxa, India, Geshe Tegchok went to Varanasi, where he received his Acharya degree and taught for seven years. He then began teaching in the West—three years in England and ten years at Nalanda Monastery in France. In 1993, His Holiness the Dalai Lama appointed him as abbot of Jé College of Sera Monastic University in India. After serving as abbot for six years, he taught at Land of Medicine Buddha in California for several years, and then taught the masters program at Istituto Lama Tzong Khapa in Italy. Khensur Jampa Tegchok Rinpoche is the author of *Transforming Adversity into Joy and Courage: An Explanation of the "Thirty-seven Practices of Bodhisattvas"* and *The Kindness of Others: A Commentary on the Seven-Point Mind Training.*

BHIKSHU STEVE CARLIER (Thubten Sherab) was born in the U.K. and has been studying Buddhism since 1977. He first met Lama Thubten Yeshe and Zopa Rinpoche in 1978 and was ordained as a Buddhist monk by Zopa Rinpoche in 1979. He received full ordination from Serkong Tsenshab Rinpoche the following year. Ven. Steve studied for eleven years at Nalanda Monastery in France, and from 1993 to 2004 was one of only a few Westerners to study Buddhist philosophy at Sera Monastery in India. He has been a student of Khensur Jampa Tegchok since 1979 and for many years has served as this great master's interpreter. Ven. Steve currently resides at Land of Medicine Buddha, teaching the intermediate level courses, leading retreats, and also teaching at the Dharma centers in the area.

BHIKSHUNI THUBTEN CHODRON became a Buddhist in 1975 after attending a course given by Lama Thubten Yeshe and Zopa Rinpoche. She became a nun in 1977 and received full ordination as a bhikshuni in 1986.

She has been resident teacher at Amitabha Buddhist Centre in Singapore and at Dharma Friendship Foundation in Seattle. Active in interfaith dialogue, she also does Dharma outreach in prisons and teaches the Dharma worldwide. She is founder and abbess of Sravasti Abbey, a Buddhist monastery in eastern Washington State. She became a student of Geshe Jampa Tegchok in 1982 and studied under his guidance since then. In addition to editing his book *Transforming Adversity into Joy and Courage*, she is the author of *Buddhism for Beginners* and other Dharma books. Please see www.thubtenchodron.org and www.sravastiabbey.org.

About Wisdom Publications

Wisdom Publications is dedicated to offering works relating to and inspired by Buddhist traditions.

To learn more about us or to explore our other books, please visit our website at www.wisdompubs.org.

You can subscribe to our e-newsletter or request our print catalog online, or by writing to:

Wisdom Publications
199 Elm Street
Somerville, Massachusetts 02144 USA

You can also contact us at 617-776-7416, or info@wisdompubs.org.

Wisdom is a nonprofit, charitable 501(c)(3) organization, and donations in support of our mission are tax deductible.

Wisdom Publications is affiliated with the Foundation for the Preservation of the Mahayana Tradition (FPMT).